Doing More with Less
in the Delivery of Recreation
and Park Services:
A Book of Case Studies

Doing More with Less in the Delivery of Recreation and Park Services:

A Book of Case Studies

John L. Crompton

Venture Publishing, Inc.

Production Supervision by Bonnie Godbey
Cover Design by Sandra Sikorski
Design by Marilyn Shobaken
Editorial Assistance and Keyboarding by Susan Lewis
Desktop-Publishing Assistance by Vincent Lewis
Library of Congress Catalogue Card Number 87-82087
ISBN 0-910251-19-3

"The state of the art in this field is in practitioners' heads."

This book is dedicated to park and recreation practitioners whose enthusiasm,
commitment to the field, and consistent ability to innovate
has enabled them to do more with less

Contents

Acknowledgements

The author's role in compiling this book has primarily been that of collecting ideas rather than initiating them. The success of the effort depended upon the willingness of many practitioners to contribute material, to discuss and elaborate on it, and to comment on and proofread the cases after they had been written. The author is particularly appreciative of the assistance provided by the following: Leon Younger, Director, Jackson County Parks and Recreation Department; Rick Dodge, Assistant City Manager, St. Petersburg; Fred Blumberg, Operations Manager, Guadaloupe-Blanco River Authority; Howard L. Bogie, Concession Coordinator, Seattle Parks and Recreation Department; Bill Cowan III, Director of Aquatics, City of El Paso; Marie Dixon, Manager of Cultural and Special Events, Long Beach Department of Parks and Recreation; George Eib, Superintendent of Forestry and Landscaping, Kansas City Parks and Recreation Department; Lou Falley, President, Falley's Inc., Topeka; Christopher "Kit" Gillem, Nature Specialist, Anaheim Department of Parks, Recreation and Community Services; Richard Hickman, Marketing Manager, St. Petersburg; Jeff Hollis, Manager of Golf, St. Petersburg Leisure Services Department; Christopher K. Jarvi, Director, Anaheim Department of Parks, Recreation, and Community Services; John Koros, Director, Mercer Arboretum and Botanic Gardens, Houston; Kim McAdams, Director, Brazoria County Park Commission; Ray Murray, Chief, Division of Planning Grants, National Park Service Western Region, San Francisco.

A disproportionate number of cases emanate from two sources. Those are Leon Younger, formerly Superintendent of Recreation in Johnson County, Kansas, and currently Director of Parks and Recreation for Jackson County, Missouri; and Rick Dodge, formerly Administrator of the Department of Leisure Services at St. Petersburg, Florida, and currently Assistant City Manager in that city. The author has regularly interacted with Leon Younger and Rick Dodge in a number of contexts over a period of many years, and has marvelled at the flow of innovations which they have implemented.

The assistance of Sheila Backman, Jill Decker, Mark Havitz, and Susan Orton, who were graduate students working with the author at Texas A&M, in preparing some of the cases is also gratefully acknowledged. The contributions of Ms. Jill Decker were particularly important in completing this effort. During the summer of 1986, Ms. Decker, who was working on a masters degree in recreation and parks at Texas A&M University under the author's guidance, served an internship as Leon Younger's assistant in Jackson County. This provided an opportunity for Jill to comprehensively document many of the innovations that Leon Younger has introduced. Jill Decker's case write-ups constitute a central contribution to this book and the author is most appreciative of her enthusiastic support for the project.

Thanks are tendered to Dr. Carson Watt, Leader of the Recreation and Parks Project Group in the Texas Agricultural Extension Service, who generously assisted by providing resources for the manuscript to be produced. A big "thank you" is proffered to Ms. Susan Phillips for typing the manuscript and tolerating the repeated amendments and revisions, which she made with warmth and good humor.

Finally, my thanks go to Liz, Christine, and Joanne for the constant support and encouragement which they give to my writing endeavors.

Introduction

The decreased availability of tax support for park and recreation services in the past decade has served as a stimulus for innovation. It has encouraged members to be proactive rather than reactive. Innovation means more than espousing creative ideas. These ideas must be accompanied by persistence and professional acumen to bring them to fruition. Many of the concepts discussed in this book are not new. Rather, they "piggyback" on established ideas. Creative managers constantly think in this fashion, looking for ways to adapt a program which works in one locale to their own environment. For this reason, the cases presented in this book stress implementation. There is a large difference between having a creative idea and implementing it. By carefully detailing each case, it is hoped that managers will be encouraged to enact some of the ideas presented.

The role of the public recreation and park manager has changed from that of being an administrator primarily concerned with the allocation of government funding to that of an entrepreneur who operates in the public sector with minimal tax support. He or she is charged with the responsibility of aggressively seeking out resources for the agency and exploiting them to ensure that client groups receive maximum possible satisfaction.

Many park and recreation managers have embraced this new role with enthusiasm. They have responded to the challenge, and this collection of case studies describes some of their successes. Three criteria were used to select these cases:

(1) The author must have been aware of them.

(2) The ideas must be distinctive. Many so-called innovative approaches in this field were innovative in 1980, but have since become "mainstreamed" as part of the normal way most agencies do business.

(3) The idea must have reasonably wide applicability. Its usefulness must not be confined to solving a unique problem faced by a particular agency.

Some of the cases reported here describe innovations which were initiated two or three years ago. Consequently, the environmental circumstances or the personnel cited in a case may have changed. Indeed, in some cases the innovation is no longer operating, either because the key person responsible for it has left the agency, or because conditions in an agency's environment have changed. Nevertheless, these cases are included because the ideas have not been widely disseminated and they are capable of being implemented by others elsewhere.

The park and recreation field suffers from a lack of information dissemination. There are two reasons for this. First, practitioners rarely document or publish their "success stories," and there appear to be relatively few people in the academic community who are prepared to perform this journalist-type service. Second, compared to other fields, there are relatively few outlets available through which information can be disseminated. The recreation and parks market for

magazines, journals, and books is too small to attract major commercial publishers. For this reason, the author is very appreciative of the willingness of Venture Publishing, Inc., to publish and disseminate this book of cases.

Some of these cases, written by the author, have previously appeared in a wide variety of outlets, but many appear here in published form for the first time. The depth of treatment of the cases varies. This is a function of both their different degrees of complexity and the amount of information the author was able to glean from personnel at the agencies involved. Most of the cases were compiled from conversations with agency personnel and any support materials which they were able to supply. The information sources for each case are footnoted.

Section 1

Innovative Revenue-Producing Services

When an agency moves aggressively into launching a range of revenue-producing services, the temptation often is to plunge ahead and implement some offerings that it hopes will produce revenue. The first case in this Section — "Is Your Department Ready to Implement a Comprehensive Revenue Generation Program?" — points out that this approach fails to recognize that a comprehensive thrust in this area cannot be successfully launched until the agency has been prepared for it and has attained a state of readiness. The article identifies and describes those elements which together constitute agency readiness. Only when these elements are in place are the particular programs likely to be successful.

The remaining cases in this section offer specific examples of revenue-generating programs. These include travel services, group picnic services, four ideas from public golf courses, two cases describing exhibitions, and five revenue-producing recreation program ideas.

1

Is Your Department Ready to Implement a Comprehensive Revenue-Generating Program?

For a comprehensive revenue-generating program to succeed, the operating environment must change to accommodate it. This chapter identifies and discusses nine elements that you should consider to determine whether or not an agency can successfully implement such a program. If you attempt to implement an aggressive revenue-producing agenda without ensuring that the agency has been prepared for it, then frustration and failure are likely to result.

This chapter assumes that some people in a department recognize that a comprehensive revenue-generation program is (or should be) a legitimate and desirable objective of a public recreation and park agency. This is not intended to imply that such a program must supplant other objectives, but rather that it should supplement and complement them. The philosophical position is that recreation and park agencies should not operate as businesses, but rather as social service providers seeking to adopt business methods as appropriate. You should not view a thrust to generate revenue as incompatible with a social service orientation. Instead you should view it as a means of assisting and contributing to that effort by making more funds available to achieve an agency's social service goals.

The three NRPA Revenue Service Management Schools, which convene annually at Oglebay Park, Estes Park, and La Jolla, were specifically established to share and disseminate information on revenue-producing programs and facilities. They have been extraordinarily successful in accomplishing this objective, and literally dozens of excellent revenue-generating ideas typically emerge from each of the annual programs offered by these schools.

Sometimes these ideas are accompanied by participant frustration. These practitioners recognize the worth of the revenue-generating ideas that emerge and are excited by their potential, but doubt that they will be able to implement them immediately when they return to their agency. They realize that an agency has to be in a state of "readiness" before these revenue producing ideas can be set in motion.

A group of approximately eighty experienced managers at the La Jolla school discussed what conditions had to be met in an agency before a comprehensive revenue program could be implemented. These practitioners suggested nine major elements which together constitute an agency's readiness to generate revenue. In this chapter they are discussed and their likely priority suggested.

The set of elements identified were:

PRIORITY 1:
(1) Internal Marketing To:
    a. Top Management
    b. Elected Officials
    c. Staff
(2) Development of an Information Base

PRIORITY 2:
(3) Appointment of a Task Force to Develop a
    "Revenue Readiness" Plan

PRIORITY 3:
(4) Establishment of a Policy

PRIORITY 4:
(5) Development of an Infrastructure for Revenue-
    Generating Services
(6) Formation of Project Teams
(7) Creation of Organizational Slack

PRIORITY 5:
(8) External Marketing

PRIORITY 6:
(9) Sustaining Personnel Morale

   "Strategy" is derived from a Greek root meaning
"generalship," and these elements constitute a checklist
to consider when you formulate a general plan that
guides and directs the agency to a state of readiness for
implementing a comprehensive revenue-generating
program. Concern is with identifying the actions and
processes necessary for an agency to institutionalize
and integrate its revenue-generating efforts into its
long-term corporate culture and operating ethic. Everyone in the public sector should enthusiastically
endorse such a plan.
   The role of each element discussed in this paper will
vary according to the unique environment within which
each agency operates. The time frame for successfully
achieving "readiness" depends on the prevailing
political and financial environment. For example, if
substantial revenue shortfall causes a crisis, then three
months may be a realistic goal. However, if there is
no sense of urgency then creation of readiness may take
two or three years.
   Similarly, suggested sequencing of elements varies
among agencies. The groups' participants reached a
consensus that the sequencing presented here reflected

when the *major thrust* on each of these elements was
most likely to occur. They also recognized that some
preliminary work with low-priority elements may be
done in the early stages.

PRIORITY 1:
INTERNAL MARKETING AND DEVELOPMENT
OF AN INFORMATION BASE

Before you can adopt a coherent action plan or policy
for revenue generation, the concept of revenue generation has to be enthusiastically embraced by three major
audiences: top management, elected officials, and staff.
Securing their support requires a comprehensive
internal marketing effort. Too often, proponents fail
to recognize the critical role of internal marketing. An
important part of that marketing effort involves
demonstrating the impact of revenue generation. This
can only be done if you have developed an information
base. Thus internal marketing and the creation of an
information base are the first tasks you must
undertake.

INTERNAL MARKETING

Internal marketing views employees as internal
customers and endeavors to satisfy their needs and
wants while addressing the objectives of the agency.
The central principle of marketing is exchange; that is,
two parties agree to trade resources. For example,
citizens may pay a fee and receive a service from the
agency in return. The exchange that takes place
between and agency and its various clientele is
commonly recognized, but those that occur among top
management, elected officials, and other agency
personnel are no less real.
   Top managers, elected officials, and staff are all affected by the implementation of a comprehensive revenue generation program since it may have political
consequences, involve major policy, organizational, or
procedural changes, require changes in managerial responsibility, and/or lead to changes in methods of accountability.
   The key question that each of these three groups asks
is "What's in it for me?" They are likely to seek different answers to this question, hence proponents of

the concept must prepare three different marketing strategies. These should be sequential. First you should gain the support of top managers since they are the gatekeepers who control access to elected officials. You can then direct the second phase of your internal marketing effort at elected officials. Staff cannot initiate a revenue-generating program without the support of top management and elected officials, so you must secure the endorsement of these two groups before the final internal marketing effort directed at all staff is likely to be effective.

Top Management. For a revenue-generation program to be successfully implemented, the staff of an agency must perceive the program's director and senior management team as personally committed to supporting it. Unfortunately, some directors are unable or unwilling to attend learning forums such as the NRPA Revenue Schools, even though they permit deputies or middle managers to participate. Lower-level managers are then in the position of having to convince top management of the merits of a revenue-generating program. The magnitude of their task is compounded if the agency is not in immediate need of revenue since the benefits of embracing a major policy change may not be immediately apparent to senior managers. It is in this type of context that the need for internal marketing is most apparent.

The internal marketing task becomes easier as the number of program proponents on the staff increases. It is likely that you will need more than a single advocate in any agency with a full-time staff of over twenty before top management is convinced. Therefore proponents should seek out other managers in the agency who may be supportive and educate them. When the support base has been expanded in this manner, then you should present the case to top management.

The experience related by one middle manager who was at the Pacific Revenue Sources School from a large city appeared to be fairly typical of successful approaches used by others:

> After my first year at Revenue School, I went back to the Department and met a brick wall. There was no interest. However, during the year I did manage to persuade one of our senior managers to attend the school the following year. After the second year, the two of us went back and persuaded the top three

people in the Department to give us three hours of uninterrupted time during which we presented our case and suggested a general strategy for moving forward. There were 15 ideas we got from the school that we wanted to implement. At that meeting we got the go-ahead to implement 5 of them in the next year. In the three years since that initial meeting 13 of those 15 ideas have been implemented.

A site visit to another agency that has a successful revenue program may also be an effective approach to marketing the concept to senior management and elected officials. Nothing is more exciting than viewing success firsthand.

Why should senior managers accept the risks associated with initiating a revenue-generation program? What is in it for them? The following are some benefits to which they may respond favorably:

— provides increased resources which can be directed to favored projects for which there would otherwise be no funds
— lauded by elected officials because tax support is reduced (or services are increased/enhanced without a tax increase)
— offers a wider range of services to citizens without increasing taxes, thus enlarging the department's citizen/political constituency support
— enhances political strength which may in turn provide revenue from non-tax sources
— enhances reputation as city innovators/leaders
— increases incentive for staff to offer high-quality and relevant services. Pricing services builds in accountability. These services must meet a real need and their quality must be good or people do not pay for them.
— offers staff a new challenge and thus creates an atmosphere of vitality, energy, and excitement within the agency.

Elected Officials. When top management embraces the concept, internal marketing efforts shift to focus on elected officials. Part of this focus may be directed at commissions and/or advisory groups since their support may be a prerequisite to eliciting the support of elected officials. Often such advisory groups are comprised of representatives from user-group clientele, and at least some of the points discussed in the subsequent section of this paper under external marketing are likely to apply here.

Why should elected officials accept the political risks inherent in a policy shift to encourage revenue generation? What's in it for them?

— increased voter support because taxes are reduced and/or the number of services offered increases without raising taxes
— a policy consistent with the prevailing political philosophy of limiting tax revenues and the prevailing concept of equity that users should pay
— new services due to more available money
— more recreation and park services, which reflect positively on elected officials
— decreased service termination since a revenue-generation program softens the impact of tax cuts.

Staff. The goal of internal marketing for staff is to secure support from everyone in all divisions. There are likely to be considerable misgivings about launching a revenue generation program among some proportion of an agency's personnel. As part of the internal marketing process, it is essential that those misgivings be voiced.

Even though some divisions in an agency may be more directly involved in raising revenue than others, it is a mistake to isolate them as "the revenue group." They must interact with other divisions in the agency to achieve their goals, and unless these other sections are empathetic, there is likely to be conflict. The revenue ethic must thus permeate the whole department. Everyone must understand and support what you are trying to accomplish.

If staff have reservations and do not verbalize them, then senior management has no opportunity to eliminate that inward resistance. Thus, while they are required to accept the revenue-generation program, they may contribute to it only tentatively and with reluctance. If agency personnel are not committed to this new thrust, they are likely to transmit their lack of enthusiasm to their clientele quickly. Indeed, there have been instances in which agency personnel have actively encouraged client groups to resist a revenue-generation program. Internal marketing to staff should be done on a personal or small-group basis. One director who successfully launched a comprehensive revenue-generating program in an agency with no pre-

vious experience in this area described the process he used as follows:

I blocked out one full month and held individual 15 minute interviews with every member of our 189 full-time staff. I listened to their assessment of the concept, reassured them so they wouldn't feel threatened by this new direction, and received their input as to what they perceived would be the opportunities and problems which the new comprehensive revenue-generating program would offer.

What is in it for staff?

— more responsibility, and an opportunity to further career experiences and development, so staff are more qualified for promotions, whether within the department or in another agency
— enhanced job security because positions are protected by the revenue stream and are not subject to the vagaries of tax allocation decisions
— more opportunity to introduce services because more sources are made available by the new revenue
— a more challenging job which offers bottom-line accountability as one feedback measure of success or failure
— the satisfaction of producing a better product (assuming the fees are used for product enhancement).

DEVELOPMENT OF AN INFORMATION BASE

You should develop an information base or feasibility study that offers data supporting the need for a comprehensive revenue-generating program. Demonstrating the impact of additional revenue, along with the agency's resource capability to implement the program, is likely to be an essential part of a successful internal marketing effort.

This feasibility study may include projections of future budgets by extrapolating the budgets of the last few years forward for three to five years. This is likely to be particularly effective if the tax allocation in real dollar terms is not increasing. Similarly, the income stream anticipated from the new revenue programs should be projected over the same three-to-five-year period. The implications of these data for sustaining or upgrading existing services and introducing new services should be emphasized.

PRIORITY 2:
APPOINTMENT OF A TASK FORCE TO
DEVELOP A "REVENUE READINESS PLAN"

A small task force with representatives who are recognized and accepted as leaders from different divisions in the agency should be appointed and given responsibility for creating a "Revenue Readiness Plan" and building acceptance for it. The design of the plan must be a participative effort. *The process of securing commitment and ownership by all groups in it is at least as important as the suggested actions which emerge from it.* Senior management must provide general direction, but input from operational staff must be incorporated so there is an understanding and common acceptance of the intended direction throughout the entire agency. Without the input, judgement, participation, and enthusiastic endorsement of operational managers, a comprehensive revenue-generation program is likely to fail. However, the director must provide guidance or the Revenue Readiness Plan may delineate unacceptable courses of action and frustration will result.

You must specifically charge the task force with identifying what has to be done to (1) establish a revenue-generation policy; (2) develop an infrastructure which is responsive to the different internal administrative needs required by revenue-generating services; and (3) form project teams to implement particular services. Each of these three tasks is discussed in subsequent sections.

In addition to delineating the specific actions that will accomplish these three major tasks, the task force has a number of other decisions to make at this point. These concern: (1) the creation of a training program for staff; (2) the timing of implementation; (3) the impact of the revenue-generating program on the agency's existing mission statement and objectives; and (4) the magnitude of initial revenue-generating efforts.

Training sessions for staff are essential to convey the scope and objectives of the revenue-generating program described above. Such sessions also offer an opportunity for staff to acquire the marketing and financial tools necessary to make the program a success and alert them to new administrative processes that the program may require. These sessions should also encourage people to express their ideas and verbalize any problems or difficulties that they foresee.

There are three types of occasions at which the introduction of a revenue-generation program may be most opportune. In the annual cycle of events, it is most likely to receive serious attention if it is introduced at the beginning of a new budget cycle since that is when financial concerns and the need to fund new programs dominate the thinking of senior management staff and elected officials.

The second opportune time occurs when newly elected officials replace incumbents or senior management changes within the agency. The agency is likely to expect that these personnel changes may be reflected in new operating philosophies or program alterations. At the same time, new leaders are likely to be searching for new ideas to help them establish their reputation.

The third opportunity arises after a staff member returns from revenue school and prepares a report for top management on what he or she has learned. This may serve as the catalyst for action.

The objectives of a new revenue-generating program need to be clearly articulated so everyone understands their intent, but they must also be consistent with the agency's mission and overall goals. This does not necessarily mean that they must conform with existing agency objectives. Rather, the new thrust may serve as a catalyst for reexamining the appropriateness of these objectives and exploring the trade-offs in narrowing or expanding them.

Ideally, revenue-generating efforts should be incrementally phased-in and where possible introduced on a relatively small scale or as a pilot program. Error and inefficiencies are likely in early efforts as part of the learning process. If a comprehensive effort is launched from the outset, it may cause frustration and have demoralizing repercussions. As skills and confidence evolve, the scope of the revenue-generating program can be expanded. Once positive results emerge, managers are likely to be more enthusiastic about broadening and extending the program.

If there is some staff resistance, even after the internal marketing effort, early projects should involve supportive staff and seek to demonstrate the success of the program to others. Early projects might include revenue-generating special events that garner substantial favorable media attention. Early successes are important, for they build credibility, establish momentum, and increase the level of support within the agency. This support is necessary not only to build commitment from those staff who remain skeptical, but also to strengthen the case with senior management and elected officials for investing more resources in the program.

PRIORITY 3:
ESTABLISHMENT OF POLICIES

Before you take any programmatic action, you need to resolve three issues. First you must affirm the compatibility of proposed actions with existing enabling legislation and ordinances. This sounds obvious, but it is easily overlooked in the excitement of moving into a more aggressive revenue-generating mode. A second key policy issue to address is how the economically disadvantaged will be served so they are not excluded when increasing emphasis is placed on revenue production.

The third issue is the establishment of an enterprise fund system. A comprehensive revenue-generating program is predicated on an enterprise fund system that is already in place, or at least an equivalent less-formal understanding that revenues will be used to sustain and nurture the programs which yield them. Without this there is likely to be opposition from user clientele: "Why should I pay all this money for this service when it goes into the general fund to subsidize some other service from which I may receive no benefits?" Similarly, agency staff are likely to voice opposition by asking, "Why should I bother with the hassle and costs of collecting revenue if it all goes downtown and doesn't come back into my program?" Without the approval of the enterprise fund concept, a successful comprehensive revenue-generating program is unlikely. Enterprise funds or trust funds offer the following advantages:

— revenue does not get deposited in the general fund to be used for other public services. Instead it enhances or sustains the services which generated it.
— expenditures become more flexible since enterprise or trust funds can be carried forward from one fiscal year to the next. Similarly, such funds permit more latitude in purchasing equipment and supplies, along with hiring personnel, since they can be set up to operate outside the normal bureaucratic procedures for performing these tasks.

— it is easier to determine exact direct costs of operating an enterprise facility and to charge indirect maintenance costs and other special expenses to the enterprise fund.

PRIORITY 4:
DEVELOPMENT OF AN INFRASTRUCTURE FOR REVENUE-GENERATING SERVICES

You must create an organizational infrastructure for success. This involves establishing efficient channels and smooth procedures to accommodate the flow of monies into and out of these services, which include purchasing requirements, personnel hiring and termination, and evaluation. Give careful thought to where proposed revenue-generating services best fit within the agency; the other divisions and/or personnel from within the department with whom they have to interact; and other departments whose cooperation has to be acquired.

Internal reorganization may be necessary to facilitate better integration. For example, in one agency, the Concessions and Contracts Division was under Administration and Special Services. With the commitment to a comprehensive revenue program, it was moved under the Recreation Division since it had to be closely integrated with the services offered by the Recreation Division.

Relationships with other departments may also have to be reformulated. One director had the following experience:

> The toughest problem we had was dealing with purchasing and personnel. Purchasing couldn't understand that money would be collected at the start of classes and there would then have to be an immediate purchase order to acquire supplies for the start of those classes. It took at least ten meetings with them before they finally agreed to the system. The support of the County Chief Executive and elected officials was crucial to us obtaining the cooperation of the Purchasing Department.

This director had similar problems with the Personnel Department, which was reluctant to cooperate in a timely fashion by hiring and terminating the large number of seasonal workers that would be necessary for a comprehensive revenue-generating program. This was resolved by the Park and Recreation Department agreeing to take on this work so that no extra burden would fall on the Personnel Department.

This case illustrates the role of two crucial factors in gaining the cooperation of other departments. First, elected officials were presented with a list of organizational relationships which crossed departments that had to become involved before a revenue-generating thrust could begin. Their endorsement of these mechanisms made it difficult for the other departments to resist. The second factor was the effort to make it as easy as possible for the other departments to cooperate by minimizing the extra workload they received.

Particular attention needs to be focused on the budget and finance officials of the city. Since they control the processes of city financing, these individuals can be particularly strong allies it they are brought on board at an early stage. Conversely, they are in a position to frustrate a successful revenue program if they oppose it in both direct and subtle ways.

An alternative strategy for securing the support of other departments whose cooperation you need — like personnel, purchasing, and finance — is to voluntarily pay them an administrative fee in return for their help with the new revenue thrust. This enables those departments to hire more people, and the fee can be written off as overhead in the enterprise funds.

You must include an evaluation process as part of the infrastructure. If the continuance of a service is predicated on the income received from user fees or concessions to cover its costs, then constant monitoring of the price-value relationship and level of customer satisfaction is imperative. Immediate and ongoing feedback is necessary to identify any failings in a program before they become sufficiently pronounced that the program fails by a large margin to meet its revenue projections.

FORMATION OF PROJECT TEAMS

To bring the revenue-generating thrust to fruition, project teams should be formed and charged with completing clearly defined, specific program tasks. You should give them the responsibility and authority to implement programs. The success and failure of their efforts is likely to be judged against what was expected of them. Thus optimistic expectations should be tempered and reasonable and modest goals

established so that success is more widely perceived to have been achieved.

In a fairly large agency, these teams may involve six to eight people and should include representatives from purchasing, accounting, personnel, and other divisions or departments involved in implementation. These teams should be comprised of people who are enthusiastic about the revenue-generating thrust, and who represent all levels of management.

One director who has had extensive experience in establishing a comprehensive revenue-generation program in two different agencies stresses the importance of keeping membership in these project teams fluid and spreading leadership responsibility throughout all management levels:

> Everyone wants the opportunity to be a project manager. It brings prestige from peers and offers excitement and the challenge of leadership. Many of our teams are led by middle managers even though senior managers are assigned to the team to play a minor role. All my senior managers are very conscious that they are Indians on some project teams, and they must respect the team leaders as Chiefs in these particular situations and not undermine the leadership. There is more than enough for all of our managers to do, and by spreading the leadership around we avoid burnout. The determination of middle managers to demonstrate they can do a good job of leadership creates incentive for excellent follow-through which is the key to success.

CREATION OF ORGANIZATIONAL SLACK

Organizational slack is the difference between the resources committed by a department to carry out its basic functions and the total resources it has available. Success requires that project team members have the time and resources to plan well. If they are fully extended, applying all of their efforts to carrying out existing commitments, it is unlikely that the revenue-generating program will succeed. This slack may be created either by retrenchment efforts which reduce their involvement with existing programs or by elected officials or top management providing additional resources as a seed investment to develop the comprehensive revenue-generation program.

PRIORITY 5:
EXTERNAL MARKETING

External marketing involves using the traditional set of marketing activities (market research, target marketing, product development, price, distribution, and promotion) to encourage potential client groups to take advantage of a service. The critical questions which users will ask are likely to be, "What's in it for us? Why should we be supportive of price impositions or increases for this service?" You have to convince affected groups that the money they pay is going to be used for their benefit. Therefore acceptable responses to these key questions may include the following.

First, more funds improve the quality of a service in the form of better facilities, equipment, staff, or officials. This claim is likely to be convincing only if an enterprise fund is established which ensures that user money is reinvested for this purpose.

Second, a service generates more dollars if it can be better tailored to meet individual needs; that is, smaller, more carefully defined target markets can be accommodated. For example, a separate program may now be offered to beginning, intermediate, and advanced participants, whereas previously one program had been offered to all, because extra revenue is now available to cover the additional costs which this involves.

Third, users can be given some control over how their money is spent. This becomes practical if the money is in an enterprise fund, whereas it is not feasible when it goes into the general fund. The costs of delivering a service should be identified and shared with users' representatives. They can be invited to make decisions as to the quality of service they want. If they want to reduce costs, they can determine what components of a program should be reduced, and they can similarly decide whether or not they want to pay the additional amount for any improvements they desire.

Listen to the concerns of affected clients and try to resolve problems by pointing out the benefits of a revenue-generation program in advance of price increases. This is crucial to acceptance.

PRIORITY 6:
SUSTAINING PERSONNEL MORALE

Although this component is sequentially listed at the end of this discussion of agency readiness, it is obviously critical to sustaining the success of a comprehensive revenue-generating program after it has been launched.

At least some agency personnel are likely to feel insecure because they lack knowledge and self-confidence about the process and content associated with a new revenue-generating program. Further, new ideas and increased sophistication are required to sustain momentum. Consistent investment in employee training is necessary to resolve these concerns, and its availability is likely to influence the level of sustained personnel enthusiasm.

The new thrust is likely to be accompanied by some mistakes and failures. These must be anticipated, accepted, and not penalized. This does not mean that sloppy work, poor planning and implementation, or incompetence should be excused; it simply means that risk is inherent in a new thrust of this nature and some failures are inevitable. Too often, agency personnel are averse to new programs because the personal cost of failure is judged to be greater that any gains they accrue from success.

CONCLUDING COMMENTS

When you move into a comprehensive revenue generation program, the temptation is often to plunge ahead and implement some offerings that you anticipate will produce revenue. This approach fails to recognize that a comprehensive thrust in this area cannot be successfully launched until the agency has been prepared for it and has attained a state of readiness.

To implement this major change successfully, the environment within which it will operate must be changed to accommodate it. Attempting to implement a revenue-generation program in an alien, non-revenue-oriented environment is likely to be futile. The elements described above constitute agency readiness.

2

Implementing a
Travel Program

Traditionally, travel programs have been considered the arena of the private sector. Some public agencies are less involved with these because they cater to specific clientele groups such as senior or special populations. Typically, such programs have been small-scale and are limited to day excursions in the local area. This case describes a large-scale broad-based travel program initiated by a public agency. It suggests that there are major opportunities for public recreation and park agencies in the travel market.

The Jackson County Parks and Recreation Department started a year round travel program in 1984. Two years later it featured ninety-eight trips which ranged from one-day "Look Around Your Town" visits to a seven-day bear-hunting excursion to the Canadian outback. The travel program began with local area one- and two-day tours for senior adults. From these the agency has expanded into a series of high-adventure trips which focus on such activities as skiing, fishing, biking, or rafting down the Colorado River. These tours are offered through three separate divisions of the Department: the Senior Adult Division, the Recreation Division, and the Outdoor Recreation Division. The department also plans a series of trips for their museum arts patrons that will involve going to historical sites for behind-the-scenes and "hands-on" activities. These excursions will be offered through the Heritage Programs and Museums Division.

Travel is viewed as a feeder to all the rest of the agency's programs, which is the main reason for offering it. It may serve to introduce some patrons to the department, or it may emerge as an outgrowth of a class, e.g., scuba class trips to off-coast waters. Travel should usually be either a teaser to attract people to the program or an extension of the program. Tours improve image and increase the visibility of the department; thus they are an integral part of the department's total program.

The department originally went out to obtain bids on their trips from travel agents. The staff insisted that one agent bid for a number of trip packages together since administrative planning would become too complicated if each journey originated from a different agency. Because most travel agencies did not want to take the time to plan so many tours or meet the department's careful specifications for their clientele, few bids were received. As a result of the private sector's lack of interest in packaging, each division now plans and packages its own trips, except in a few cases where a travel agent or outfitter is better able and willing to complete these tasks. Travel agents and media have not reacted adversely to the department creating its own travel program because they are invited to become involved when appropriate.

The travel program in each division operates through an enterprise fund. All trips are priced to cover expenses and make a small profit for the division. In addition to its small profit margin, each division adds an eighteen-percent administrative fee to all of its enterprise programs to cover administrative costs. For each trip a minimum and maximum occupancy is determined. Minimum occupancy is the number of people necessary to cover the fixed costs of the journey and the variable costs associated with that number. If the trip does not fill to minimum occupancy by the time deposits are due, it will not cover its costs and will be cancelled. The maximum occupancy is the greatest number of people who can be comfortably accommodated and supervised on the trip. The fees paid by each additional participant over the minimum number covers their own variable costs and, since the fixed costs are already covered, generates a surplus which is recycled into the program.

Therefore, to set the price of a trip, fixed costs for services such as transportation, guide or escort, and staff time are calculated and divided by the minimum occupancy. (See Figure 1.1.) This number is the fixed cost per person. The total cost per person is determined by adding the variable cost per individual to the fixed cost per individual. Variable costs include such items as equipment, sightseeing fees, accommodations, meals, all gratuities, and lift tickets and lessons on ski trips. The eighteen percent administrative fee is added to the total cost per person to determine the price set for the trip or tour. The administrative fee is expected to cover administrative expenses associated with the travel program such as telephone calls, printing and mailing brochures, advertising, and secretarial costs. All surplus remains within the division and is used to purchase additional equipment and improve existing programs or begin new ones. The total 1987 travel budget for all three divisions is approximately $833,000, all of which will be revenue-generated.

The department arranges trips a year or more in advance so that they can set registration deadlines far enough ahead of the trip to cancel reservations without a penalty if the roster does not fill. This is particularly important for longer excursions and those requiring airline reservations. No refunds are made for registration cancellations unless the department cancels the entire trip. In advance of each journey, staff also

FIGURE 1.1

Price Calculation for Mini Getaway to Lost Valley Dude Ranch

September 3-8, 1986
32 Minimum/40 Maximum

Fixed Costs

Transportation	$3000.00
Tour of Air Force Academy & Cadet Chapel	60.00
Staff Escort/Staff Time	464.00
TOTAL FIXED COSTS	3524.00
FIXED COSTS PER PERSON (32 min. occ.)	$ 110.02

Variable Costs Per Person

Hotel Accommodations (5 nights, double)	$189.88
Round Trip Cog Railway Tour to Pikes Peak Summit	60.00
All Entertainment at Lost Valley Ranch	75.00
Meals (Continental Breakfast)	6.00
(Dinner at Casa Bonitas-Denver)	12.00
(Family Style Meals at Lost Valley Ranch)	45.00
Baggage Handling	10.00
TOTAL VARIABLE COST PER PERSON	397.88
TOTAL COST PER PERSON	508.00
ADMINISTRATIVE FEE (18%)	91.44
PRICE OF TRIP ROUNDED TO	599.50
Potential Profit = $110.12 x 8 people =	$880.96

hold a meeting with participants to encourage social interaction, introduce the tour guide, answer questions that people may have about such things as appropriate dress, itinerary, or accommodations, and provide information about the destination with slides or videos solicited from hosts. This pre-trip meeting eliminates the need for the department to independently respond to identical questions that participants may have and "whets the appetite" for what lies ahead. After each trip, the department throws a reunion party. In addition to sharing slides and reminiscences from past trips, participants are introduced to future tours that they may be interested in taking. There is a high proportion of repeat users on these trips.

SENIOR ADULT TRAVEL PROGRAM

The department's Senior Adult Division offers a wide variety of tours especially designed for active persons aged fifty-five and over. The program gives older people the opportunity to travel at group rates with friends of similar ages. Tours are comfortably paced and provide the sense of security which is important to this age group.

The 1986 senior travel program consisted of over twenty one-to-three-day "Mini Getaways," eight one-day "Look Around Your Town" trips, a week-long New England cruise, and two ten-day Hawaiian Cruises. Figure 1.2 lists the 1986 Senior Adult Travel Schedule. The local one- or half-day excursions may be to sample a new restaurant, attend a play at the Waldo Astoria dinner theatre, or enjoy a relaxing evening at the Ice Capades. Mini Getaways take seniors to such destinations as the "Rose Festival" in Richmond, Indiana, or the Lost Valley Dude Ranch in Colorado.

The department employs two full-time staff members to coordinate and plan every aspect of the Senior Adult Travel Program. Their salaries are paid out of money generated by all Senior Adult Programs, of which the trip program is the major part. They must be creative and knowledgeable about places to visit and events to attend both locally and across the country. Essentially, they serve as in-house travel agents since they arrange for transportation, accommodations, sightseeing tours, restaurants, escorts, etc. The department contracts a motor coach company which they use for all road tours. Staff send

FIGURE 1.2

Senior Adult Travel Schedule

Look Around Your Town Trips

April 12	Imagery on Ice
May 8	A Theatrical Legend: Billy the Kid
June 4	Afternoon of Broadway: *Arsenic and Old Lace*
June 24	Picnic with a Lakefront View
July 23	Paddlin' the Mighty Mo
August 13	Afternoon on Broadway: *The Sound of Music*
November 5	The Green Machine (Tour Federal Reserve Bank)
December 20	*Nutcracker* Ballet

Mini Getaways

June 7	Fort Scott (Fort Scott, MO)
June 14	Council Grove (Council Grove, KS)
June 18-19	Oklahoma (Tahlequah, OK)
June 25	Arrowrock (Missouri)
June 27-30	Rose Festival (Richmond, IN)

July 9-19	Expo '86/Canadian Rockies (Calgary, Alberta)
July 25-27	St. Louis — Amtrak (St. Louis, MO)
July 30	Nebraska City (Nebraska City, NE)
August 2	Czech Fest (Wilbur, NE)
August 7-10	Chicago/Venetian Regatta (Chicago, IL)
August 16-17	Relax at the Elms (Excelsior Springs, MO)
August 28-29	Mt. Pleasant (Mt. Pleasant, MO)
September 3-8	Lost Valley Dude Ranch (Denver, CO)
September 6	Plattsburg/Trenton (Trenton, MO)
September 20	St. James (Rolla, MO)
September 27	Lincoln (Lincoln, NE)
October 1-3	Ozarks (Lake of the Ozarks area, MO)
October 4	Hiawatha (Hiawatha, MO)
October 11	Winterset (Winterset, IA)
October 16	Weston (Weston, MO)
November 29	Elk Horn (Elk Horn, IA)

Vacation Cruises

September 13-21	New England Cruise
November	Cruise Hawaii
December	Cruise Hawaii

bid specifications to interested firms and choose the one that provides the best service for the lowest cost. Some transportation companies produce their own brochures and literature, and the department is often able to negotiate for space in their literature in return for the exclusive contract and visibility the companies receive in the travel brochures distributed by the department.

One staff member usually acts as an escort on each trip. On occasion, the department may contract an escort to supervise the tour, particularly if it is in a specialized area of interest. This person must have formal training in CPR and First Aid. Because it is operated through an enterprise fund, staff can travel extensively and be out of the office for long periods of time without difficulty.

A travel agency external to the department arranges cruises since it is better equipped to negotiate with airlines and cruise lines. The staff again establish criteria such as first-class travel, AAA accommodations, etc., for the number of seniors expected to register for the cruise. Three travel agencies are then invited to submit a package and price to the department. The department chooses the agency with the superior package.

Promotion is a major part of the senior travel program. Sixty percent of participants are repeat trip goers, so direct mail is important. Each January, the department mails a Mini Getaway Guide to approximately 2,700 senior adults who have previously participated in the department's travel program or one of its other senior programs. The guide contains a description and the details of every Getaway offered during the year and a postcard insert with a list of the trips. Recipients are asked to check the trips that interest them and return the card to the department. A few weeks before registration opens for each of those trips, an individual trip brochure is mailed directly to those who indicated interest free of charge.

The department also prints and mails a monthly newsletter to all senior citizens who have participated in any senior program, whether it be trips or classes. The yearly travel schedule and highlights of several trips are printed each season in the departmental tabloid. This publication is mailed directly four times each year to approximately 50,000 county residences and distributed through libraries, government offices, and other public buildings. Finally, the seniors' social calendar, a brochure which describes local outings, is distributed to area residents. It is usually mailed with the "Getaway Guide." The Senior Adult Division spends approximately fourteen thousand dollars a year for printing and postage associated with its travel program.

The 1987 senior adult travel budget is approximately 510,000 dollars. Surplus revenue from this program funds the department's entire range of senior-citizen services: center activities and special events receive no tax support.

OUTDOOR RECREATION DIVISION

The outdoor recreation travel program began as a series of high-adventure trips that offered physical and mental endurance challenges and has since embraced an additional market segment that sought science and nature and/or solitude. The program now offers twenty-four day trips, including Little Blue River float excursions, cross-country ski tours, bicycle tours, and bird and wildlife refuge visits as well as twenty-four "Weekends in Missouri" that feature such programs as Ozark float trips, backpacking, spelunking, camping trips, and trail rides. The 1986 outdoor travel program also offered four major "Adventure Vacations." These included a canoe trip in Minnesota's Boundary Water Canoe Area, a dude ranch vacation in Jackson Hole, Wyoming, and a Colorado white-water raft trip.

The program is run by a highly qualified outdoor recreation specialist with twenty years of experience. The recreation specialist plans, organizes, and personally leads every trip with the exception of those for which an outfitter can be contracted at less cost. Many hours of research are needed to plan trips around animal and waterfowl migration and low-use areas. Scientific trips dealing with archaeology, ornithology, and ecology are tax deductible, and others are offered for college credit. These trips are contracted to certified outfitters and require an added forty-dollar fee.

The outdoor recreation division offers outdoor equipment rental. Sleeping bags, tents, cross-country skis, backpacks, personal flotation devices and climbing gear are some of the items individuals may rent at low rates for various trips.

The mode of transportation varies with the length of the trip and the size of the group. For small groups, transportation consists of a county-owned van. If a group is larger and the trip takes less than five hours, a school bus is rented. For drives of more than five hours, the department charters a bus. If the trip takes over twenty hours of driving time, then transportation is by air at group rates.

Outdoor trips are also promoted through the departmental tabloid and directly mailed tour catalogs and single-trip brochures. Written press releases and radio advertisements obtained through trade-outs can promote individual excursions in advance of registration day.

Recreation specialists also occasionally have the opportunity to do guest spots on a local PBS station.

The 1987 outdoor recreation trip program was operated on an enterprise budget of approximately 100,000 dollars. Budget breakdown is shown in Figure 1.3.

FIGURE 1.3

1987 Outdoor Recreation Travel Budget

EXPENSES:

POSTAGE
Mailing flyers that advertise
trip program — 3000 x $.22

$ 600

TRAVEL EXPENSE
Travel advances for trip leaders
for misc. expenses & emergencies
  4 major trips @ $100   400
  24 weekend trips @ $50   1,200
                        TOTAL 1,600

ADVERTISING
Newspaper advertising of trips   2,300

Printing
20 flyers x $200 @   4,000
Seasonal brochures   2,400
                        TOTAL 6,400

RENT - AUTO EQUIPMENT
1. Rental of school buses —
   10 trips x $350 @   3,500
2. Charter of bus for adventure
   vacations — $2,500 x 4 trips 10,000
                        TOTAL 13,500

RENT — MISCELLANEOUS
Rental of outdoor equipment
1. Canoes
   (12 trips x 12 canoes x $36)   5,184
2. Canoe trailers for Little
   Blue floats
   (6 weekends x $40)   240
                        TOTAL 5,424

LAUNDRY SERVICES
Clean-up of supplies after trips   100
Cleaning of rental sleeping bags   150
                        TOTAL   250

ADMINISTRATIVE SERVICE
(minimum $32,495 x 18%)   5,849

OTHER CONTRACTUAL SERVICES
1. Contracts for outfitting
   4 major trips (4 trips x
   24 persons x $350)   33,600
2. Camping fees for 10 weekend
   trips (10 trips x 22 persons
   x $10)   2,200
                        TOTAL 35,800

REFERENCE BOOKS AND PUBLICATIONS
Outdoor Recreation & Trip
Literature   100

FIGURE 1.3   (CONTINUED)

GASOLINE
For van and leased buses   1,000

FOOD
For float trips, backpacking, camping trips
— (20 trips x 5 meals x 20 people x $2.50)
5,000

RECREATION SUPPLIES
Recreation supplies & equipment as needed
1. for trips   600
2. for rental equipment   400
                              TOTAL 1,000

OTHER OPERATING SUPPLIES
Other supplies as needed for trips   244

MOTOR OIL & LUBRICANTS
For van   120

SMALL TOOLS AND MINOR EQUIPMENT
Complete tool kit to keep on trip vehicles   150

OUTDOOR RECREATION STAFF
Outdoor Recreation Specialist

(full time)
Outdoor Recreation Intern
(3-month seasonal summer)   19,073

TOTAL $98,470
REVENUE:

LEASES & RENTAL CHARGES
50 rentals x $ 5   250
50 rentals x   10   500
50 rentals x   20   1,000
                          TOTAL   1,750

PARK FEES
24 day trips x 18 persons
x $15 (average price)   6,480
24 weekend trips x 24
persons x $105 (average price)   60,480
4 adventure vacations x 24
x $310 (average price)   29,760
                          TOTAL $96,720

TOTAL $98,470

SPORT RECREATION DIVISION

Finally, the department operates a travel program in the Sports Recreation Division. This program operates on a budget of approximately 224,000 dollars and in 1986 consisted of thirteen downhill ski trips to areas such as Steamboat, Beaver Creek, the Summit, Copper Mountain, and Tahoe, and four Canadian fly-in black-bear hunting and outpost fishing trips. The Canadian trips included round-trip transportation from Fort Frances, Ontario, to the drop-off point, a boat, motor, gas, license, canoe, tent, life jackets, food and cooking utensils, and all other necessary equipment. These trips are packaged by Canadian outfitters, though the department receives a basic fee or commission for assembling groups to go on these trips. They also work closely with the outfitters to arrange discounted rates. The five- to seven-day trips range in price from 295 dollars to 675 dollars per person.

The downhill ski trips are packaged by a full-time recreation division staff member and include transportation by bus or plane depending on the trip, accommodations, two staff supervisors, lift tickets, and optional equipment and lessons. Prices range from 185 dollars for off-season trips to 645 dollars for the Tahoe ski trip. The average trip price is about 325 dollars.

The department rents all of the ski equipment from a local ski shop. In return, the ski shop supplies a copy of their mailing list. The shop previously sold packaged ski vacations and advertised the department's ski trips in their own brochure. The retailer no longer wanted to be in the ski-trip business and invited the department to take over this service. As part of this agreement, the department contracted with the shop owners to rent ski equipment exclusively from them In this arrangement the department also received substantial discounts on condominiums which the retailer had accrued through several seasons of high-volume support. The ski trip budget increased from 60,000 dollars in 1986 to 150,000 dollars in 1987.

The department promotes recreation trips through single-trip posters, advertisements in the travel section of local newspapers, the quarterly tabloid, and direct mail brochures. The department also gives away ski trips as promotional trade-offs with a local radio station. About one month before the registration deadline, staff present two free trips to the radio station. One is for a dee-jay and the other is offered over the air. In return, the radio station gives the department free air time and permission to announce themselves as the sponsor of the free trip.

Some radio stations enhance their involvement by doing live remote broadcasts from resort sites. As part of this promotion, they typically include a radio contest to give the trip away. As people call in during the contest, a name and address list is compiled. The station awards the trip about three weeks before the registration deadline and the department receives the list of those who express interest by calling in. Then they call each person on the list to encourage them to sign up for the tour. They also add them to the mailing list for future trips. The dee-jay talks on the air about how much fun he or she had on the ski trip, which provides additional promotion for upcoming excursions.

CONCLUDING COMMENTS

Staff who supervise or lead tours or trips are on duty twenty-four hours per day for the duration of the trip. Their expenses are paid but they receive no overtime pay. They have the incentive to arrange fun, exciting trips and organize them well because they can then enjoy themselves and not be bothered with administrative or planning problems during the trip. Travel liability is covered by the county as part of its self-insurance program. The organizations and agencies involved who offer tour services must provide liability insurance for those services.

The major difficulty encountered in launching this travel program was getting the purchasing and budgeting departments of the county to work with the department. They had to be made to understand the need to turn money around quickly. The department has to be able to take money in advance and reimburse it promptly should the trip be cancelled for any reason. There is also some risk involved in travel because many things can go wrong and the government is traditionally a low risk-taker.

The key to success is having people who know the travel business. Jackson County sends its travel staff regularly to training programs and travel shows to ensure that their knowledge is current. The program was started slowly to gain the confidence of the purchasing department and county officials, and to demonstrate that public support for the program exists. The department's travel program is still relatively new and growing, but approximately eighty-five percent of the planned trips have come to fruition. The Jackson County Parks and Recreation Department is considering a second phase to their travel program — packaging tours from the outside to come to Jackson County!

SOURCE:

Jackson County Parks and Recreation Department
22807 Woods Chapel Road
Blue Springs, Missouri 64015

3

Offering Group Picnic Services

Many groups have picnics in the parks. Some agencies now offer to organize these picnics for a fee, which relieves group members of the responsibility for organization. This case describes how one agency successfully operates this service.

Fleming Park in Jackson County, Missouri, near Kansas City has been the site of various group outings for many years. The park has fourteen shelter structures, a day-camp facility, and a swimming pool all sited in semi-private areas around the 960-acre lake. These shelters are equipped with restrooms, running water, and electricity, and are often reserved several months in advance for thirty dollars a day for such events as family reunions, civic or church picnics, and many other types of group socials.

The Jackson County Parks and Recreation Department identified an opportunity to capitalize on this resource by providing a group picnic service. The department borrowed the idea from Sacramento County, California, which began offering group picnics to community businesses and community organizations during the summer of 1984. The department offers complete planning and organization of large group picnics which are individually tailored to the needs of each group. Picnic packages may include park shelter and swimming-pool reservations, complete catering, picnic games for children and adults, clowns, magicians, sporting tournaments, awards, prizes,

balloons, the Jackson County Parks Department's "fun pak," banners, host staff, clean-up, and any other services that a group may request.

The group picnic service is targeted toward corporate picnics, church outings, family reunions, and club picnics. There is no size limit, and the special-events coordinator selects the site most suitable for the needs of the group. The department offers the service during the summer months from May 17 through September 21.

PUBLICITY

A brochure is printed containing detailed information about the group picnic service. This brochure is distributed in September to other county departments, service clubs, churches, and convention planners, as well as through the department's registration office. Groups who have reserved shelters in previous years and companies on the department's corporate mailing list receive the brochure through direct mail.

The group picnic service is also promoted through public-service announcements on the radio and in area newspapers. Interested groups are encouraged to respond quickly because the shelters are in high demand.

ORGANIZING STEPS

The department sends out a Group Picnic Planning Menu in response to initial inquiries. (See Figure 1.4.) This package contains a checklist of all available services, including food and beverage items, activities, entertainment, and specialties. The group is responsible for making selections from the list, providing information on dates, times, and numbers, and returning the planning menu to the special events coordinator no less than eight weeks before the intended picnic date.

FIGURE 1.4

The Group Picnic Planning Menu

Please complete this planner to help us design a picnic especially for your group!

Group Name _____

Contact Person _____

Address_____

City _____

Phone_____

Picnic Date _____

Approximate Attendance: Children _____Adults_____

AVAILABLE SERVICES

A variety of programs and services are available to make your picnic a success! Please check the services desired.

Catering:

Main Course	Salads	Beverage
____Rib-eye Steak	____Potato Salad	____Soda
____Chicken	____Baked Beans	____Beer (keg)
____BBQ Ribs	____Cole Slaw	

All picnics include chips, breads, condiments, dessert, and choice of three salads.

ACTIVITIES

Softball	Volleyball	Horseshoes

Free Play
_____

Tournament
_____

Officials
_____

Awards
_____

# of Teams
_____

_____Swimming	_____Bingo	_____Pony Ring
_____Face Painting	_____Carnival Games	_____Children's Games w/ prizes
_____Petting Zoo	_____Moonwalk	_____Adult Picnic Games

ENTERTAINMENT

_____Singing Telegram	_____Magician
_____Deejay & Sound System	_____Cartoonist
_____Clown	_____Puppet Show
_____Hot-Air Balloon Tether	_____Skydiver

SPECIALTIES

_____Helium Balloons	_____Raffle	_____Theme Party
_____Banner w/ group name	_____Party Favor	_____Photographer

Other:
_____
_____
_____

Please call with any questions. (816) 795-8200

Return completed form to: Mary Campbell
                         Special-Events Coordinator
                         22807 Woods Chapel Road
                         Blue Springs, MO 64015

The picnic planner must be received eight weeks prior to picnic date.

When the picnic planner is returned, the picnic is discussed in more detail by phone or, for larger picnics, in a meeting with the contact person. The coordinator then begins to develop a working budget. This includes catering, entertainment, staff, facilities, and any special purchases required such as awards and prizes. The cost of each picnic depends on the size of the group and the services provided. A nineteen-percent profit is also added into each budget. (See Figure 1.5.) The department has set a minimum surplus requirement of eighteen percent on all programs such as this, which it operates through an enterprise budget.

FIGURE 1.5

A Sample Group Picnic Budget

ST. JOSEPH HOSPITAL

June 21, 11am-7pm

Facilities		$ 755.00
8' Banner — SJH Celebration	$ 50.00	
Shelter 14	30.00	
40 x 60' Tent	475.00	
Signage	20.00	
Portable Toilets (6)	180.00	

Staffing		822.00
Rec. Leaders, Supervisor, Coordinator	$782.00	
Rangers	40.00	

Entertainment		2,415.00
Petting Zoo — 4 hours	$250.00	
Pony Ring — 4 hours	350.00	
Carnival Games—6 games/3 hours	540.00	
Mouse Races	350.00	
Clown and Mini Car — 2 hours	200.00	
Tether — 2 hours	400.00	
Moonwalk — day	200.00	
Jacob's Ladder — day	125.00	

Games		800.00
Stilt Races		
Balloon Toss		
Lap Sit		
Caterpillar		
Bug Tug		
Knots-So		
Tug of War		
Horseshoes		
Volleyball		
Softball		
Parachute		
Fun Pak		
Prizes		$800.00

19%		$4,792.00
		910.48
TOTAL		$5,702.48

FIGURE 1.6

Group Picnic Services Agreement

Jackson County, Missouri

THIS AGREEMENT made and entered into this
_____day of _____, 19 ___ by and between the COUNTY OF JACKSON, hereinafter "County," and

_____
hereinafter "Group."
1. TERM
The term of this Agreement, a description of the services, compensation, time of payment, amount of insurance, and such other terms and provisions pertinent hereto is specified in EXHIBIT A attached hereto and by this reference is fully incorporated herein.

2. PREMISES, EQUIPMENT & SUPPLIES
Jackson County Parks and Recreation will furnish all equipment and supplies as listed in EXHIBIT A for operation of services as agreed.

3. TERMINATION
Group understands that County may cancel this Agreement at any time, should facilities become unavailable, payment to County is not on time, or Group defaults on any of the terms or conditions of this Agreement.

4. CANCELLATION
No cancellations shall be made less than 96 hours prior to the picnic. In the event of cancellation less than 96 hours, Group will be liable for all costs incurred by County including catering services, supplies, and staff.

In case of rain, the group may postpone the picnic without penalty provided, however, that one full working day notice is given. It is Group's responsibility to notify the county before 10:00 am one working day prior to the picnic's postponement due to rain. If an acceptable postponed date cannot be found through no fault of Group, a full refund will be given.

5. COMPENSATION
Group agrees to make payment in full to Jackson County not more than fifteen (15) days after the picnic in the amount stated in EXHIBIT A.

6. MAINTENANCE & REPAIR OF EQUIPMENT
Group shall repair at their expense any and all loss or damages to county property caused by Group, their agents or employees.

IN WITNESS WHEREOF, the parties hereto have caused this Agreement to be executed this day and year first above-mentioned.

BY:_____

Director, Department of
Parks and Recreation

_____
Company or Group

_____
Authorized Signature
&Printed Name

_____
Title

_____
Address

_____
City, State, Zip Code

"EXHIBIT A"
GROUP OR COMPANY PICNIC AGREEMENT
COUNTY OF JACKSON
DEPARTMENT OF PARKS & RECREATION

1. This agreement is for picnic services to be provided _____, 19 ___ at _____ County Park from the hours of _____ to _____

2. On the above date, the County shall provide the following catering services at the specified time:
_____
_____
_____

3. On the above date, the County shall provide the following activities:
_____
_____
_____

4. On the above date, the County shall provide the following supplies to conduct activities or as requested by the group:
_____
_____
_____

5. Compensation for the above services shall be paid by the group as follows:

_____

_____

6. All sound-producing devices or loudspeakers must have prior written approval of the Director of Parks & Recreation Department. The following sound devices will be used:

_____

_____

Once a group has confirmed that they will use the service, the staff reserves a shelter and has a group picnic service agreement signed. This legally binding agreement contains a description of the services to be provided and the terms of cancellation, insurance provision and payment.

The actual picnic coordination and arranging begins approximately two weeks prior to the picnic. The caterer is booked and arrangements made with entertainers and equipment suppliers. During the final week, the department reserves a park vehicle for staff use, produces banners and directional signs, and makes necessary purchases such as awards and prizes. Picnic staff members are contacted to confirm the hours that they will work. They arrive at the picnic site two hours prior to starting time with all necessary supplies.

STAFF

The special-events coordinator hires two types of staff for group picnics: a group picnic supervisor and recreation leaders. Each picnic requires one supervisor and between two and six recreation leaders, depending on the number of people attending and the types of activities planned. The supervisor, under the jurisdiction of the special events coordinator, is responsible for hosting the picnics. He or she directs the caterer, entertainers, contractors, and recreation leaders to the designated areas and facilities, oversees all picnic activities, and supervises programs offered by recreation leaders. This position requires enthusiasm, creativity, and good leadership skills. Qualified supervisors must have completed sixty semester hours at an accredited university in recreation and leisure

services, or a related field, or two years of full-time paid or volunteer experience in an organized recreation program, and must have a valid driver's license. Supervisors are compensated at the rate of $4.90 an hour, and must be available to work thirty to forty hours during the weekends.

Recreation leaders, under the guidance of the supervisor, are responsible for leading children's and adults' group games during the picnic. They set up the game area, organize teams, lead games, award prizes, and assist with clean-up. Leaders must have completed thirty semester hours in a recreation field or have one year of experience in an organized recreation program. They must also possess basic skills in organizing and leadership to oversee games and sports contests for large groups. A valid driver's license is a must as well. Recreation leaders receive four dollars an hour and must be available on most weekends from May to September.

Job announcements are sent to area colleges and universities by February. Recreation and leisure service departments also advertise positions through public announcements and at the Missouri Parks and Recreation Association's annual conference. The department holds interviews during the Easter break and follows these with training sessions in park regulations, CPR, First Aid, and picnic games in late April. Meetings are held during the summer as necessary.

CATERING

A major part of any picnic is food. To provide a reliable service, Jackson County enters into an exclusive contract with a catering firm for all county needs each year. Staff hold a pre-conference bid to apprise interested area caterers of the specific service criteria which are expected under contract. (See Figure 1.7.) The caterer must have the capacity to handle multiple group picnics on the same day and reschedule a picnic with a minimum of six hours' notice. They must also be able to accommodate any group size. The catering contract allows the special-events coordinator to quote a price to the group before contracting the caterer. The firm which best meets the requirements is awarded the contract.

FIGURE 1.7

Catering Requirements for Group Picnic Contracts

Caterer must meet or exceed service within each of the following criteria:

1. All menu listings as they appear on the Group Picnic Services (G.P.S.) menu must be available from caterer on a regular basis as a standard menu selection available to any catering client. Any discrepancies in menu-listing description and actual preparation must be noted and labeled "Attachment A," e.g., liquid smoke/barbecue sauce poured over meat is not the same as hickory-smoked meat.

2. Prices must be consistently representative of menu selection per group number. Prices may not fluctuate by season or group.

3. Caterer must offer a standard a la carte menu on a regular basis. This menu must include each individual item listed on the G.P.S. menu. Include a complete a la carte listing and prices as "Attachment B."

4. Picnics will be one-meal affairs unless otherwise determined by G.P.S. coordinator. Service time shall not exceed 1 1/2 hours for a group of 500 or less and shall not exceed 2 hours for a group of 500-1,000. Labor charges for additional serving time per person should be listed as "Attachment C."

5. Caterer must have a minimum of 3 serving attendants for groups of 300 or less and an additional attendant for each 100 additional guests unless determined unnecessary by G.P.S. coordinator in the instance of a self-service event only.

6. All catering attendants must be consistently attired and maintain a well-groomed appearance. Long hair must be pulled back, with no frayed jeans or short shorts allowed. Caterer is responsible for ensuring that staff maintain a high standard of personal hygiene.

7. Caterer must arrive no less than on (1) hour prior to picnic-serving time as determined by G.P.S. coordinator.

8. Caterer will have the capability of handling multiple group picnics on the same date. List two dates within the past fifteen months in which a multiple picnic booking occurred, the companies booked on those dates, the company contact, and the phone number to call. Label "Attachment D." Information will be kept confidential.

9. Caterer must be capable of rescheduling a picnic with a minimum of six (6) hours notice prior to scheduled serving time at no charge if an affair is rescheduled. Offer supplemental information, labeled "Attachment E," that specifies recovery costs if rescheduling does *not* occur within a specified length of time

   A.   6 hours
   B.   10 hours
   C.   12 hours
   D.   18 hours
   E.   24 hours
   F.   36 hours
   G.   Other

10. Caterer must offer complete picnic reference information. Submit a minimum of two references per group range that includes the number in the group and a picnic date that falls within the last 15 months.

    A.   200-500 guests
    B.   500-1,000 guests
    C.   1,000-2,000 guests

    Label as "Attachment F." Information will be kept confidential.

11. Caterer will offer separate consultation and quotes for each event on an on-call basis and will be accessible to County personnel twenty-four hours daily, seven days a week. Submit contact name(s) and phone number(s) as "Attachment G."

12. Price quotes shall include (at minimum):

    A.   Two (2) entree choices
         Three (3) salad choices
         One (1) bread choice
         One (1) dessert choice
         Two (2) beverage choices
         as determined by group and as chosen from G.P.S.menu.
    B.   Complete delivery, buffet-table covering, buffet set-up, service, and clean-up.
    C.   All paper goods and utensils.

D. All condiments (mustards, mayonnaise, ketchup, relishes, pickles, salad dressings, etc.)

13. Supply proof of inspection and licensing as "Attachment H."

14. As a supplement, attach a list of any other specialty items or services not mentioned above that would also be included in quoted prices as "Attachment I."

15. The caterer shall carry Jackson County as an additional insured party on their liability coverage. A certificate of insurance shall be required 10 days after notice of award to successful bidder. Attach proof of current coverage as "Attachment J."

ENTERTAINMENT/ACTIVITIES

Recreation leaders initiate and guide activities. The department provides the equipment for badminton, volleyball, softball, whiffleball, bingo, and horseshoes. Leaders may use relay races, treasure hunts, and new games to separate children from their parents so both may enjoy the outing. The department can contract out for other equipment and activities such as balloon walks, Jacob's ladders, carnival games, mouse races, or a petting zoo or pony ring to be operated during the picnic if a group desires. These and all other types of entertainment such as bands, clowns, and magicians are personally viewed by the special-events coordinator prior to contracting. Arrangements must usually be made approximately two weeks in advance to ensure booking.

EVALUATION

The final action in the group picnic service is evaluation. The department mails surveys to each group or company with their final invoice. (See Figure 1.8.) This gives guests the opportunity to rate location, food service and quality, and program and activity content. They can also make suggestions for improving picnic services. Such evaluations provide valuable input for special-events coordinators, who use them as a basis for continually upgrading services.

FIGURE 1.8

Group Picnic Services

Evaluation

Thank you for utilizing Jackson County Parks and Recreation Group Picnic Services.

Please take a few minutes to complete this brief evaluation and return it to:

Group Picnic Services
Jackson County Parks & Recreation
22807 Woods Chapel Road
Blue Springs, MO 64015

In the future, our program will be expanded to offer more activities and entertainment. Your comments will help us determine the needs of groups like yours so we may better serve you.

Group Name:_____

Please return this evaluation by:_____

Please rate the following by circling one (1) letter:

1. How was _____ as the location of your picnic?

    A. Excellent
    B. Good
    C. Adequate
    D. Fair
    E. Poor

    Why?

    _____

    _____

2. How was the service and quality of food provided?

    A. Excellent
    B. Good
    C. Adequate
    D. Fair
    E. Poor

    Why?

    _____

    _____

3. How was the leadership and program content of the children and/or adult activities?

   A. Excellent
   B. Good
   C. Adequate
   D. Fair
   E. Poor

   Why?

   _____
   _____

4. How was the program schedule for the picnic?

   A. Excellent
   B. Good
   C. Adequate
   D. Fair
   E. Poor

   Why?

   _____
   _____

5. What additional services would you like us to offer at your next picnic?

   _____
   _____

6. How can we make your picnic more convenient?

   _____
   _____

7. Will you use our Group Picnic Services again next year? _____ If not, why not?_____

   _____
   _____

8. Please list any additional comments or suggestions below. We appreciate your input!

   _____
   _____

Thank you for your cooperation!

Mary A. Campbell
Special-Events Coordinator
Jackson County Parks & Recreation Department
22807 Woods Chapel Road
Blue Springs, MO 64015
(816) 795-8200

CONCLUDING COMMENTS

The group picnic provides a valuable service to companies and other visitors while benefitting the department at the same time. Programs create awareness of the county park system, encourage positive public relations with businesses and other influential groups, increase use of picnic areas, and generate revenue through services provided. What makes the picnic service so popular? Staff relieve visitors of the burden of organizing the affair, entertaining the children and cleaning up the mess. The group's only obligation is to have a good time.

The Group Picnic Service organized a total of twelve picnics in the summer of 1986, which was its first operating season. These included outdoor affairs for corporate employee associations, a hospital, and a political rally and ranged in size from approximately one to fifteen hundred people. (See Figure 1.9.)

The first year of operation for all enterprise programs in the department is considered experimental. This was essentially a test-market exercise on a relatively small scale. The response from participating groups convinced the department to retain the program. In 1987, it anticipated arranging thirty-five picnics.

FIGURE 1.9

1986 Group Picnic Service Schedule

Date	Group	Attendance
June 7	Scholley, Inc.	125
June 14	General Instrument, Inc.	200
June 21	St. Joseph Hospital	1000
June 22	Waddell & Reed	250
July 19	Yellow Freight	1200
August 2	The Labor Council	1500
August 16	K.C. Missouri Credit Union	150
September 6	Missouri Public Service	1020

September 7	Realex Corporation	270
September 19	Missouri Lottery	180
September 20	DITMCO	500
September 27	Kansas City Peterbilt	120

SOURCES:

Jackson County Parks and Recreation Department
22807 Woods Chapel Road
Blue Springs, Missouri 64015

County of Sacramento
Department of Parks and Recreation
3711 Branch Center Road
Sacramento, California 95827

4

Golf-Course Revenue-Generating Ideas from Four Public Agencies

The four golf-course revenue ideas described in this case include two different approaches to sponsoring individual golf holes adopted in Jackson County and Topeka, a special golf event which generated publicity and new business in Seattle, and two innovative programs for increasing pro-shop revenue in St. Petersburg.

JACKSON COUNTY'S GOLF-HOLE SPONSORSHIP

The Jackson County Parks and Recreation Department has implemented an annual golf-hole sponsorship program to help fund improvements and general operation at the new Longview Lake Golf Course, along with clubhouse facilities which the department operates. Staff have targeted these sponsorships toward local businesses who benefit from the exposure and other promotional benefits they receive as hole sponsors.

The golf-hole project is part of the comprehensive sponsorship program which the department operates in all its divisions. Staff make an effort to match the interests and target markets of local businesses with the socio-demographic make-up of the golf course clientele. Located in a scenic area adjacent to the Longview Lake, the course attracts a middle- to upper-middle-class clientele from a large surrounding area A

list of prospective sponsors is compiled from this market area. The list includes such businesses as banks, restaurants, beverage companies, savings-and-loans organizations, and automobile dealerships.

Each year the department develops a sponsorship proposal that outlines the details of the golf-hole sponsorship program and the promotional opportunities associated with it. The proposal is then mailed to approximately fifty targeted businesses. This method of soliciting golf-hole sponsors has two major advantages; businesses are more likely to sponsor a golf hole when they are personally invited to do so, and the department does not incur the expense of a promotional campaign. Interested businesses are asked to phone the department to reserve their golf-course hole. By offering the sponsorships on a yearly basis, the department is free to make changes in the program as the golf course and its target markets change. The department believes that it is able to generate more funds for the golf course over a period of years with an annual program such as this one, which requires a relatively small investment, than by offering long-term sponsorships that demand relatively large contributions.

Costs and Benefits. A one-year golf-hole sponsorship requires a six-hundred-dollar commitment from the sponsoring company. In return, companies receive the publicity generated through the sponsorship. The department produces photographs of company representatives at their sponsored hole for the company's use and prominently displays a sponsor board in the clubhouse. A photo display is designed for the sponsor's business. Staff also attach sponsor name plates to tee markers of respective holes. (See Figure 1.10.) Sponsors are ensured widespread visibility through both media-covered celebrity golf tournaments and the number of golf rounds played by public golfers during the year. Finally, sponsors are recognized in the departmental program tabloid that is distributed quarterly to approximately 100,000 homes in the Kansas City area.

The sponsor commitment of six hundred dollars is comparable to prevailing local rates for similar exposure. The department obtains current advertising rates for small billboards and signage based on the number of people expected to view them. The golf course is expected to average approximately fifty thousand rounds of golf per year. Staff then base required sponsor investments on current advertising rates for that amount of exposure. The six-hundred-dollar solicitation request is described not as a fee for advertising but as a tax-deductible contribution to a non-profit agency. The department offers the sponsor an opportunity to enhance the company's public image while contributing to the public golf course.

Each of the twenty-seven holes were sponsored within thirty days after the first annual sponsor proposal was mailed, generating 16,200 dollars for the golf course. The department uses these funds to make continuous improvements to the golf course and related facilities.

TOPEKA'S ADOPT-A-GREEN PROGRAM

The Topeka Parks and Recreation Department in Kansas has instituted a lifetime golf-course sponsorship program to raise funds for the development of an additional nine holes and to expedite the rebuilding of the eighteen existing greens on the only city-owned public golf course in Topeka. The city owns the land designated for the additional holes and had budgeted for the replacement of the existing greens over a ten-year period. However, it lacked the resources necessary to develop the additional holes. Instead Mr. Lou Falley,

FIGURE   1.10

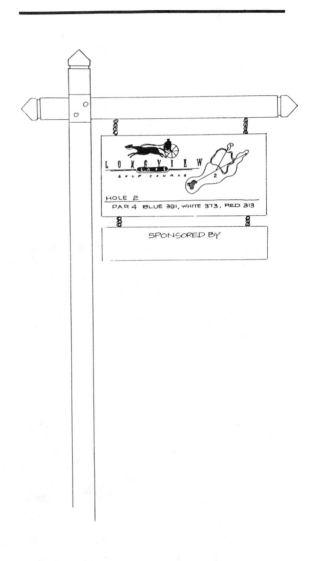

a leading citizen in Topeka with a personal interest in the golf course, took the initiative and developed the Adopt-a-Green golf-course sponsorship program.

The Adopt-a-Green program is administered through the Topeka Parks and Recreation Foundation, a non-profit 501 (c) (iii) charity under the direction of a nine-member board of trustees who work with the department to identify needs and seek contributions. As a prerequisite, a lifetime golf-course sponsorship requires a five-thousand-dollar contribution from an individual or corporation. The incentives for adopting a golf green include tax benefits and the associated public-relations boost. All contributions to the foundation are tax-deductible, and staff place a brass plaque that displays the name of the sponsor near the tee marker. Golf-course sponsors are also recognized in the department's catalog of programs, which is distributed twice a year to thousands of area residents.

The Adopt-a-Green program is promoted primarily through the personal efforts of Mr. Falley. One of the original builders of the golf course, he is involved in many community projects. This makes it easy for him to personally contact individuals and corporations in search of golf-course sponsors. Staff also promote the program through the foundation brochure and the department's catalog.

The revenue generated from the sponsorship program speeds renovation of existing greens. Over a period of ten years, money budgeted for green rebuilding will replace the expanded sponsorship revenue and help to develop nine additional holes. To date, various corporations and individuals have sponsored twenty greens. Eleven have been rebuilt. (See Figure 1.11.)

SEATTLE'S SEVENTY-FOOT PUTT CONTEST AND GOLFER VOLUNTEERS

Each year the Seattle Parks and Recreation Department arranges the Seventy-Foot Putt Contest for a two-week period. The event takes place from 10 am to 6 pm each day at two of the city's golf courses in conjunction with celebrity golf tournaments. Anyone can answer the challenge, including children and non-golfers, whereas the more usual hole-in-one competitions are limited to serious golfers.

In the 1986 contest, all who participated received a free drink from Coca-Cola. Anyone who successfully holed a seventy-foot putt was eligible for a free large

FIGURE 1.11

Companies Involved in Topeka's Adopt-a-Green Program

Nestle Foods, J.P. McCarthy	Green #5A
North Plaza State Bank, Richard Campbell	Green #6B
Highland Park Bank & Trust, Allan Rolley	Green #2B
First National Bank, Tom Clevenger	Green #9B
Merchants National Bank, Don Spencer	Green #5B
Kent Brown Chevrolet	Green #4B
Charles Bennett	Green #7C
Fidelity Bank	Green #3C
Fairlawn Plaza State Bank, Russ Watkins	Green #4C
Noller Ford, Inc. Laird Noller	Green #8C
Falley's, Inc., Lou Falley	Green #3A
Mass Merchandisers, J.D. Erwin	Green #4A
Vic Blakely	Green #1C
Ed Bozarth	Green #1A
Capital Distributors, Bill Renbarger	Green #2C
Fleming Company, Joe Noble	Green #2C
Lapeda, Inc., Eldin Danehauer	Green #1B
Palmer News, Joe Lumpkin	Green #3B

Commerce Bank & Trust,
    Emery Fager   Green #9C

Southwestern Bell Telephone,
    Ed Whitaker   Green #2A

pizza from Shakey's, a local pizza parlor. They were
also invited back to participate in a shoot-out final at
the end of the two-week period. Forty-five people
qualified for the final, and they brought family and
friends to watch. During the contest, all had the same
opportunity to win. Thus, if five people were successful in round one, those five made it to round two and
the contest continued until a single winner emerged.

The entry fee is three balls for a dollar. In 1985 the
winners received a vacation at a Mexican resort, sponsored by a travel agency. In 1986 the prize at one
course was a trip to a new golf resort in Phoenix, Ari-
zona, and at another it was an electric lawn mower,
Leonardo golf bag, and a year's free supply of Coca-
Cola. Each of these events raised two thousand dollars
and introduced many new people to the golf courses.

Considerable media coverage also resulted. Two local radio stations agreed to broadcast the names of people who holed the putt each morning in their sports
shows. Similarly, local television carried not only
extracts of the shoot-out, but preliminary teaser pieces.
The stations even hosted the organizers of the event on
talk shows.

At the city's Jackson Municipal Golf Course, the
fairway of the first hole was a major concern because
of the presence of many potholes. The pressure from
use was so great that it was unrealistic for the city to
consider closing the hole for the several days it would
take its relatively small golf-course crew to fix the five
hundred potholes scattered along it. Golfers had been
justifiably dissatisfied for several years.

To resolve the problem, the city closed the course
between 5 am and 8 am for one morning. Then they
worked with course golf organizations who invited
golfers to come at this time and donate their labor to
solve the problem, after which they were invited to
play at no charge in a tournament. Over seventy-five
golfers volunteered and the damage was repaired.

INCREASING REVENUE AT ST. PETERSBURG'S PRO SHOP

The pro shop at the City of St. Petersburg's Mangrove
Bay Golf Course is operated directly by the city. The
city's golf-course manager, Mr. Jeff Hollis, has introduced two innovative programs which have successfully built a clientele for the pro shop, increasing its
turnover and profitability.

Hollis implemented the first program at selected
tournaments. It involves designating a 150-yard, par-
three hole as a "target hole." Golfers face the challenge
of driving the ball into a circle with a fifteen-foot ra-
dius that has been drawn around the tee. This challenge is magnified by the opportunity to make wagers
on the outcome.

Originally, Hollis invited golfers to pay one dollar
to take part in this program. If they successfully hit
the target zone they won a sleeve of golf balls. This
plan was not very profitable. At the suggestion of the
golf professional at the course, Steve Hasselbring,
Hollis altered the procedure. He invited players to
invest any amount they wished between five and fifty
dollars. If players failed to hit the target zone, they received vouchers valued at the same amount they invested that they could redeem at the pro shop. If they
hit the target zones, they received a similar voucher,
but its value was double the amount they had invested.

From a player's perspective, this is a no-lose situation that offers every incentive to invest in the wager.
From management's point of view it is an all-win situation. Typically, when the wager hole is used at a
one-day tournament, golfers invest about seven hundred
dollars while the department pays out only forty dollars
worth of "double value vouchers." Thus the majority
of players are unsuccessful but still keep their five-to-
fifty-dollar voucher, which they can redeem at the pro
shop. By paying out the double-value vouchers to
players, management does not simply donate forty
dollars worth of goods; the vouchers are redeemed at
the shop's retail prices, which are substantially greater
than the price of goods at cost. In addition, the
program generates traffic beyond the value of the
vouchers because once golfers are attracted into the pro
shop to redeem their vouchers, they often either buy
additional goods or use the voucher as partial payment
for more expensive goods.

The second program is called Club Day. Introduced
for the first time in April, 1986, it was so successful

that it will become an annual event. Five leading manufacturers of golf clubs — Wilson, Hogan, Spalding, Titlist, and Pro Group — were invited to send their representatives to the Mangrove Bay Course to participate in this special event.

Staff provided tables at the course's driving range for each of the companies to display their range of golf clubs and promotional material. The golfing public were then invited to come and try out this equipment at no cost. Salesmen who manned the tables were able to answer questions on design, length of club, shaft type, and so on. The city invested a thousand dollars to promote the event by placing advertisements in the St. Petersburg daily paper for two successive Saturdays, and posting fliers around the clubhouse for a month in advance of the event. In addition to promoting the demonstration, the city provided the range and supplied free balls.

Over five hundred people attended Club Day. All the demonstration clubs were available for purchase through the pro shop. The pro shop had a major sale in association with the event at which clubs and other goods were discounted. On the day of the event, sixteen sets of clubs were sold. This total rose to fifty sets in subsequent sales that were directly attributable to customers' experiences at Club Day. The sets retailed for between three hundred and five hundred dollars.

Pro-shop sales that weekend were fifteen thousand dollars whereas normal sales volume for the pro shop for the whole month of April had been ten thousand dollars in previous years. In addition to direct sales, another benefit that resulted from Club Day included attracting new people to the Mangrove Bay facility. Some were sufficiently impressed to become regular users. Others who had played on the course before had never been aware of the pro shop and the range of products it offered. Thus the event also brought long-term benefits to the course.

SOURCES:

Jackson County Parks and Recreation Department
22807 Woods Chapel Road
Blue Springs, MO 64015

President
Falley's, Inc.
Topeka, KN 66603

Concession Coordinator
Seattle Parks and Recreation Department
Room 210, Municipal Building
Seattle, WA 98104

Manager of Golf
875 62nd Avenue, N.E.
St. Petersburg, FL 33702

5

Raising Revenue from Exhibitions

Some park and recreation agencies have become in-
volved in fairs or exhibitions. By sponsoring a fair or
exhibition, an agency serves as broker. The event
offers an opportunity for clientele groups with a spe-
cific interest to interface with exhibitors whose prod-
ucts and services cater to them.

Opportunities for agencies to sponsor exhibitions
and fairs are substantial because appropriate themes or
topics embrace the full spectrum of leisure activities.

The example discussed here is a large-scale Garden
Show Exhibition. It illustrates that in addition to
offering a valuable service, sponsorship of fairs and
exhibitions can become an additional source of
revenue.

ORGANIZING A FLOWER, LAWN AND GARDEN SHOW

"Suddenly it's Spring" — or so it seems for Kansas
City residents each February as Bartle Hall comes alive
with the annual Flower, Lawn and Garden Show, a six-
day exhibition spectacular featuring horticulture-related
displays, demonstrations, sales, and live entertainment.
Exhibitors and visitors from a four-state area crowd
into the two-square-block Kansas City Convention
Center to experience one of the country's largest garden
shows.

The show, which has been in existence since 1961,
was purchased by the Kansas City Parks and
Recreation Department in 1983 for 175,000 dollars.

The department had been involved with the show for
many years, designing and setting up the feature display for a fee. The owner, a private businessman who
wished to sell the business and retire, approached the
Kansas City Parks and Recreation Department with an
offer. Under the terms of the agreement, the department
purchased the name and rights to the show, and the
purchase fee was paid in installments from the profits
accruing from their first three shows. The department
made the final purchase payment and retained over
forty-five thousand dollars after their third show in
1986, thus acquiring rights at no cost to the taxpayer.
Total income generated by the show comes from two
sources: sale of floor space and sale of admission
tickets.

Exhibits and Commercial Booths. Bartle Hall contains approximately 200,000 square feet of exhibition
space. This space is partitioned by a floor plan and
portions are sold to businesses and groups for booths
and exhibits. Income from these sales comprises approximately one-half of the show's total revenue. The
sale of space begins in July. The department hires a
salesperson to recruit exhibitors and conduct sales. It
also donates space to non-profit horticulture-related
organizations.

Show participants fall into two basic categories:
those who sell home-, yard-, and garden-related
merchandise and those who set up displays and exhibits
or conduct demonstrations. Approximately eighty to

ninety percent of show participants sell their wares. Commercial booths designated for those marketing particular kinds of merchandise are uniformly ten by ten feet or ten by twelve feet. These are arranged in rows separate from the exhibits. Rates for these spaces are three dollars a square foot. The department charges an additional fifty dollars for corner booths because they provide extra exposure.

Non-selling exhibitors comprise the remaining ten to twenty percent of show participants. These groups set up various displays and demonstrations for educational and informational purposes or for advertising exposure. The 1986 show featured 175 exhibits. Exhibit spaces are laid out in a variety of shapes and range in size from three hundred to four thousand square feet.

Exhibits are categorized into four classes according to how they relate to the flower, lawn, and garden theme. Class One exhibits are most related while Class Four are least related. Figure 1.12 lists the show categories. The price per square foot of exhibition space is based on the class. (See Figure 1.13.) Consequently, Class One exhibits are the least expensive while Class Four are the most expensive with Classes Two and Three falling between them. The department offers volume discounts for Classes One through Three. Class One exhibitors purchasing over a thousand square feet of space receive a discount of fifteen cents per square foot. Class Two and Three exhibitors who purchase over nine hundred square feet receive discounts of twenty-five and fifty cents per square foot, respectively. The 1986 show grossed 130,743 dollars from the sale of floor space.

Exhibitor Agreements. All show participants are required to sign a legally binding agreement with the Flower, Lawn and Garden Show to follow the rules adopted for the conduct of the show. (See Figure 1.14.) Each exhibitor must show proof of insurance and surrender the right to make liability claims against the show or the department. Backdrops and electricity are provided for non-commercial exhibitors if they request them. Spaces may not be sublet to other businesses without permission from the department. The agreement provides for master passes given to representatives of each exhibit. Exhibitors sign these agreements when they purchase the space.

FIGURE 1.12

1986 Flower, Lawn and Garden Show Categories

CLASS ONE: NURSERIES - GARDENS - FLORAL DISPLAYS - AND LANDSCAPE DEMONSTRATIONS

Garden Centers
Flower Shops
Nurseries
Landscape Contractors

CLASS TWO: GREEN INDUSTRY - In the lawn on the lawn but not landscaping

Pavers	Fertilizers	Ties
Seeds	Cut Flowers	Grills
Irrigation	Sod	Furniture
Rocks	Play Equipment	Flower-Shop Sales
Books*	Fences	Potted Flowers
Gazebos	Statues	Ceramics

CLASS THREE: TOOLS - Tools and equipment to take care of the garden

Garden Tools	Mowers	Decks
Tillers	Chain Saws	Patios
Tractors	Pools	Driveways
Spas		

CLASS FOUR: ON THE HOUSE - IN THE HOUSE - IN THE GARAGE

Porches	Wine	Potpourri
Art Work*	Wood Stoves	Siding
Sun Lamps	Crafts	Trailers
All-Terrain Vehicles	Awnings	Tours
	Plant Hangers	

* Horticulture-related material

FIGURE 1.13

Exhibitor Fees for Flower, Lawn and Garden Show 1986

Floor Space Sales - Price to Exhibitors

Class I	$1.50 sq. ft.
	over 1,000 sq. ft., $1.35 sq. ft.
Class II	$2.00 sq. ft.
	over 900 sq. ft., $1.75 sq. ft.
Class III	$2.50 sq. ft.
	over 900 sq. ft., $2.00 sq. ft.
Class IV	$3.00 sq. ft.
	No volume discount
Commercial Booth	$3.00 sq. ft.
(10 by 10 &	Plus $50.00 per corner
10 by 12)	

Admissions. Ticket sales provide the second source of income for the Flower, Lawn and Garden Show. Available individually or in group packages, they come in a range of different prices. (See Figure 1.15.) General admission fees account for approximately ninety-seven percent of ticket revenues. Prices range from $1.50 for children aged six to twelve to $4.00 for adults. Discounts are offered to students aged twelve to twenty-one and senior citizens aged sixty and over. Staff also distribute coupons for fifty cents off an adult ticket through local businesses. Coupons for a dollar have previously been printed in the Kansas City newspapers for use during the first two days of the show. Traditionally, these two days attract the fewest number of visitors, so this helps distribute visitors more evenly over the six days of the show.

Groups like garden clubs, Golden Age organizations, and schoolchildren are admitted for single fees of twenty-five and fifteen dollars. Garden clubs are in-vited to sell tickets for the show in return for a portion of the revenue from each ticket.

Dealer tickets are sold to horticulture-related retailers for two dollars and fifty cents each. Dealers may then use the tickets to promote their businesses by offering them as premiums or giving them away to customers who come into their stores. The 1986 show attracted 45,000 to 50,000 visitors and grossed 137,000 in ticket revenues.

Food and Entertainment. Food and entertainment are almost as important to the event as the exhibits. A corner area of approximately thirty-five-hundred square feet is reserved for a local restaurant that contracts with the department to provide food and beverage service during the show. Contracted and assuming their own liability, concessionaires also operate stands during the show.

The Flower, Lawn and Garden Show features a continuous flow of live entertainers, including stage bands, walk-around Dixieland bands, pianists, FTD (Florist Transworld Delivery) flower-arrangement demonstrations, and various other amusements. Performers are booked for various lengths of time and paid a wide range of fees. The Kansas City Zoo sponsors an elephant act free of charge.

Promotion. The promotional effort behind the Flower, Lawn and Garden Show is substantial. In fact, the fifty thousand dollars spent on advertising is the greatest single expense incurred by the department in connection with the exhibition.

An advertising firm is hired to handle the advertising campaign. This firm develops advertisements for use on television, radio, newspapers, and signboards. They also print discount coupons and display them in stands located in various flower shops, gardens, and other related businesses in Kansas City. These coupons and others offered in newspapers are offered during the first two days of the show and serve a promotional function.

The department itself promotes the show through on-site activities. Live broadcasts air over local radio

FIGURE 1.14

Contractual Agreement with Show Participants

Full Price of Space ....
Total Sq. Footage...
Deposit Required (25%)..
Dec. 1, 1986 (25%)...
Jan. 15, 1986 (25%)..

1987 KANSAS CITY FLOWER, LAWN AND GARDEN SHOW
Offices at: 5605 E. 63rd Street, Kansas City, Missouri 64130 / 816-523-2784
Make checks payable to: Flower, Lawn & Garden Show, mail to above address
AGREEMENT made this..day of..............................., 19...........,
by and between KANSAS CITY FLOWER, LAWN AND GARDEN SHOW, hereinafter called the Licensor and
....
....
.... hereinafter called the Exhibitor, party of the second part, WITNESSETH:

That the said Licensor, for and in consideration of the payments and agreements on the part of the Exhibitor to be made and performed, hereby grants to the Exhibitor the right to use space in .... **BARTLE EXPOSITION HALL** .... designated as **SPACE** .... on the diagrams of **KANSAS CITY FLOWER, LAWN AND GARDEN SHOW** .... Date .... **FEB. 17 thru 22, 1987**..for the exhibition of
.... on the following terms and conditions:

First: The use of said space shall be subject to said Rules and Regulations and to all further rules and regulations now or hereafter adopted for the conduct of said show, which are hereby made a part of this agreement and to which the Exhibitor agrees strictly to conform.

Second: The Licensor will issue to the Exhibitor a maximum of four (4) exhibitor credentials (master passes) for a one booth display, six (6) for a two booth display and pro rata to those Exhibitors whose displays occupy bulk space. The credentials will be issued in the firm name. THE EXHIBITOR AGREES NOT TO PERMIT CHILDREN TO USE HIS CREDENTIALS.

Third: The Exhibitor will hold the Licensor harmless from any damage, expense, or liability arising from any injury or damage to said Exhibitor, his agents, servants, employees, the general public, or to the property of said Exhibitor, occurring in the Hall, the approaches and entrances thereto, by virtue of his occupancy hereunder or anything connected with said occupancy.

Fourth: The Exhibitor agrees to pay for the right to use said space the sum of ....
.... ($.................................)
dollars, payable as follows, viz: Twenty-Five percent (25%) deposit to accompany contract; Twenty-Five percent (25%) **December 1, 1986**; Balance of Fifty percent (50%) **January 15, 1987**. No refunds will be made. EXHIBITOR CREDENTIALS CANNOT BE ISSUED UNTIL SPACE IS PAID IN FULL.

Fifth: If the Exhibitor fails to make either of said payments at the time appointed therefor, all rights of the Exhibitor hereunder shall cease and terminate, and any payments made by him on account hereof prior to said time shall cease and terminate, and any payments made by him on account hereof prior to said time shall be retained by the Licensor as liquidated damages for the breach of this agreement as aforesaid, and the Licensor may thereupon resell said space.

Sixth: This license may be terminated by the Licensor at any time on the breach of any other of the conditions hereof by the Exhibitor, and thereupon all his rights hereunder shall cease and terminate, and any payments made by him on account hereof prior to said termination shall be retained by the Licensor as liquidated damages for such breach, and the Licensor may thereupon resell said space.

Seventh: The Exhibitor hereby names...as his duly authorized representative in charge of his exhibit.

Eighth: The Exhibitor shall not assign this license, or sublet, or license the whole or any part of the space hereby contracted for, unless expressly approved by management.

Ninth: The Exhibitor agrees not to install, or cause to be installed, any special or additional signs, apparatus, shelving or standards which will protrude more than eight (8) feet from the floor along the rear of a 10 x 10 foot booth or more than three (3) feet from the floor along each side of the booth, or install, or cause to be installed, any merchandise which will obstruct the view of other exhibits. (The Director of Exhibits will advise Exhibitors in this respect. This applies only to diversified section.)

Tenth: This agreement shall be binding upon the parties hereto and their respective executors, administrators, successors and assigns.

IN WITNESS WHEREOF, the parties hereto have hereunto set their hands, the day and year first above written.

KANSAS CITY FLOWER, LAWN, AND GARDEN SHOW

By...

_____Phone #
_____Business
_____Home

Exhibit Name...

Signed By..

Please sign and return to our office. Exhibitor's copy will be returned by mail.

FIGURE 1.15

Admission Fees for Flower, Lawn and Garden Show 1986

General Admission

Adults	$4.00
Adults w/coupons	3.50
Students (12 to 21)	2.50
Golden Age (60+)	3.00
Children (6 to 12)	1.50

Other Tickets

Dealer Tickets	2.50

Group Tickets

Golden Age	$25.00
Garden Clubs	25.00
School Groups	15.00

Garden Club

Discount Tickets	3.50 Sale Price
	3.00 Turn-In Price

stations with well-known radio personalities and horticulture extension agents speaking from the floor of the show. The department also gives away hanging baskets and a riding lawn mower donated in alternate years by John Deere and Kubota. Additionally, the department spends nearly ten thousand dollars a year on its own feature exhibit, justified as a contribution to general horticulture education. This promotes their work of beautifying the Kansas City environment.

Staff-contracted Services. The Flower, Lawn and Garden Show is produced by independent contractors and temporary employees under the direction of the Superintendent of Forestry and Landscaping and his assistant. These two full-time staff members work an average of one hour per day all year to organize the show. They hire a temporary employee to begin selling floor space in July. This person receives a salary and a commission from sales as an incentive. The department contracts for an exhibition decorator to provide the decor for the show, a floor manager to coordinate exhibitor move-in and move-out, a paramedic to be present during the entire event, and ticket takers for the door. Temporary secretaries also type name tags, answer phones, and handle mail and other correspondence. The department's organizing staff attends the Philadelphia Flower Show each year to solicit ideas for the Kansas City show.

CONCLUDING COMMENTS

The Flower, Lawn and Garden Show generates many indirect dollars for the local economy of Kansas City by attracting outside visitors and thousands of dollars in net income for the department. The financial statement shown in Figure 1.16 summarizes the income produced and the expenses incurred to produce the 1986 show.

The show operates with an enterprise fund budget. The department must carry over approximately fifty thousand dollars each year as start-up funds for the next year's show. Since the department has made a final purchase payment, they anticipate a substantial increase in profits from future shows. Profits generated from the Flower, Lawn and Garden Show are used solely for funding horticulture-related products.

FIGURE 1.16

1986 Flower, Lawn and Garden Show Income and Expenses

INCOME:

Tickets 136,963.50

Floor Space 130,734.05

Total Show Income. 267,706.55

EXPENSES:

PRODUCTION

Advertising/Promotions 52,699.78

Production 22,390.70

Entertainment 4,850.00

Printing (tickets). 2,987.96

Feature Garden Display 11,385.54

Total Production Expense 94,313.98

SELLING:

Salaries (Space Salesperson) 15,290.00

Commission (Space Salesperson) 15,988.90

Rent (Downtown Office) 1,625.00

Phone 2,602.88

Electricity 48.11

Total Selling Expense 35,554.89

BARTLE HALL RENTAL:

Rent ($5,000/day) 30,000.00

User Fee 5,636.30

Equipment Rental 232.50

Total Bartle Hall Rental 35,868.80

Missouri Sales Tax 7,544.07

Total Show Expenses 173,281.74

Total Show Income 267,706.55

Total Show Expenses 173,281.00

Final Purchase Payment 48,975.21

Retained Earnings 45,449.60

SOURCE:

Kansas City Parks and Recreation Department
5605 East 63rd Street
Kansas City, MO 64130

6

Five Recreation Revenue-Producing Programs

The five programs discussed here do not produce large amounts of revenue, but they enable an agency's range of service offerings to be expanded without cost to the agency, and they are readily adaptable to all types of communities. The sale of discount books to client groups generates direct revenue for the agency, while coupons encourage people to try out services and help build clientele. Providing a birthday-party service meets the needs of working parents. Featuring local park scenes on Christmas cards can both publicize the park and generate revenue, as can a food-tasting special event promoted in a park. Video offers an efficient means of delivering instructional services to clients.

DISCOUNT CARDS
AND COUPON BOOKS

The Johnson County Park and Recreation District in Kansas solicited discounts from all local businesses who had connections with the agency's athletic programs — like sporting-goods stores, eating establishments, and fitness centers. The discounts were inserted as coupons into a booklet. The department then sold these booklets for five dollars exclusively to people who participated in the county's programs. The value of the discount coupons exceeded five hundred dollars. Athletes received a good value, stores discovered an efficient way to persuade a valued target group to try their products, and the program generated about

ten thousand dollars net per annum for the department, as well as enhancing rapport with both businesses and clients.

A variation of this theme was the discount card, which the department either sold to program participants for five dollars or offered free as an incentive to sign up for selected County programs. The card offered discounts of two to twenty-five percent at selected businesses. Where coupons were designed to get people to sample a store, the card was intended to encourage them to continue patronizing one.

Every participant received an introductory letter explaining the program, accompanied by the "invitation to purchase" form and a brochure listing participating businesses. (See Figure 1.17.) Instructors and team captains handed out forms to participants, but they had to be mailed back, and no other handling mechanism was provided. Then the coupon book or card was mailed to participants. They were required to exhibit their membership card for all purchases, and upon request had to provide at least one piece of identification to prove authenticity.

Businesses were solicited by mail. The department set up two mailing periods in June and December to send out a form and a letter. (See Figure 1.18.) Their enrollment in the card program covered a one-year period, after which it had to be renewed. Sports shops were enthusiastic because their products were targeted directly at the clientele they sought to attract.

FIGURE 1.17

Brochure Showing Participating Businesses

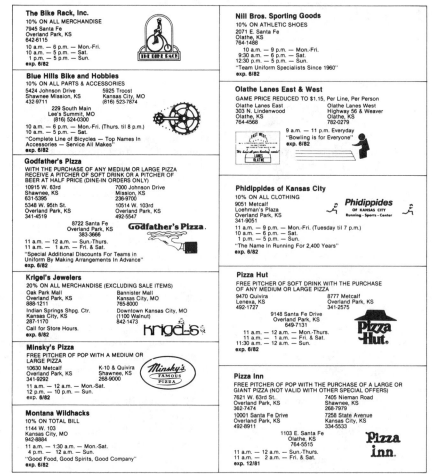

ENROLLMENT IN THIS WELL-RECEIVED PROGRAM IS NOW OPEN TO LEAGUE PARTICIPANTS IN SOFTBALL, BASKETBALL, VOLLEYBALL, FOOTBALL, SOCCER AND GOLF. REGISTRATIONS RECEIVED NOW THROUGH DECEMBER 31, 1981 ARE VALID THROUGH JUNE 30, 1982. A SECOND ENROLLMENT PERIOD WILL BE HELD IN DECEMBER WITH AN EXPIRATION DATE OF DECEMBER, 1982. A SUPPLEMENT WILL LATER BE DISTRIBUTED TO ALL MEMBERS, AS NEW MERCHANTS WILL BE ADDED TO THE RAPIDLY GROWING LIST.

THESE PARTICIPATING BUSINESSES ARE OFFERING INVALUABLE SAVINGS TO YOU

(listed below in alphabetical order):

The Bike Rack, Inc.
10% ON ALL MERCHANDISE
7945 Santa Fe
Overland Park, KS
642-6115
10 a.m. — 6 p.m. — Mon.-Fri.
10 a.m. — 5 p.m. — Sat.
1 p.m. — 5 p.m. — Sun.
exp. 8/82

Blue Hills Bike and Hobbies
10% ON ALL PARTS & ACCESSORIES
5424 Johnson Drive   5925 Troost
Shawnee Mission, KS   Kansas City, MO
432-9711   (816) 523-7874
          229 South Main
          Lee's Summit, MO
          (816) 524-0300
10 a.m. — 6 p.m. — Mon.-Fri. (Thurs. til 8 p.m.)
10 a.m. — 5 p.m. — Sat.
"Complete Line of Bicycles — Top Names In Accessories — Service All Makes"
exp. 6/82

Godfather's Pizza
WITH THE PURCHASE OF ANY MEDIUM OR LARGE PIZZA RECEIVE A PITCHER OF SOFT DRINK OR A PITCHER OF BEER AT HALF PRICE (DINE-IN ORDERS ONLY)
10915 W. 63rd   7000 Johnson Drive
Shawnee, KS   Mission, KS
631-5395   236-9700
5348 W. 95th St.   10514 W. 103rd
Overland Park, KS   Overland Park, KS
341-4519   492-5547
          8722 Santa Fe
          Overland Park, KS
          383-3666
11 a.m. — 12 a.m. — Sun.-Thurs.
11 a.m. — 1 a.m. — Fri. & Sat.
"Special Additional Discounts For Teams in Uniform By Making Arrangements In Advance"
exp. 6/82

Krigel's Jewelers
20% ON ALL MERCHANDISE (EXCLUDING SALE ITEMS)
Oak Park Mall   Bannister Mall
Overland Park, KS   Kansas City, MO
888-1211   765-8000
Indian Springs Shpg. Ctr. Downtown Kansas City, MO
Kansas City, KS   (1100 Walnut)
287-1170   842-1473
Call for Store Hours.
exp. 6/82

Minsky's Pizza
FREE PITCHER OF POP WITH A MEDIUM OR LARGE PIZZA
10630 Metcalf   K-10 & Quivira
Overland Park, KS   Shawnee, KS
341-9292   268-9000
11 a.m. — 12 a.m. — Mon.-Sat.
12 p.m. — 10 p.m. — Sun.
exp. 6/82

Montana Wildhacks
10% ON TOTAL BILL
1144 W. 103
Kansas City, MO
942-8884
11 a.m. — 1:30 a.m. — Mon.-Sat.
4 p.m. — 12 a.m. — Sun.
"Good Food, Good Spirits, Good Company"
exp. 6/82

Nill Bros. Sporting Goods
10% ON ATHLETIC SHOES
2071 E. Santa Fe
Olathe, KS
764-1488
10 a.m. — 9 p.m. — Mon.-Fri.
9:30 a.m. — 6 p.m. — Sat.
12:30 p.m. — 5 p.m. — Sun.
"Team Uniform Specialists Since 1960"
exp. 6/82

Olathe Lanes East & West
GAME PRICE REDUCED TO $1.15, Per Line, Per Person
Olathe Lanes East   Olathe Lanes West
303 N. Lindenwood   Highway 56 & Weaver
Olathe, KS   Olathe, KS
764-4568   782-0279
          9 a.m. — 11 p.m. Everyday
          "Bowling is for Everyone"
          exp. 6/82

Phidippides of Kansas City
10% ON ALL CLOTHING
9051 Metcalf
Loehman's Plaza
Overland Park, KS
341-9051
11 a.m. — 9 p.m. — Mon.-Fri. (Tuesday til 7 p.m.)
10 a.m. — 6 p.m. — Sat.
1 p.m. — 5 p.m. — Sun.
"The Name In Running For 2,400 Years"
exp. 6/82

Pizza Hut
FREE PITCHER OF SOFT DRINK WITH THE PURCHASE OF ANY MEDIUM OR LARGE PIZZA
9470 Quivira   8777 Metcalf
Lenexa, KS   Overland Park, KS
492-1727   341-2575
          9148 Santa Fe Drive
          Overland Park, KS
          649-7131
11 a.m. — 12 a.m. — Mon.-Thurs.
11 a.m. — 1 a.m. — Fri. & Sat.
11:30 a.m. — 12 a.m. — Sun.
exp. 6/82

Pizza Inn
FREE PITCHER OF POP WITH THE PURCHASE OF A LARGE OR GIANT PIZZA (NOT VALID WITH OTHER SPECIAL OFFERS)
7621 W. 63rd St.   7405 Nieman Road
Overland Park, KS   Shawnee, KS
362-7474   268-7979
10001 Santa Fe Drive   7258 State Avenue
Overland Park, KS   Kansas City, KS
492-8911   334-5533
          1103 E. Santa Fe
          Olathe, KS
          764-5515
11 a.m. — 12 a.m. — Sun.-Thurs.
11 a.m. — 2 a.m. — Fri. & Sat.
exp. 12/81

Johnson County Park & Recreation District and the cooperating merchants in this brochure are hopeful you will consider the value of these discounts which players are afforded through participating in the Athletic Association. The program is being offered as a benefit to all players in Johnson County Park & Recreation District leagues. The district is not, however, endorsing these businesses and emphasizes that if a merchant should decide not to honor a discount as stated herein, the Johnson County Park & Recreation District cannot be held responsible. All offers are subject to change without notice and are invalid on sale items and other specials.

FIGURE 1.18

Johnson County Park and Recreation District Athletic Association

1. Contact person if other than on the enclosed letter:

_____

2. Phone number during the day:

_____

3. When is the best time to reach you at this number?

_____

BROCHURE INFORMATION

1. Full name of business as you would like it to appear in the brochure:

_____

2. List below the address and phone number of the location offering the discount. If more than one location is offered, please list:
   ADDRESS (include street, city, state, zip)

_____

PHONE NUMBER

_____

If any additional space is needed, please use back.

3. Description of discount:
   Example A: 10% on all merchandise, excluding sale items
   Example B: 15% off all food items

_____

4. Expiration date if other than June 30, 1982:

5. Slogan or brief statement describing your business (optional):

_____

6. Logo: Please return a logo (accompanied by this form), preferably 1 x 1", if available, to include in the brochure. If you do not have a logo in this size, send what you have and we will attempt to reduce it to the desired size.

7. Number of brochures desired:_____

8. HOURS _____ to _____M-F;Sat.
   _____Sun. _____

9. _____
   signature   date

10. Please return the form and logo to:

   _____
   _____

A caveat accompanied these discount programs with the following statement: "Please note that we are not endorsing these businesses and that Johnson County Park and Recreation District is not responsible for merchant default in recognizing discounts."

The City of Seattle Parks and Recreation Department took advantage of an existing citywide coupon book compiled and distributed commercially by a company called Entertainment. This book is published annually and contains many hundreds of pages of coupons. Divided into color-coded sections according to service — restaurants, sports, hotels, etc. — the book contains coupons that offer discounts with savings of up to fifty percent.

It costs nothing to put coupons in the book, and the company takes care of all artwork and printing. The Seattle Department had thirty-two coupons in their 1985 book and were well-satisfied with the new and down-time business that they generated. In a follow-up study of coupon users at their golf course, the department discovered that seventy-eight percent of them had not used the city's golf courses in the previous six months and that fifty-two percent had never used their courses before at all. These golf coupons admitted two people for the price of one. However, once inside the facility, these patrons made additional purchases of balls, cart rentals, food, beverages, etc., thus generating additional revenue for the city.

Entertainment sells sixty thousand of these books in Seattle and charges thirty dollars for them. The city distributes them through its recreation centers and earns a seven-dollar commission on each book sold. It is anticipated that a thousand will be sold in this way this year.

Seattle has also inserted its coupons into similar books which the same company produces in

Vancouver, British Columbia, and Portland, Oregon, in an effort to attract visitors from these cities to the department's facilities when they visit Seattle. In the first six months of 1985, the public redeemed four thousand coupons from these two cities at the Seattle Zoo or Aquarium.

Entertainment now produces these books in seventy-five major cities across the United States. Advantages of their program are identified in their brochure, part of which is reproduced in Figure 1.19. Park and recreation departments are increasingly making use of them. Seattle's experience suggests that they are a successful means of attracting a new clientele to facilities.

If this particular company doesn't operate in your city, link up with a coupon distributor who does. Almost every city has one.

BIRTHDAY PARTIES

Many mothers today work and find it difficult to arrange birthday parties for their children. To meet this need, the Johnson County Park and Recreation Department in Kansas hired a full-time staff member as a children's birthday-party specialist. She organized and led birthday parties for children from three to eleven years old.

The parties lasted forty-five to ninety minutes. The specialist visited with parents ahead of time to discuss the type of party they wanted, the kind of house in which to hold it, and the types of activities parents permited in their house. She encouraged parents to hold the party at one of the Johnson County recreation facilities since they offered more space, gave her more time to set up for the party, and provided more activity options.

The specialist made special arrangements with suppliers such as caterers to provide birthday cakes and pizza. A per-child cost of three to six dollars was established for this service depending on the type of party requested. The specialist brought along a wide repertoire of party activities appropriate for any particular age, along with articles like hats, streamers, food, party favors, and prizes.

It took about six months for this business to become established. Annual revenues ranged from 35,000 to 40,000 dollars. The problem with this type of service is that once it is established and doing well,

the specialist may decide to leave the district and offer the same service as a private venture, taking clientele away from the district. This did happen in Johnson County.

Although this program was established for children, you may need to create a similar offering for senior citizens.

CHRISTMAS CARDS FOR SENIORS

The Jackson County Park and Recreation Department in Missouri operates 26,000 acres of park land. Each year it enters into an agreement with Hallmark Cards based in Kansas City to use a park scene and develop it into a Christmas card. One of Jackson County's facilities is Missouri Village, an historical recon-structed old town park with structures representing Missouri in 1855. When snow falls in November and December, Hallmark arranges for deer and other animals to be brought to the site. Then they shoot pho-tographs from which they select a card for the follow-ing Christmas season.

Hallmark gives Jackson County fifty percent of the profit that accrues from the sale of that card. They also give the county the card artwork. This is used to re-produce a postcard that is then sold at Jackson Coun-ty's facilities. Typically, Jackson County receives 7,500 to 10,000 dollars per card from this arrangement. The venture creates excellent publicity for the park system and in some instances focuses attention on the aesthetic attractions of some the lesser-known parks.

BITE OF SEATTLE

A promoter put this event together in Green Lake Park, which is Seattle's biggest. He charges fifty restaurants 2,500 dollars each to participate. Each restaurant may sell only one entree for no more than four dollars. The event takes place from a Friday evening to a Sunday in mid-July. In 1985 it grossed 600,000 dollars, and the city received six percent of the gross, i.e., 36,000 dollars. The promoter pays all costs for set-up, clean-up, police, fire, or whatever. He or she also provides entertainment, but this must be approved by the city.

FIGURE 1.19

Entertainment Brochure

HERE'S HOW TO FILL EMPTY SEATS:
PUT THE ENTERTAINMENT˚ INCENTIVE TO WORK.

ENTERTAINMENT® is the easiest, most effective means of attracting customers—and more profits.
Why does it work so well?
People refer to the ENTERTAINMENT® book as a guide that tells them where to find the best places for well-produced, exciting events. Your offer of one complimentary admission with a full-price purchase is a strong incentive for these patrons to attend.

You see the results in more seats sold to people who normally wouldn't be there. Thousands of businesses have used the ENTERTAINMENT® method of cost-free advertising. Since 1962, this effective and proven concept has added to the profits of Theatres, Shows, and Sports, by filling empty seats when they've needed it most.

LET ENTERTAINMENT˚ BRING THE CROWDS TO YOU.

No performer wants to play to an empty house. Everyone benefits from the thrill of excitement that a full house generates.
With ENTERTAINMENT®, you tap into a fresh new market that wants to try new activities. Watch the electricity that happens. The performance sparkles.

The audience is drawn to the performance—and into your house. Concession sales increase. And your reputation is enhanced. Best of all, these new prospects quickly become your repeat customers, helping boost your ticket sales, year after year.

EVERYTHING TO GAIN AND NOTHING TO LOSE.

Most of your overhead is fixed, regardless of attendance figures. With our new patrons filling the house, you'll see a dramatic rise in your profits. Remember: ENTERTAINMENT®'s programs cost you nothing. It's the

perfect no-cost promotion that brings you increased volume and greater profit. The perfect equation gives you everything to gain with nothing to lose.

entertainment.
A quarter-century of profit-building programs.

All the major restaurants in the city feel obligated to participate in order that citizens can inexpensively sample their food. No alcohol is permitted to be sold. At the same time, an adjacent community center holds an arts-and-crafts fair, selling booths for a hundred dollars each to capitalize on the traffic.

USING VIDEO

Jackson County produces and offers for sale or rent approximately thirty "how-to" video-tape programs. These half-inch VHS tapes may be rented for three dollars for three days. If the tape is broken or damaged, borrowers are required to pay for it. However, the expense is frequently covered by homeowners insurance. The program generates about ten thousand dollars gross revenue per year.

Some of the tapes are purchased by the county and feature nationally known professionals demonstrating techniques, e.g., Pele on soccer, Billie Jean King on tennis, Jane Fonda on fitness, and Willie Mosconi on billiards. In these cases, the county operates only as a retail service similar to that of any store.

However, the county also produces a number of video tapes featuring their own instructors. These tapes are produced on a trade-out basis. One individual does the taping in exchange for a free golf pass. Another individual pays all the costs of producing the tapes and receives fifty percent of all revenues which accrue to Jackson County from their sale or lease. These videos are promoted in the county's literature and are available directly from the county. They are also sold in Missouri by three video chain stores and promoted on local-access cable television stations. The county puts "how-to" tapes on the cable as samplers. That way, if people miss them, they can obtain copies from the district.

The tapes cover such topics as golf instruction, how to build a canoe, how to teach children to swim in a backyard pool, backyard-pool maintenance, competitive swim strokes, fly-tying, cooking, weaving, growing herbs, and so on. In some instances, tapes are produced as an educational tool. For example, a tape of golf etiquette is shown in the snack bar of the golf club, so while golfers are eating or taking a break, they are informed of the cost incurred when they fail to replace divots or damage the course. Instructional tapes are also shown in the snack bar.

County instructors enjoy doing the tapes. Since many of them subcontract for classes, they also recognize that the increased visibility they derive from the video tapes, which focus on basic skills, may translate to more participants in their classes. This is because people who view them become sufficiently interested in moving on to more advanced skills.

Other related uses for video include the following. First, the county has made tapes available to a hotel in the area that offered to run them as a pilot test on its internal system. That way guests are made aware of recreation opportunities in Jackson County. The success of this pilot test is still being evaluated. Second, the county provides exclusive rights to sponsors to videotape softball games. Hence a local bar that sponsors a softball event may tape the game and replay it later that evening in the bar. This is popular with players and attracts business to the bar. Players are required to sign releases permitting this when they register in the league.

SOURCES:

Jackson County Parks and Recreation Department
22807 Woods Chapel Road
Blue Springs, MO 64015

Johnson County Park and Recreation District
6501 Antioch Road
Shawnee Mission, Kansas 66202

Concessionaire Coordinator
Seattle Parks and Recreation Department
Room 210, Municipal Building
Seattle, WA 98104

Section 2

Acquiring Donations

Acquiring donations for park and recreation projects has never been more difficult. Recent tax reforms have reduced the level of corporate and individual taxes dramatically. This has had the effect of removing most of the tax incentive for making donations. Now contributions are more costly to make.

At the same time that tax incentives have been substantially reduced, the retraction of federal grant programs and the reluctance of local governments to incur residents' wrath by increasing local taxes have forced many agencies to more actively solicit donations to maintain their services. The competition from other public services and the non-profit sector for funds is acute. Public agencies such as education and health organizations have been proactive in the donation arena for much longer than parks and recreation. They are sophisticated in their approach to fund-raising.

The cases included in this section are intended to offer hands-on guidance and success stories about acquiring donated money or resources. The first case offers a systematic approach to soliciting corporate resources. This approach consists of six stages and suggests angles and insights that agencies have found useful in persuading the corporate sector to buy into park and recreation projects. In the second case, William Penn Mott, director of the National Park Service, relates how he solicited a large contribution from a reluctant donor when he was superintendent of parks for the City of Oakland. Mott's vignette is analyzed, and the general principles underlying the success of his solicitation effort are discussed so they can be adopted by others.

Case 9, the third in this section, describes the systematic process implemented by the City of Anaheim for soliciting contributions from corporations. Cases 10 and 11 detail St. Petersburg's imaginative launching and implementation of a bequests program, along with two examples of financing capital projects by persuading people to buy a personalized brick.

Case 12 documents four examples of how agencies have acquired donated trees and made constructive use of dead Christmas trees. The final case here describes how Anaheim took a highly successful proactive approach to stemming vandalism in parks by involving school groups in the maintenance and development of parks. The program has created a strong, positive feeling of stewardship in the students.

7

Six Steps to Soliciting
Corporate Support

Persuading the corporate sector to buy into park and recreation services is emerging as a primary means by which many agencies are able to expand their number of offerings or improve the quality of their existing services. This paper suggests a practical systematic approach to soliciting corporate resources.

Corporate entities can contribute either monetary or "in-kind" resources. There are three types of in-kind resources that an agency may solicit. First, it may request a loan of manpower from a business that has expertise that the agency needs. For example, a business may loan people for a fixed period of time to assist in establishing a cost-accounting system, developing a new computer system, formulating a marketing plan, or training managerial personnel in new techniques. Second, a business may give equipment or facilities to an agency. Third, it may enhance its reputation by endorsing an agency's program. This institutional support may add visibility and credibility to a particular service. Such contributions make it possible to view every business in a community as a potential contributor to the agency.

Efficiency and effectiveness in soliciting corporate support are likely to be a function of (1) the philosophy which underlies an agency's approach; (2) the extent to which the approach is systematically organized, and (3) the staff and volunteer resources allo-

cated to it. Discussion here is limited to the first two of these factors.

A marketing approach to solicitation involves carefully targeting specific companies or types of companies, identifying their motivations for giving, and designing marketing programs that bring about mutually satisfying exchanges over an extended period of time. Agency personnel who accept this philosophy and use it to guide their actions are likely to view themselves as brokers who are concerned with furthering the welfare of the potential support organizations by encouraging them to buy into the agency's services. They seek situations in which both the business and the agency win. The intent is to persuade potential companies to invest some of their resources in a program from which it is anticipated they will derive at least equivalent benefits.

A systematic approach to soliciting corporate resources involves six steps. They are: prospecting and targeting, preparation, presentation, handling objections, closing, and follow-up.

PROSPECTING AND TARGETING

The first two stages in a systematic approach are prospecting and targeting, along with preparation. These stages address the first part of a well-known sales aphorism, "plan your work — and then work your plan." Typically, too little thought is given to planning a solicitation effort. This is often the difference between its success and its failure.

Two tasks are involved in identifying particular businesses that should be targeted. The first is to compile a comprehensive list of all local businesses, and the second is to prioritize these prospects based on how likely they are to be responsive to requests for resource support.

Developing a List of Prospects. A list of businesses in a jurisdiction is likely to be available from the Chamber of Commerce. In larger cities it may be useful to limit the list to a manageable length by establishing a minimum size criterion. The minimum size will vary according to the number of businesses in the community and the magnitude of the contributions being sought. For example, in Dallas, Texas, an appropriate minimum size may be businesses that employ over five hundred people because there are almost four hundred businesses that meet this criterion. In a city of 15,000 people, an appropriate criterion may be businesses that employ more than ten people.

Agencies may consider adopting not only a minimum size, but a maximum one. This may enable them to find a niche or market segment in which there is not as much competition for corporate support. It is likely that the largest business enterprises will also be identified as prospects by many other non-profit organizations. Thus, in the case of Dallas, an agency may find more responsive prospects among those businesses that employ 250 to 500 people since there may not be as much competition for their resources as there is in the segment comprised of the largest companies.

Targeting. A campaign-oriented agency targets its efforts at "everybody" while a marketing-oriented agency aims at "specific somebodies." Once the prospect list has been developed, businesses should be assigned to one of three prospect categories: "hot," "medium," and "cold." Their assignment should be based on four criteria: (1) the size of the business; (2) its image in the community; (3) its past proclivity for working with public agencies; and (4) the extent to which a corporation's interests, products, and target markets match the make-up of the clientele likely to participate in a program.

Larger businesses have greater potential for investing resources in recreational and park services. In addition, their senior managers are more likely to be "big people" with a broader view of the world and a more sensitive community conscience.

Businesses that have a negative image may be responsive because of their need for good publicity. Recreation and park agencies generally have a wholesome, positive image, and linkage with them may help a business redeem its public image. However, an agency has to be careful that support from such sources does not tarnish its own image. The emerging debate over the appropriateness of public agencies accepting sponsorship of their events by the manufacturers of adult products such as beer, liquor, and cigarettes is an example of this dilemma.

If a company has worked with a public agency in the past, even if it was not the recreation and parks department, then it is likely to be a prime prospect. Such businesses are aware of the benefits to be gained from supporting public-agency programs, so recreation and park personnel have only to persuade them that they will receive a better return on their investment in this field than from other agencies that they have supported in the past.

For a company to be a "hot" prospect, a program's target markets must match a company's product and target markets. Thus a key question staff must ask about each program for which corporate support is being solicited is "What kinds of companies can use this program or event to improve their business, given the target market it is likely to draw?"

PREPARATION

After a list of the most probable prospects has been derived, the next stage is to prepare an approach tailored to each of these prospects. The preparations commitment is time-consuming but essential. Success at soliciting support is more likely to result from good preparation than from good presentation techniques. Three questions should be addressed in the preparation stage: (1) what is in it for them? (2) who in the business enterprise should be contacted and what is their role? and (3) what is the appropriate time to contact that person?

What Is in It for Them? The marketing approach requires an agency to identify what companies are likely to want in return for investing their resources in a program. This information forms the basis for developing a presentation for each prospect. Tailoring the presentation is probably the most important phase in the entire solicitation process. Too often, agency personnel spend too much time thinking about their own needs and not enough time considering what their prospect, the potential investor, wants. The managers of a business have no mandate to give the company's money away in donations to needy causes. A business makes contributions because it believes that it is in its selfish interest to do so. Managers are required to invest company funds only in projects that will bring a return from that investment to stockholders.

Businesses select projects that offer them the best return from the large array of investment opportunities that are available. A company's "problems" should be the focal point of a solicitation effort. The challenge confronting an agency is to suggest how the benefits that a project offers can contribute to alleviating these problems. There are four overlapping categories of benefits which businesses may seek: (1) enhanced image and visibility; (2) community developments; (3) employee morale; and (4) product trial.

Enhanced Image and Visibility. The visibility that companies seek can take several forms. They may seek recognition that is of long duration. For example, XYZ Corporation may donate the XYZ Park that will always be there for the community to see and use, and give it long-term visibility. An alternative way in which companies may seek extended recognition beyond the immediate target audience is through media coverage.

Some managers believe that failure to visibly respond to social concerns damages their public image. They view contributions to public agencies as a means of positively responding to criticisms that their business is not a good neighbor or is "profit hungry," that business serves no social good, and that it does not distribute its resources equitably among those who generate them.

Community Improvements. A second major benefit that recreation and park agencies offer to businesses is

the opportunity to contribute to making their community healthy and attractive. If a community is healthy, then its business climate is also likely to be healthy. Urban customer-service businesses such as retailers and financial institutions are particularly sensitive to the need for an ordered, attractive environment. If the quality of life in the service area in which they are located deteriorates, the financial health of their businesses is also likely to do so. Improvement in the health of society will mean, in the long term, improvement in the profits of business.

In addition, an area must be an attractive place to live and work in order to entice desired employees to a business. Hence companies must be prepared to invest in projects that contribute to this end. It is difficult to persuade people to relocate because of the relatively high-interest mortgage rates and the social upheaval that move inflicts upon families. An environment that offers superior amenities and quality of life is often a more effective incentive in enticing highly skilled and sought-after people to move than monetary incentives.

Employee Morale. Supporting public recreation and park programs may be perceived as a means of building employee morale. Shell Oil Company alludes to this concern in its donations policy statement:

> Our programs of charitable giving are related to the civic responsibilities of employees of the sponsoring Shell companies. In a sense, the Company regards itself as their partner in citizenship. For this reason, most charitable support is made on a local basis where Shell people live and work.

Product Trial. Companies are continually trying to find ways of persuading potential customers in target markets to try their products. Trial enables non-users to evaluate a product and is perceived by companies as the most effective way to convert a non-user to a user. If a recreation event can offer a target audience to a company that sells consumable products, and the company is permitted to give out samples at the event, then the company is a prime prospect as an investor in the event.

These four types of benefits overlap; they are not mutually exclusive. They represent a broad framework to guide agencies' thinking. When the benefits most likely to appeal to a targeted company have been determined, the agency then asks the next preparation question: "Who in the business enterprise should be contacted and what is their role?"

Who Should Be Contacted?   In small businesses this question is easily resolved, but in large companies it often requires a surprising amount of effort to find out who should be contacted. If the benefit offered is primarily enhanced image and visibility or product trial, the key decision-maker is likely to be in a company's marketing division. However, if the benefit is improvement in community or employee morale, the location of the decision-maker in the company may be more difficult to ascertain. For example, the author spent some time identifying the contact person responsible for investments in such projects in eight major companies in Houston. The titles of these eight individuals were: community and employee relations manager; manager of contributions and public relations; public relations director; director of civic affairs; vice-president in charge of human resources; director of communications; director of donations for the Houston region; and vice-president of advertising.

Once the contact person has been identified, that individual's role in the decision-making process has to be ascertained. There are likely to be several corporate actors who play a role in the decision process, and they fall into three categories: gatekeepers, influencers, and decision-makers. However, one person may fill more than one of these roles.

It is most probable that the contact person in a large company will be a *gatekeeper*. This person may simply receive the request for resources and forward them to others who make the decisions through the company's established channels. Alternatively, the gatekeeper may be assigned the role of a "first screener" who eliminates some requests and forwards a selective list to the decision-makers. The manner in which a gatekeeper passes along a request may be critical. If he or she is not personally supportive, the information may be relayed less accurately and with fairly evident disapproval. Thus the gatekeeper is a key person in determining the response to a request and must be "won over." Agency personnel should try and persuade gatekeepers to permit them to present their cases directly to the decision-makers. This ensures that the proposal is presented in its best light and that there is an

opportunity to respond to any questions or objections the decision-makers may have.

An *influencer* is a person whose views or advice help shape the attitudes of decision-makers and who thus exerts some influence on final decisions. The third type of actor is the *decision-maker*, who decides whether or not to accede to the request. The decision-maker may be either a member of an in-house committee comprised of executives from a variety of divisions who meet periodically to review resource requests or an individual. If an individual is sole decision-maker, he or she may only be authorized to make a limited contribution. For example, managers at local and regional levels may be permitted to invest resources of up to, say, two thousand and five thousand dollars, respectively, and amounts over these limits may have to be forwarded to corporate headquarters for approval.

Requests for resources should be directed at the highest level to which an agency can gain access because it has been observed that "top level managers are paid to say yes, while middle-level managers are paid to say no." Senior managers generally have a broader perspective and a more acute social conscience. For these reasons, they are most likely to be responsive to contribution requests. Too often there is a mistaken tendency to confine personal contacts to employees at lower levels because agency managers feel less intimidated and more comfortable with them. They merely hope that the request will filter up to key decision-makers.

An important adage in soliciting contributions for a park system is that people give to people first and needy causes or organizations second. This is also true of corporate executives. Success is more likely to spring from personal chemistry than the worthiness of the cause.

This makes it imperative that an agency search for links between its personnel and the gatekeepers, influencers, and decision-makers in a targeted company. The key questions are: "Who on the staff knows any of the key corporate actors?" and "Who can we enlist as an ally?" The best types of links are personal acquaintances, but if these don't exist then it becomes necessary to seek referrals. Are there any mutual contacts who could introduce agency personnel to key company officials? The more intimately an agency's personnel are interwoven into the community structure, the more likely it is that either personal acquaintances or referral opportunities develop.

The agency's task is to learn as much as possible about the individuals who are gatekeepers, influencers, and decision-makers, and to match their backgrounds with senior agency personnel who have similar training. A substantial body of empirical research suggests that positive interaction between the potential contributor and agency representatives is greatly facilitated if their experience, personalities, interests, and lifestyles are compatible. The greater the perceived similarities, the stronger the mutual attraction or affinity between them is likely to be.

PRESENTATION

An effective presentation explains all aspects of the agency's proposition as it relates to the benefits sought by each prospective contributor. The first minute of a presentation can be the most critical part of it even though it represents only a miniscule percentage of the total presentation time. You only have one opportunity to make a first impression. This often determines the receptivity of the potential resource supporter to the substance of the presentation.

While there are many ways of making a presentation, the best approach is interaction, with the prospect performing as an active communicator. This approach begins by exploring the client's needs: "What results would you want to see from a contribution that you made?" The primary task of the agency representative during this stage is to listen and to suppress any premature urges to talk about what the agency has to offer. During the listening phase, the agency representative should consider the features, advantages, and benefits (FAB) of the agency's services that are relevant to the potential contributor's needs.

After the prospect has explained his or her needs, an agency representative using the FAB approach begins explaining the outstanding and unique features of the service or project. The advantages portion of the presentation addresses ways in which the service or project is superior to other investment opportunities available to the potential contributor. The benefits section transforms features and advantages into benefits and addresses the important question, "What's in it for you?"

HANDLING OBJECTIONS

If the presentation is to yield the anticipated result, it is necessary to draw out any objections that prospects may have. Objections should not be dreaded, but welcomed. They provide valuable feedback and are the prospect's way of explaining how to make the presentation successful. Answering objections removes barriers, and the objections themselves provide clues as to the best tack to take for the remainder of the presentation.

Quiet prospects who hold questions and reservations in their minds and give few clues about their inner resistance are likely to be least influenced by the presentation. If they raise no objections, it means either that the prospect was prepared to respond positively at the start or that the prospect is not sufficiently interested to raise an objection.

Over a period of time, agency personnel are likely to hear any objection that can possibly be raised and eventually will not be surprised by any of them. They should "keep track of the flack;" that is, document the objections received and determine the best way to handle them.

CLOSING

At the closing stage, the agency representative typically summarizes the major benefits on which there has been agreement, addresses anticipated objections or reservations about taking the action sought, and requests that the prospect take specific affirmative action. Many people find that closing is the most difficult part of a presentation. They feel guilty or lack the self-confidence to ask for a commitment, or they have not thought about how they will orchestrate the closing to obtain a commitment from the prospect ahead of time.

You can use many approaches to closings. Three of the most common are illustrated below.

— Obtain agreement on a major benefit and then build upon it. "If I understand you correctly, Mr. Smith, you are most interested in increased visibility from your investments." "Yes." "An investment of five thousand dollars would enable us to . . . "

— Ask an open question and pause: "Mr. Smith, you've seen the benefits this investment could provide. What are your reactions?" or "How should we now move ahead?"

— Use the "based-on" technique that refers to a major point which you previously agreed about and build on it: "Based on your desire for maximum visibility, I'd like to suggest an investment of five thousand dollars, which would give you high visibility in the community."

On occasion a prospect may not be prepared to invest in a project at the level the agency seeks when the question is asked at closing. However, there may be a willingness to invest either in a different project at that level, or in the same project at a lower level. Therefore it is desirable for any agency to have more than one project and more than one investment level in mind. Then, if the main investment opportunity is rejected, the agency representative can present other options.

FOLLOW-UP

The success of the initial personal interaction with a prospect should not be viewed in the immediate context of whether the resource will be forthcoming or not. Rather, you should regard it as the beginning of a long-term relationship. A period of time may be needed to consolidate personal relationships before resource support is given. Early efforts may yield relatively little, but you should make them anyway in anticipation of increased return in the future as the acquaintance and confidence in the agency are nurtured.

The way that the follow-up is handled determines the likelihood of receiving future support from investing companies. In the follow-up stage, you should enhance relationships that have already been established. A key to a successful on-going resource effort is not securing new supporters, but retaining previous investors. An old marketing adage says, "your best customers are your best prospects." If investors are pleased with the results of their support expenditures, they are likely to be receptive to future support requests. They are also likely to be valuable sources of testimonials and referrals to others.

If the solicitation effort has been successful and resource support is forthcoming, an agency has two main responsibilities. The first is to keep investors informed and to provide periodic progress reports to them on the status of the project or service. These should identify its present status, outcome, and projected future. Presentation of the outcome in some objective form that measures the effectiveness of contributions is particularly important because business executives need a scorecard to justify their investment to their stockholders and superiors. Developing a short video about the project's highlights and the company's role in the project is an excellent way to accomplish this.

An agency's second responsibility is to make investors feel appreciated as part of the team, and to make sure that they are thanked and recognized in a way they deem appropriate. Some businesses may not seek public recognition and visibility because this exposes them as prime targets for more financial requests.

However, most businesses are likely to seek recognition, particularly in cases where donations rather than sponsorship are being sought. Therefore an agency should have a recognition program. Such a program should be structured in the shape of a pyramid to increase the incentive to invest in order to receive more recognition.

Smaller agencies can use the same principle scaled down to their level. For example, the former director of the recreation and parks department in Grand Island, Nebraska (population 33,000), described their recognition program in the following terms:

Everyone was recognized no matter how small the gift. Gifts of $15 or more were acknowledged with a certificate of thanks and a paperweight with the parks and recreation department logo. A paperweight was selected because it sits on top of a desk and is a very visible symbol of the donation. People who donated over $100 got a personalized plaque etched in gold. The plaque was presented at a formal ceremony by the mayor if the donation was over $100. Any donations over $1,000 rated a presentation by the council, complete with media coverage. If the donor was a member of a local civic or business group, the presentation was made in front of the group by council members to maximize felt importance and to get others in the group excited about making a contribution. After the presentation ceremony, an 8 x 10" color photograph of each donor was posted in the "Hall of Fame," located in the lobby of City Hall, where it stayed for a month.

When projects are turned down, it is often not because a business cannot benefit from them, but rather because their timing is not right for the company. Polite persistence pays off. Thus, immediately after an unsuccessful effort, send a thank-you letter to let prospects know that the time they spent visiting with agency personnel was appreciated. The agency should keep in touch with these people and proceed on the assumption that their company may be a prime prospect for resource support at a future time.

8

How to Solicit a Donation:
A Case Study

William Penn Mott has had a distinguished career in the parks and recreation field. He was superintendent of parks for the City of Oakland, California; general manager of the East Bay Regional Park District; director of the California State Parks system; executive director of the California Parks Foundation; and director of the National Park Service. Throughout his career, he has been known for his perceptive vision, innovation, and a leadership quality which others find inspiring. One of his peers has observed that

> *He makes things possible that wouldn't happen otherwise . . . . Because he has such a great belief in what he was doing himself, he has the ability to inspire others to do more and to do better work than they would otherwise . . . He is a truly great leader in the field with an ability to bring people along with him who wouldn't have come otherwise.*

Mott aggressively solicited private donations in all his positions, long before it was widely acknowledged as being an important management task. He left the City of Oakland in 1962. One of the attractions he added in Oakland was Children's Fairyland. In the following anecdote, he relates how he persuaded Victor Burgeron, founder of the Trader Vic restaurant chain, to make a 25,000-dollar donation to Children's Fairyland. The anecdote was included in a presentation which William Penn Mott gave at the National Recreation and Park Association Annual Congress in Dallas, Texas, in 1975.

This vignette is included here because it illustrates many key ways to successfully solicit a donation. The reader is invited to identify key factors which contributed to Mott's success in acquiring the contribution he sought. A discussion of these factors is included after the story.

WILLIAM PENN MOTT TELLS HOW HE SOLICITED A MAJOR DONATION FOR CHILDREN'S FAIRYLAND IN OAKLAND (CIRCA 1960)

I want to make some points about how to solicit a donation by using an illustration which I think that you will enjoy.

If you are going out to raise funds, whether you do it or somebody else does it, you have to know the person from whom you are going to raise the funds. You have got to do research in advance whether it is a person, a corporation, or whatever. You have to study that organization or individual and understand his background and his interests, and identify his particular concerns.

In Oakland we built Children's Fairyland, and I think a lot of you are familiar with it. It is an animated three-dimensional interpretation of children's stories. I decided that one of the sets I would like to build would be Robinson Crusoe. I wondered where to get the funds, because in Children's Fairyland the whole construction cost was donated and all its operations costs came from the revenue it generated. That was the only way we could get it done.

The thought occurred to me that I would try to get the money from Trader Vic. Some of you may be familiar with the Trader Vic restaurants that expanded out of California around the country. Trader Vic is Victor Burgeron. He is quite a large man, has a limp leg and is what you would visualize as an old gruff sea captain. That's the kind of person that he is. He had never up to that point made a contribution of any kind to the city of Oakland, even though he got his start in Oakland with his Trader Vic restaurant. So I decided that is the man I am going to tackle for Robinson Crusoe because Trader Vic restaurants are built around a Polynesian theme and have some of the kinds of artifacts that were needed for a Robinson Crusoe set.

I researched his whole background and found that he went to the South Seas every year sailing and to collect artifacts; that he was very much interested in Polynesian art and that type of thing; that his wife was particularly interested in children's hospitals and in children. I knew from Trader Vic's background that I couldn't get him to Children's Fairyland under any conditions. But I thought I could get him there through his wife because she was interested in children and the Children's Hospital.

Although I didn't know either one of them, I decided to call Mrs. Burgeron and I told her what I had in mind. I would like her to see Children's Fairyland. I knew she was interested in art. Children's Fairyland was done with an artistic flair and it was designed and developed by an artist with whom she was familiar. I used his name and said, "I would appreciate it very much if you would visit Children's Fairyland and bring your husband so he could see what Children's Fairyland is like, and I could get some counsel from him in connection with the development of the Robinson Crusoe set." She agreed to that.

I got to Children's Fairyland a little after they got there. To get into Children's Fairyland, you have to stoop down to go through the instep of the Old-Lady-Who-Lives-in-a-Shoe entrance. This is so that all adults are at the same level as children when they come into Children's Fairyland psychologically as well as physically. Trader Vic is quite a big man as I told you, both in height and width. He had to stoop down to go into Children's Fairyland. When I came through the gate, I introduced myself. He said to me — and I

am going to use his language now — "What in the heck am I doing here?" and he has a gravelly, gruff voice that you can hear a mile away.

I said, "Well, I decided that I would like to develop a set to interpret Robinson Crusoe for the kids in Oakland. I know that you have a great deal of interest in the art forms of the South Pacific and have spent a great deal of time down there. I know that you sail down there. I need a dug-out canoe; I need some bamboo; I need some goat skins; and I need some parrots and alligators. I thought possibly you would be able to at least get for me a small dug-out canoe that would be in scale with what I'm doing here at Children's Fairyland."

He looked me straight in the eye and he said, "Young man, you don't know anything about the Robinson Crusoe story. Robinson Crusoe was in the Caribbean, not in the South Pacific, and I don't know anything about the Caribbean."

When he made that statement, I knew that he was on my side. He had corrected me. I knew Robinson Crusoe wasn't in the Caribbean all the time. He had corrected me so he was then trapped into assisting. You understand this; he was then ego-involved and became committed.

We talked a little bit and then he said, "I have got to get out of this place, but I will get you the dug-out canoe. I'll do that much for you. I'm going to the South Seas next week."

As he was walking out, I said, "You have a tremendous artist that does the decor for your restaurants. Could he help me a little bit on the design of this?"

Victor Burgeron said, "Sure, talk to him. I'll tell him that you are coming."

Now that the project was moving I had the man who made our models make a beautiful model of what the Robinson Crusoe set was going to look like.

When Victor Burgeron returned from his South Seas trip, he had a beautiful little dug-out canoe right to scale. He had some goat skins which he had brought for me; some bamboo; and he had made arrangements for parrots to be sent. I showed him the model of the set, which was really beautifully done, and I said, "This is what we are going to do. There is your dug-out canoe. This is the way we are going to use the goat skins, the bamboo, and so forth."

He was quite pleased and said, "Well, that's a very nice model. You have done a nice job."

Then I said, "I'm now going out to raise the money to finish this and I appreciate very much what you have done for me in getting this dug-out canoe and the other materials."

He said, "Who in the heck are you going to get the money from?"

I said, "Well, I don't know at this point. I'm going to talk to different people."

He said, "I started this durn thing. I will finish it."

That is exactly what he said. You could hear him all over the restaurant.

I said, "Gee, that's great. If you are going to do that, I sure appreciate it."

I didn't tell him how much it was going to cost. I said, "You want me to go ahead and finish this set?"

He said, "Yes, go ahead and finish it."

I finished the set. I was scared to death as to how I was going to break the news to him of what this thing cost. At that time, in Oakland and throughout California there was a TV series on which they talked about business and what it did for communities. The program had a tremendous rating — everybody was watching it. So I went to them and said, "How about doing Trader Vic's restaurant and his success and relating it to the Robinson Crusoe set in Children's Fairyland?" I took the producer over to the site and he got all excited about the photographic possibilities.

The opening of the set was scheduled so it could be covered by the show. Of course Trader Vic got tremendous publicity. A couple of weeks after the show was aired, I went down to Trader Vic's for lunch and said, "Well, the set is all finished. I hope you appreciated all that TV publicity and promotion."

He said, "It was just tremendous. I am getting letters from all over the state about it. It was just great."

I said, "Well, here is the bill for the set." It was 25,000 dollars. Children's Fairyland is small, and the Robinson Crusoe set is no bigger than a corner of an average-sized room.

When he got the bill and looked at it, you could hear him bellow all the way to the City Hall in Oakland. He gave me a check for 25,000 dollars right there and then and said, "Get out. I never want to see you again."

I have seen him since many times and he always reminds me about this. He really is a great guy.

FACTORS CONTRIBUTING TO THE SUCCESS OF MOTT'S SOLICITATION EFFORT

In the author's view, each of the following points contributed to the success of Mott's solicitation effort. They are not prioritized in order of importance.

1. Mott *targeted* Victor Burgeron for this donation for two reasons. First, the Robinson Crusoe set reflected the atmosphere and public image of Trader Vic's restaurants. Second, the theme also tied in with Victor Burgeron's leisure interest of sailing round the South Sea Islands. Since there were two good complementary approaches to arouse Victor Burgeron's interest, Mott tailored his presentation to these.

2. Mott *prepared thoroughly by investing effort in researching* Victor Burgeron's professional and leisure interests, and those of his immediate family, before making his approach. As a result of this research, the initial contact was made with Mrs. Burgeron because of her known interest in children. She served as the *gatekeeper*, and it was her influence that persuaded Victor Burgeron to view Children's Fairyland. Her presence at the initial site visit and her sympathy for the project presumably made it more difficult for her husband to reject Mott's initial request for artifacts.

3. The approach was *carefully timed* to coincide with Victor Burgeron leaving on a South Seas vacation the following week. This was the ideal time to launch the project and gain momentum by persuading Victor Burgeron to commit himself to active assistance and involvement in acquiring artifacts.

4. Mott *cared deeply* about Children's Fairyland. He was a "product champion" espousing his cause. His conviction, sincerity, and enthusiasm were conveyed to Victor Burgeron.

5. Mott provided *a clear idea of what was envisioned.* The initial visit with Victor Burgeron was on-site — not in an office — so he could clearly see the quality of the other sets and the context of the planned Robinson Crusoe attraction. A model of the set was built so its potential could be easily appreciated. As

the artifacts were acquired, they were incorporated into the set. This way their visibility helped sustain momentum.

6. Victor Burgeron *gradually acquired "ownership"* in the set, so eventually it became his project. Mott did not ask for the 25,000 dollars at the outset. The link and emotional involvement were built slowly and progressively. Mott's initial request was for counsel and advice, then a few artifacts, then the use of the company's artist, then the use of a model to illustrate how the initial artifacts fit in and what remained to be done. Finally, Burgeron identified so much with the project that he offered to finance the whole set.

7. *Extensive and extended media coverage* emerged from the project, giving Trader Vic's restaurants enhanced image and visibility. The commercial value of this publicity far exceeded the 25,000 dollars that Trader Vic invested in the project. Mott did not present the bill until after his establishments got this publicity, so Burgeron was able to place the cost in the context of the economic value of the media coverage of his business.

9

Systematic Solicitation of Contributions from Corporations

The City of Anaheim established a corporate contract office, manned primarily with trained volunteers, to solicit corporate donations. They have developed a systematic approach that includes using targeted lists of companies and recording the outcome of each contact made. This case was first published in a Texas Agriculture Extension Service publication, Developing and Using a Gifts Catalog.

The City of Anaheim, California, established a corporate contact office in the Department of Parks, Recreation, and Community Services. Its purpose is to solicit contributions of money or in-kind services, manpower, and materials to supplement the department's existing resources.

Organizers had three objectives when they established the corporate contact office. These were:

1. To initiate a five-year plan to encourage large corporations and service organizations to "adopt a park" or subsidize a program, such as the Therapeutic Recreation Center, on a continuing basis.

2. To secure corporate contacts for annual programs, such as the Volunteer Recognition Program, Therapeutic Golf Tournament, and Walkathon, to raise money for the Senior Day Care Program.

3. To generate approximately 100,000 dollars worth of gifts for the department's programs through the community by donations of services, manpower, materials, and supplies.

The office was formed in 1982. Until that time, each division within the department had its own independent program for soliciting donations. Often there was no communication between divisions on fund-raising. Whenever one division conducted a fund drive for specific projects, it did so independently of the rest of the organization. There was no coordination between individual campaigns.

Staff members recognized that this lack of coordination impaired the fund-raising effectiveness of the department as a whole. For example, no records were kept that tracked the companies who gave, those who did not, or why. Every year, each division started from scratch with its own fund-raising effort. The department committed itself to a more ambitious, coherent approach to fund-raising that would integrate the efforts of all divisions in the agency. This led to the establishment of the corporate contact office within the department.

This office is managed and supervised by a corporate contact program coordinator. It was staffed by volunteers from 8 am to 5 pm Monday through Friday. The program coordinator is responsible for the scheduling and training of all volunteer staff. Department staff develop project priorities for the office annually. These are approved by the director. (See Figure 2.1.)

When leads are developed which seem likely to involve contributions valued at 5,000 dollars or more, then the department's executive staff becomes involved in the effort. All independent contacts made by staff on behalf of their programs are reported to the corporate contact office. This includes copies of correspondence and reports of verbal interactions.

The time invested in the solicitation effort is primarily volunteer time. A key principle of the corporate contact program was the creation of a data base that included records of fund-raising activities department-wide. Information entered into the data base serves as the foundation for all future efforts to attract resources. Each division serves as a node in the information-gathering network. Every time a staff member contacts a potential prospect, a record of the meeting is entered on a "contact sheet." Contact sheets include who was contacted and when they were contacted, a list of actions detailing the degree of success of the solicitation effort, and the total amount raised. (See Figure 2.2.)

The corporate contact office maintains the following reference and resource materials:

A Master Log of Business Contacts which lists the name of each company contacted, its address, phone number, and contact person. This log is updated each time a staff member contacts the company.

Mailing Lists of Industries are developed so separate lists of companies in each industry are available. This facilitates targeting for specific services which may be required for a particular project — food, for example.

Standard Forms and examples of solicitation letters which can be personalized are available (Figure 2.3), together with such items as contact sheets, presentation folders, certificates, and photograph folders.

Corporate Strategy Notebooks are compiled which document all actions related to previous solicitation campaigns for projects such as the volunteer recognition banquet, Therapeutic Recreation Golf Tournament, wheelchair basketball game, and celebrity basketball game. They include a comprehensive evaluation that contains specific information on business contacts, correspondence samples, promotion, and records of successes and failures. An example of such an evaluation is shown in Figure 2.4.

FIGURE 2.1

Corporate Contact Priorities — 1983-1984

Project (Type of donation and months contacts made)	Priority	Target Amount	Corporate Office Responsibilities	Department Staff Responsibilities
Anything-Goes-ATHON — in-kind donations, financial contributions to seniors (Aug.-Oct.'83)	1	$20,000	Assisting in developing new strategy (research, calls,corresp.) Corporate - 120 hrs.,Recreation Services Manager - 24.Train and supervise volunteers.	Jan Kleeman to organize and implement program. Businesses and community organizations to be involved.
Senior Day Care Center - Major financial donations	1	$10,000	Assist in developing strategy for pursuing donations of $300 scholarships, and grants.	Jan Kleeman to organize and implement.

FIGURE 2.1 (CONTINUED)

Foundation memberships	1				Chris Jarvi
Youth in Gov't Day Sponsorship - in-kind and financial (Jan.-Apr.'84)		$5,000	Provide training and resources to staff and volunteers as requested.		Youth commissioners to make most contacts. Prepare correspondence/ portfolio.
Teen Center Openings - sponsorship, membership sales. (Contacts made Nov. 1983 to June 1984.)		$10,000	Same as before.		Teen center staff to make most of the contacts,prepare corresp. and promotional info. Contact industries benefiting from youth market.
Anaheim Softball Classic - Jan. 1984. (Contacts made between Oct.-Jan. 1984.)		$2,000	Same as before.		Dave Sommers to contact Lamp Post Pizza, Boegie Sporting Goods, Cowboy and Crackers for donations of T-shirts, etc.
Saturday Lunch Program West Anaheim Senior Centre	4	$4,000	Same as before		Lynne Smith and her volunteers are making ongoing contacts for the program.
Dept. slogan/logo - in-kind service.	1	$2,000	Prepare letter follow-up calls and visits to public relations/marketing. Corp. Coord. - 5 hrs a week for 1 mo. - (4 wks.) = 20 hrs. total Rec. Serv. Mgr. 1 hr. a week = 4 hrs.		Tim Barry to assist with with portfolio and follow-up meetings with companies.
Volunteer Recognition Banquet — financial donations, in-kind products and services.	1	$15,000	Prepare letters, follow-up calls, and visits to misc. industries. Corp. Coord. 10 hrs. a week for 3 mos. = 24.		Teen,co-rec and volunteer svcs. section to organize and implement program.
Therapeutic Recreation Golf Tournament	1	$4,000	Assist with new contacts and mail portfolios. Advise about corporate strategy. Corp. Coord. 2 hrs./wk. for 3 mos. - 24 hrs.		Mary Lou Simas will prepare all correspondence, follow up on past contacts, coordinate, and implement program.

FIGURE 2.2

Sample Contact Log Sheet

Mailing   Label

Name: ABC INSURANCE COMPANY

_____
Phone Number   Name:

_____
Phone Number: Name: Address: 17570 GIVING WAY

                                                                     FOUNTAIN VALLEY, CA 92708
_____
Phone Number: Name:

                                                    Contact Person: MR. JOE SMITH
_____
Phone Number: Name:

                                                    Title: CHAIRMAN OF CONTRIBUTIONS
_____
Phone Number: Name:
                                                    Phone: 976-1122
_____

Type of Company: INSURANCE COMPANY

(Describe food, service provided):

Type of assistance they like to give or reasons why they do not:

CONTRIBUTIONS COMMITTEE IS ESTABLISHED IN EACH DIVISION.

IT LOOKS OVER PROPOSALS AND DECIDES WHOM TO GIVE MONEY TO.

VERY STRICT SOLICITATION POLICY FOR PARTICIPATION BY EMPLOYEES.

IT IS ALMOST A BLANKET NO.

Contact Log

Date	Who Called	Reasons	Comments, why called, response, follow-up needed, etc.
08/22/83	M.K.	VOLUNTEER BANQUET	SEND A PROPOSAL AND THEY'LL SEE WHAT THEY CAN DO.
09/28/83		VOLUNTEER BANQUET	RECEIVED LETTER STATING THEIR DESIRE TO GET INVOLVED,
			AND THEY SENT $150.00 TO SUPPORT THIS EFFORT.

FIGURE 2.3

Sample Solicitation Letter

Ms. Joanne Smith
Community Services Manager
ABC Information Services
100 Fifth Street
Orange, CA 92667

Dear Ms. Smith:

Enclosed you will find documentation of a community volunteer program which has won national awards — your community volunteer program!

For the past three years, we have invited local businesses to join us in recognizing the contributions volunteered by individuals and groups which enhance the environment of our community. We are now planning our 1984 Volunteer Recognition Program and would like to offer you the opportunity to join us as a major sponsor. The following are a variety of ways you may wish to invest in the promotion of community volunteerism in Anaheim:

Assist with the production of a multimedia show — "Anaheim Life. Be In It "— promoting some creative new ways to become involved in our community. This show will premiere at the April 28, 1984, banquet before seven hundred volunteers and community leaders, and will be shown for the next two years throughout the city and state. Your company would receive a great deal of visibility in this production. We need in-kind donations and sponsorships to prepare the title slides and program, along with producing the show. Our previous production, "Volunteers in Action in Anaheim," is available for your review as an example.

We need financial assistance to offset the cost of the Volunteer Recognition Banquet. As of this date, we have raised approximately 3,000 dollars toward the cost of meals for the seven hundred volunteers. We need an additional 1,000 dollars. The Anaheim Convention Center will provide a Hawaiian buffet at cost, in support of volunteerism in Anaheim. All sponsors will be acknowledged by the table signs at the banquet, in the official program, in media releases, and in our recreation program brochure, which is mailed to every residence in Anaheim. Attached for your review is a copy of last year's program.

In-kind donations are needed to print the recognition banquet programs, invitations, and tickets. Last year, this service was provided by Pacific Telephone. We wish to continue to improve our banquet program by including pictures of the volunteers in action and written descriptions of the types of services they perform. We have also written to President Reagan requesting a letter of recognition in support of our Volunteer Program, which we anticipate having reproduced in the program. Attached you will find a copy of this letter. This program will be used throughout the year to promote and publicize our community volunteer program. Your company's contribution would be acknowledged in a special section of the program.

We sincerely appreciate your consideration of our request. If you would like additional information regarding our volunteer program, please contact Marie Dixon or Annette Haynes at 999-5191.

Very truly yours,

Christopher K. Jarvi

Director

FIGURE 2.4

Example of a Written Evaluation of a Corporate Contract Effort

The Project

Each major project for which the Anaheim Department solicits gifts is evaluated. This example relates to its Volunteer Recognition Banquet. The Anaheim Department has developed a sophisticated and extensive volunteer program. Each year all individuals and businesses who have participated in the program are invited to a Volunteer Recognition Banquet. More than 700 volunteers and community leaders attend.

The banquet is held only if $15,000 is solicited in in-kind donations or monetary support. To solicit these gifts, the department developed a portfolio which included a solicitation letter, a description of the event and a copy of the previous year's program from the recognition banquet. If an individual or business expressed interest during an initial telephone contact, then the department sent a portfolio to try to translate that interest into a donation. In this Appendix, a sample solicitation letter is reproduced, together with an overall evaluation of the solicitation effort and examples of evaluations of the responsiveness of various industries who were approached.

Overall Evaluation of the Corporate Contact Effort for the Volunteer Recognition Banquet

Program or Event: Volunteer Banquet   Date of Event: April 28, 1983

Total Calls Made	Total Time Spent on Calls	Total Letters Sent	Total Companies Donating	Estimated $ Value of Donations
250	120 hrs.	185 (20 portfolios)	33	$14, 544

General Comments:
Overall, the corporate strategy for this event achieved all its planned objectives. We doubled the financial donations for this program. Prior sponsors for the past 2 years increased their support. Many new industries such as fruit, fabric, airlines, doctors, lawyers and mortuaries were pursued. We experimented with new methods of solicitation such as the use of the portfolio, return postcards for sponsors to indicate their financial donation, varied style of correspondence, and increased use of volunteers to assist in solicitations.

The cause of volunteer recognition in the City of Anaheim surged because of the emphasis President Reagan placed on volunteerism. The response of businesses for this cause was as follows:

Hotels—Overall poor response. Disneyland Hotel® always helps in some way. Hilton® helped on parking. Excellent potential from these two hotels for next year.

Printing—Outstanding response from Pacific Telephone®, Northrop®, Hughes® and Phillips Printing®. The printed banquet program and invitations should be negotiated early with these companies for 1984 banquet.

Food—The biggest in-kind donation was the discount on dinners by the Anaheim Convention Center. We need to negotiate early for dinners for 1984 to remain at $10 and confirm Anaheim Room.

Product industries were good for in-kind donations of products such as fruit. If we know the menu for next year, items of food should be solicited early. Donations should be large enough to warrant a trip to the produce section of L.A.

FIGURE 2.4 (CONTINUED)

Decor—The strategy of utilizing items received such as fabric, flowers, props for the banquet, department events, and other agency recognition programs gave us more leverage for soliciting large donations. We have a written commitment from the County of Orange Social Services Agency to assist us in solicitation in 1984. The Director of Display from Robinson's Department Store® has committed to plan and design for the 1984 banquet. She will supply materials, tools and staff time to decorate.

Evaluations of the Responsiveness of Each Industry

The overall evaluation is compiled from the responses from each industry sector which was approached. The following examples illustrate some of these specific industry evaluations.

Program/Event: Third Annual Volunteer Recognition Banquet
Date of Event: April 28, 1983   **Industry:** *Printing*

Number of Calls to Solicit	Number of Letters Following Solicitation	Number of Follow-up Calls Made after Letters	Number of Companies Actually Donating	Percent of Companies Donating after Letters	Estimated Value of Donations
10	6	10	3	30	$3,250

Comments:
•All large corporations contacted had in-house printing facilities, for example, Pacific Telephone®, TRW® and Hughes®.
•Printing is a donation that really doesn't cost the company anything out of pocket.
•Companies need at least two months advance notice and at least 2 weeks to print. Materials should be as complete as possible when taken to them. These companies are a good resource for design and layout ideas.

Industry: *Fruits*

Number of Calls to Solicit Solicitation	Number of Letters Following after	Number of Follow-up Calls Made Donating Letters	Number of Companies Actually	Percent of Companies Donating after Letters	Estimated Value of Donations
12	6	15	6	50	$1,000

Comments:
Overall, the response by the produce industry was good. E.A. Silzle® donated half a ton of grapefruit and a half a ton of oranges; Del Monte Banana Company® donated 25 cases of pineapple. The industry is mostly located in L.A.; pickups were made between 8 a.m. and noon. Detailed coordination of delivery and pickup arrangements are necessary.

Industry: *Florists*

Number of Calls to Solicit	Number of Letters Following Solicitation	Number of Follow-up Calls Made after Letters	Number of Companies Actually Donating	Percent of Companies Donating after Letters	Estimated Value of Donations
30	15	23	13	15	$435

FIGURE 2.4 (CONTINUED)

Comments:
•Poor timing with poor economic situation and Mothers Day right around the corner. (A handful of florists had gone out of business.)
•1983 florists' donations were $500 below 1982 donations.

Industry: *Fabric/Cloth*

Number of Calls to Solicit	Number of Letters Following Solicitation	Number of Follow-up Calls Made after Letters	Number of Companies Actually Donating	Percent of Companies Donating after Letters	Estimated Value of Donations
12	4	4	1	25	$200 Wholesale $400 Retail

Comments:
Retail fabric stores would not donate even "scrap" yardage. Chain outlets cannot donate from local stores—donations are made from executive offices. These people have standing charities. Wholesalers are most open to solicitation with a lot of advance notice. They will keep us informed of "seconds" that are returned to them and donate them if we call quarterly to determine what they have.

SOURCE:

Anaheim Parks, Recreation and
Community Services Department
200 South Anaheim Blvd.
Anaheim, CA 92805

10

Soliciting Bequests
in Wills

For many years, hospitals and educational institutions have actively encouraged people to leave bequests to them in their wills. In recent years, some recreation and park managers have recognized that the facilities they manage offer many of the same benefits to prospective donors as hospitals and educational institutions. These facilities are highly visible, permanent, give pleasure to many, and are central to the quality of life in a given area.

The most efficient way for a recreation and parks agency to launch a bequests program is to initiate a series of wills clinics. These provide a network of contacts and prospects that serve as a starting point. Subsequently, staff can invent individually targeted and personally tailored approaches, and people attending the clinics may also assist in identifying prospects. Staff may direct wills clinics at either laypersons or professionals.

WILLS CLINICS FOR LAYPERSONS

These are designed for people interested in setting up their own planned giving instrument or will, who are uncertain as to how to proceed. Many are apprehensive about the "legalese" involved, may not understand the range of possibilities, and don't know where to turn for help. A clinic provides the opportunity for these people to get pointed in the right direction, and to be referred to good sources of assistance.

To conduct a clinic, the agency enlists an instructor from a local law firm, law school, bank, or community foundation who can provide an overview of the process of establishing a will and discuss the many options possible.

Attendees come away with a better understanding of wills and potential beneficiary options. They also know where to turn for services. This event is scheduled and publicized as a community service. You can charge a fee to cover expenses for the clinic and suggest bequests to parks as a beneficiary concept or option during the clinic.

A variation on this theme is to bring in several lawyers to provide free, "sit-down" legal services, including drafting of wills, for senior citizens in the community. Lawyers may be willing to participate to get exposure to potential clients whom they can serve as executors. Fees are based on a state-regulated sliding scale, depending on the worth of the estate. You can present and explain the park-giving option through the park agency, friends of the park, or the lawyers themselves.

A further variation is to orchestrate a more prestigious event in which individuals are invited to a seminar of park giving and wills. Quality is the hallmark here, and a fee may not be necessary. The invitations come from a top-flight "inviter" -- a highly respected individual who is a philanthropist also willing to speak on behalf of the park system's needs. The inviter sets the tone for the seminar in the keynote speech, explaining the giving needs and opportunities along with his or her own personal commitment. The inviter then introduces three panelists recruited from the community 's leading law firm, bank, and accounting firm. Top firms want to participate since it represents good business and favorable exposure for them. They offer their best people as panelists at the clinic.

Each panelist is invited to speak for twenty to thirty minutes about changes in laws, accounting practices, and money matters related to wills, and what to watch out for. Usually it is possible to find sponsors willing to pay for invitations, refreshments, and meeting space for such a prestigious event.

WILLS CLINICS FOR PROFESSIONALS: THE ST. PETERSBURG EXAMPLE

An alternative type of wills clinic serves professionals who deal with wills like attorneys, bank trust officers, and tax consultants. Agencies should recognize that these people are gatekeepers who manage the affairs of relatively wealthy people. They can open the gate and provide access to or influence their wealthy clients.

The Leisure Services Department in St. Petersburg believed that influencing this group was the most efficient way to launch their bequests program. Accordingly, the department approached the chamber of commerce and the local bar association with a proposal to host a seminar on recent major changes in tax laws affecting planned giving. The chamber and bar association enthusiastically agreed to co-sponsor. The Small Business Council of the chamber was so impressed that a public agency was aggressively seeking outside support that they made a small grant to help underwrite the seminar. The co-sponsors and other professional organizations in St. Petersburg provided their membership mailing lists to help publicize the event.

The city leisure services director was very candid in welcoming the 110 participants to the seminar. He said the goal of the city in hosting the session was to acquaint delegates with the benefits of charitable trusts set up to benefit parks in St. Petersburg. Some of his

opening remarks were reproduced in his welcoming letter at the front of the written materials given to each seminar participant. (See Figure 2.5.)

Participants at the seminar looked on it as an opportunity to broaden their knowledge and skills at a bargain price. One attorney said, "I never thought of the the city as a potential beneficiary. The scouts and hospitals, yes. But not the city."

The seminar was presented by a nationally recognized expert in planned giving, Norman Sugarman of Washington, DC. Sugarman's fee was 5,000 dollars for the four-hour session. (Sugarman was also impressed by the city's efforts. He later donated his services in incorporating a non-profit "friends" organization for the city.) A very small fee was charged participants — twenty-five dollars, including lunch. Additional expenses beyond those covered by revenues from the seminar fee were met by a grant from the chamber of commerce.

The seminar was held at the St. Petersburg Yacht Club. As an added inducement to participate, the co-sponsors arranged five hours of continuing education credit for the attorneys and CPAs who attended.

The leisure services director and his staff each had a goal of establishing a working dialogue with at least ten of the seminar participants, so they could be made aware of the donation opportunities (or needs) afforded by the park agency. These contacts were made at the clinic. They continue to be nurtured over time so the professionals are continuously reminded of park giving options they can suggest to their clients.

The follow-up was the real payoff. Typically, an attorney or accountant asks the park director to sit in on a meeting with a client interested in a charitable trust. The director listens very carefully as the donor explains his or her desires for the trust, and follows the meeting promptly with a one-page proposal tailored to the needs of the donor. One or two additional meetings with the donor may be needed to complete the arrangement.

In the first three years after this seminar launched the program, over two million dollars had been pledged in wills to the City of St. Petersburg.

FIGURE 2.5

Welcoming Letter to Seminar Participants

Good Morning, Friends:

Welcome to our Family and Business Tax Planning Program under the new tax laws. We are offering this program for two reasons:

First, we are confident that this program will aid you and your clients in tax planning. After Norman Sugarman presents this program on the new tax laws and invites questions on specific cases in a group setting, we will all become much more up-to-date on a very complicated issue.

Second, we are involved with this program so that you will be aware of the city's need for consideration when you and your clients make charitable donations. As our budgets tighten, we must look for alternative sources of funding for the many niceties our city offers. As Reaganomics goes into operation, we must identify those programs and activities that are necessities and fund them with our resources. We must also identify programs and activities that should rightly be funded with private support. With these areas pinpointed, we must then assist private enterprise and individuals in finding ways to continue operating. Here is where we need your help.

When you are planning your business and clients' charitable gifts, we ask you to review some of our programs and activities in the same manner as you review other non-profit organizations. Our Legal and Development staff are available to assist you. Give us the opportunity to help you assist the many wonderful people of our city.

Again, welcome to our program. I look forward to working with you in the future.

Sincerely,

LESSONS LEARNED ABOUT WILLS CLINICS

1. *Make it a classy event.* Wills seminars should be imbued with quality. They should be held in attractive and dignified surroundings such as yacht clubs, country clubs, corporate conference rooms, and museum board rooms. Also, to attract top professionals or potential major donors, be sure that presenters have name recognition.

2. *Build and follow up on contacts.* Planned giving is a process that depends on nurturing personal relationships, both with financial advisors and with donors themselves. At the seminar, circulate and meet people. Stay in touch with the financial advisors you meet there. Don't hesitate to call seminar attendees from time to time to remind them of the opportunities available to give to your park system.

3. *The director should attend all follow-up meetings with potential donors.* This demonstrates the park agency's genuine interest in and need for obtaining a contribution. Many major donors want to deal directly with the top manager. Follow every meeting with a written thank-you, and respond with a brief proposal addressing the issues covered at the meeting.

4. *Get one or more respected co-sponsors.* Co-sponsors lend credibility and help attract others to attend wills seminars.

5. *For professional wills seminars, arrange for continuing education credit.* Many professionals, such as attorneys and accountants, are required to continually upgrade their skills by attending educational seminars. A wills seminar can meet that need. Local professional organizations can arrange for credit for attendees.

6. *Think about the long-term, not the short-term, return.* Even if the seminar does not break even, remember that planned giving nets long-term returns.

SOURCES:

Park and Recreation Technical Services Division, National Park Service Western Region
Box 36063
450 Golden Gate Avenue
San Francisco, CA 96102

Department of Leisure Services
P.O. Box 2842
St. Petersburg, FL 33731

11

Financing Projects with Donated Personal Bricks

Several park and recreation departments, or their support groups, have financed projects by selling personalized bricks to residents in the community. Two such projects are discussed here. They are Fair Park in Dallas, Texas, and Pioneer Square in Portland, Oregon.

FAIR PARK IN DALLAS, TEXAS

The Friends of Fair Park, a community support group organized to help out historic Fair Park, that is located in Dallas, Texas, sold personalized bricks in a special walkway of the park called the Texas Promenade. Contributions to this project help the Friends promote special events year round at the park; support park restoration and preservation, sponsor festivals and events, and plan the development of science, history, and technology museums at the park.

For a contribution of thirty-seven dollars, donors become a permanent part of Fair Park by having a personalized brick placed in the Texas Promenade, a walkway between the Music Hall and The Science Place in the park. This special walkway will be made up entirely of bricks bearing the names of "Texans" from all across the nation.

Individuals, families, and corporations can all buy personalized bricks in the walkway. The bricks are available from the Friends of Fair Park and a variety of clubs and organizations in Texas.

The Texas Promenade was an official project of the 1986 State of Texas Sesquicentennial Celebration as well as part of a comprehensive and much-needed Fair Park face-lift.

Special bricks were also available. For 250 dollars, a donor could select a "halo" brick — one personalized brick surrounded by unprinted bricks so it would stand out in the Texas Promenade.

The friends of the Fair Park promoted the "ego gratification" of having *your name* immortalized in brick, urging donors to become a part of the Texas Promenade walkway, a permanent fixture in a park with a long and rich history.

PIONEER SQUARE IN PORTLAND, OREGON

The Friends of Pioneer Square thank George Washington, who left his name on schools, parks, counties, mountains, paper money, beds, and whatnot. This tells us that it is truly American to immortalize *a brick in Pioneer Square* with our own personal one-of-a-kind name for all to see for ever and ever. Sounds simple to emulate the father of our country; is it really possible to be remembered for longer than fifteen minutes? Can you still "sneak in" the way Amerigo Vespucci imprinted his own name on two continents? Is the day gone when your graffiti can identify a cave, a sandwich, an automobile, a religion, a nation, or a lipstick?

Not an easy problem to solve; there are those among us who pooh-pooh graffiti and seem to welcome oblivion. Not the Friends of Pioneer Square. We say that each of us should go noticed. Bake your name on a brick. Better yet, have it done; the fee is only fifteen dollars.

The plan was born of desperation. The Portland City Council had approved a stunning design for a public square in the heart of Portland's central retail district. The plan involved transforming a parking lot into Pioneer Courthouse Square. High-level business opposition emerged for the open plan envisioned. The business community was concerned that an open public square would attract "street people" who would discourage shoppers from coming downtown. They cited the experience of other squares and plazas that became gathering places for vagrants. Instead they supported a design featuring an enclosed and covered public space which could be controlled and supervised. They felt this would attract shoppers downtown from the residential areas and suburbs.

The US Department of the Interior, which had awarded a 1.5 million dollar matching grant in Land and Water Conservation funds to assist in acquisition of the site for recreation open space, could not approve construction of a covered facility. An apparent impasse developed since the city could not afford the building costs without the financial support of the downtown community and the federal government.

All development ground to a halt by January, 1981, when the mayor declared the project dead. Emotions were high and the city was divided. The City Council decided that 1.6 million was needed from private sources for construction to begin and authorized a small group of public-spirited citizens to try to raise it. They organized themselves into Friends of Pioneer Square.

They could not approach major donors (many of whom opposed the square) and thus had to begin a grassroots fund-raising campaign. This campaign, in addition to raising a large sum of money, had to conclusively demonstrate public support for Pioneer Courthouse Square and thus force the city to proceed. The Friends believed that most people would like to be immortal. Failing that, they might settle for having their names live forever, or at least as long as an engraved brick might endure on the square. This idea proved valid. The identity of the individual who first

suggested imprinted bricks is lost to mythology, but smaller brick programs were newly underway in Tacoma, Washington, and Indianapolis, Indiana. They were the only sources of organizational suggestions.

However, the Friends quickly recognized the potential of the idea and threw full support behind it. Time was short. The project had to be rescued soon or die. They decided to launch the brick-sales campaign on April 6, 1981 — Portland's birthday.

The Organization. Full time, paid staff was small: a director, office manager, and volunteer coordinator. All other positions were volunteer. The executive committee (president, vice president, and secretary/treasurer) acted as a board of directors. In addition to planning policy, they were active fund-raisers. A steering committee was also formed to provide a larger forum for ideas and discussion and to assist in major fund-raising. This group was composed of business and civic leaders enthusiastic about the campaign. (The committee's effectiveness was dampened by volunteer reluctance to make calls.)

Well-organized and active, a general solicitations committee made up of mid-level management volunteers was also formed to raise money from smaller contributors. Medium and large donations took the form of "purchased" architectural features of the Square. These ranged from the amphitheater to drinking fountains, trees, and trash receptacles. This effort raised one million dollars with a largest single gift of 100,000 dollars. The "purchaser" had his or her contribution acknowledged by an appropriately inscribed bronzed brick close to the selected item. More leeway was allowed in quantity and content of the inscription on the bronzed bricks than on the regular bricks. Many were purchased as memorials.

The brick campaign was co-chaired by two city commissioners. Not only did these two lend their names and reputations to the campaign, but they actively solicited and were available for all tasks requested of them by the staff. This was a working campaign for all!

The Strategy. With 20,000 dollars in seed money provided by Portland Development Commission (a branch of city government), the Friends established an office in partially donated space, equipped it, and hired a public-relations/advertising firm to define the campaign and produce materials. The firm was so enthusiastic about the project that they cut their fee to the minimum and each partner personally donated ten percent of his or her fee.

Because of the initial lack of support from the business community, staff decided to gain such a strong platform of support from the average citizen that the program could not be denied and the city would have to go forward with the project. To make the program as egalitarian as possible, all bricks were to be randomly placed and to sell for the same amount. After estimating the costs of the program to be five dollars per brick (including imprinting bricks), a price of fifteen dollars was established. In addition to equality, the random placement made possible the low price.

The ads were stunning — evocative, witty, humorous, and effective. Good organization, excellent materials, a popular cause, and a novel idea made the campaign a natural for helpful media coverage. The campaign broke with a full page ad in the daily newspaper. Well-done PSA's followed on radio and TV. The campaign lasted almost a year, with major pushes at the beginning, Christmas ("Jingle Bricks"), Valentine's Day ("Don't Brick My Heart"). The campaign attached itself to all manner of civic celebrations: Rose Festival, Autumn Fest, ArtQuake, etc. However, staff found that while these heightened awareness, they did not generate immediate sales.

Special activities which aided brick sales included "Hit the Bricks Run." Organized and staffed by Pacific Northwest Bell, it netted 2,500 dollars. Beer gardens Friday evenings on the site featured live music, beer, wine, and popcorn. But expenses were high, and this effort only broke even. Design perspective prints were sold to raise money and publicize brick sales. The perspective was donated by the architect and most printing costs were substantially reduced by a sympathetic printer. Publicity was good and it did produce some revenue.

Selling the Bricks. The most visible part of the campaign was the sales booth. Open from 10 am until 6 pm weekdays and 11 am until 5 pm on Saturdays, this volunteer effort was maintained almost a year! Working in pairs, in shifts lasting two to three hours, volunteers explained the parameters for imprints,

supervised the filling out of forms, handed out brick buttons and ID cards, and collected money.

The sales booth was located on the construction site — a very central downtown spot — in a trailer loaned by a bank which had used it as a temporary branch office. An attractive area evolved around the booth, with a "patio" of demonstration-imprinted bricks, outdoor furniture with umbrellas, and flower-filled planters. With donations of labor and materials, including the bricklayers union, a masonry contractor, and several nurseries, this landscaping cost virtually nothing.

In selling bricks, volunteers had to explain that the ultimate position of the brick could not be specified and that imprints could not exceed twenty-four letters and spaces, could not use quotes or parentheses, and had to consist only of proper names. Proper names, however, could include names of pets, clubs, celebrities, etc. MARKET STREET PUSSY CATS was a small but active club, HOT NUTS a small business, and SWEET CHEEKS the professional name of a lady wrestler. Many canines and felines apparently also have exotic names. Upper case only was used. Questionable imprints went to the office for further evaluation and a final decision. One very important item always requested was the daytime telephone number of the brick purchaser!

While the question of how a person would eventually find his or her brick in the completed square rarely came up, campaigners felt that by the time construction was completed, an enterprising individual or group would take on the job of mapping the imprinted bricks as a way of making money. And this did happen. However, some purchasers resented having to pay another fee for finding their brick(s), and in future campaigns it is recommended that the cost of a brick finder be included in the purchase price of a brick.

Orders could be paid in cash, by check, or with VISA or Mastercard. The lead time was long enough that NSF checks were not a problem. To prevent a possible problem, however, the signature on the check was to be the same name given as the purchaser. This allowed an NSF check to be traced to the order. With very few exceptions, purchasers were found to be extremely honest. A member of the staff balanced the account from the sales booth daily — sometimes more than once a day if business was especially brisk.

Orders arrived by mail also. All newspaper ads, mailers, handouts, and forms picked up from the booth had order forms prominently displayed that carried a post-office-box address. These as well as all check orders from the sales booth went directly to a donated bank lockbox service which processed the checks and returned copies of them attached to the orders. Since the checks usually had the purchaser's address printed on them, these copies helped immeasurably when the purchaser's writing/printing was illegible.

Telephone orders with charge cards accounted for a significant proportion of the total. This was a particularly popular way for the elderly purchaser, as well as the busy executive, to place orders. The phone number was 22-BRICK. Callers received a taped message about purchasing bricks when it was not staffed. During busy seasons, four lines were constantly in use and an additional paid person became necessary. Staff also discovered that the "telephone voice" is extremely important for public relations — friendliness and accuracy are essential!

Processing the Brick Orders. Processing the brick orders to ensure accuracy, completeness, and timeliness is complex — and very important! A brick number — ranging from 000001 to 048657 in this case — followed it until placement in the square. Staff used this number for filing, owner inquiries, tracking, etc. After checking the brick order for suitability, completeness, readability, and error, staff assigned the number, then entered the order into the computer.

The computer was programmed to print a "brick certificate" — an ornate document that included the imprint, brick number, and date of computer entry. Mailing labels addressed to brick purchasers were produced in alphabetical order in the same batch. For each day's input, the computer generated an alphabetized list of purchasers showing their address, total dollar amount of purchase, and corresponding brick numbers. Also generated daily was a list of imprints, alphabetized by first letter, with their corresponding brick numbers.

With a daily batch of brick certificates, frequently two hundred to seven hundred at a time, volunteers put labels on certificate envelopes, which they kept in order, organized the certificates to go into the envelopes, and stuffed them. An accompanying note explained that the imprint on the certificate was exactly as it would appear on the brick, and that any errors had to be reported within two weeks.

Getting the right brick certificate to the right purchaser was no automatic task. If a certificate for a particular order was missing, it meant searching through all envelopes already stuffed until it was found. Checking each certificate and label against the printout before stuffing the envelope proved prudent. During the busiest times, four or five volunteers a day worked extra shifts of about three hours each, processing orders.

Certificates were mailed first class. Although expensive, this kind of postage enabled staff to control delivery and transit time. Even so, the post office failed to deliver a few.

It took about six weeks after the final certificate-mailing for correction calls to stop. Some changes were due to administrative errors, others to indecision or inaccuracy by the purchaser. A five-dollar correction fee was charged for the latter type of alteration. If an imprint request could not be honored and the purchaser declined to make a change, a refund was cheerfully given. After all corrections were made, the imprints were alphabetized by the first letter of imprint, printed by brick number onto a master list, and shipped off to the brick makers.

Making the Bricks. In simplistic terms, the manufacturing process involved using a Linotype "slug" to press the imprint into a "green" (formed but still soft) brick which was then fired. To make imprinted bricks for promotional purposes, staff frequently obtained green bricks from a friendly supplier, had Linotype slugs made at a typesetting firm, and — with the light touch of a mallet or other instrument — impressed the green brick with the desired imprint. The next step was to take them to a friend with a kiln for firing. Everyone loves to see his or her name in print, and these early promotional bricks were exceedingly well-received.

The biggest challenge for the masonry contractor was to maintain accuracy control when faced with a "book" of 835 pages with fifty-seven names per page. Smith Masonry of Clackamas, Oregon, the masonry contractor for Pioneer Courthouse Square, separated the imprinted bricks into lots of five hundred. Each lot was tagged with the pages of the book represented by the imprints it contained. The lots were then transferred to wooden pallets of fifteen hundred for shipping to the construction site. The pallets also had to be tagged in the same manner. As masons installed named bricks, they noted the imprint of any broken or deficient brick on the check-off sheet of imprints so that it could be remade and installed at a later time.

The bricks were "pavers" measuring 1 1/4 x 3 1/2 x 7 1/2". Caslon twenty-four-point type was used for the imprints in Pioneer Courthouse Square. We would recommend, however, that you use a slightly larger type so imprints can be read more easily.

Results. The sale of close to fifty thousand bricks at fifteen dollars each raised approximately 500,000 dollars, after expenses, of the campaign goal of 1.6 million dollars. Beyond the actual financial gain, however, the tremendous public support for the project ensured its completion and brought a sense of broad "ownership" to this unique block in downtown Portland. Each person whose name appears on a brick has a feeling that the square is partially his or hers. This may also have been the first fundraiser in history that people were sad to see end since they wanted to buy more bricks in the future. Indeed, the manager of the square later had no trouble selling another twelve thousand bricks at thirty dollars each to replace some unnamed bricks and to provide a start-up administrative resource.

HINTS FOR A SUCCESSFUL CAMPAIGN

1. While volunteers are necessary for nearly all campaigns, they are essential to one of this kind. Anything and everything should be done to see that their experience — daily and long-term — is positive so that they are willing to stay the course. Besides daily thank-yous and other signs of appreciation, an occasional "volunteer appreciation" event is a good investment. Never stop recruiting volunteers.

2. Decide the imprint parameters and fee schedule well ahead of opening day so everyone can be well-informed.

3. Keep the imprint guidelines simple.

4. Price the bricks at an amount that is easy to multiply and work with (e.g., fifteen dollars rather than $14.95).

5. Post information regarding imprint guidelines, corrections, receipt-keeping, certificates, etc. in the sales area.

6. Develop a system for "mapping" the bricks when in place. Include the cost of this mapping and notification of location in the original purchase price. People care where their bricks are!

SOURCES:

City of Dallas Parks and Recreation Department
1500 Marilla, 6FN
Dallas, TX 75201

Pioneer Courthouse Square of Portland, Inc.
701 SW Sixth Avenue
Portland, OR 97204

Wendy Myers Brand and Fontaine Hagedorn, "The Portland Experience," *Trends,* Vol. 22, No. 2, 1985, pp. 9-11.

12

Tree Donation and Recycling Programs

Agencies can use three complementary strategies to benefit from the massive annual purchase of Christmas trees. The first method is described in a case by Charles Murray, Superintendent of Parks and Recreation for Marshall County in West Virginia. The case shows how his department worked with a local nursery and the citizens themselves to establish their "Christmas Tree Donation Program."

In contrast to the Marshall County program, which is structured to secure live trees that can be transplanted into parks after home use during the Christmas season, the City of Austin, Texas, initiated a program targeted at acquiring dead trees thrown out at the end of the Christmas season. The second case describes how the city arranged to collect the dead trees and recycle them into mulch, which is used in gardens maintained by the parks department. Similarly, the third case describes how sand dunes were restored in Brazoria County, Texas, with discarded Christmas trees.

The final case, Operation Plant Rescue, describes a program in Houston that rescues desirable plants from development sites before they are cleared by the contractor.

CHRISTMAS TREE DONATION PROGRAM

Recognizing the ever-present need in a park environment for continuous landscaping and the accelerating cost of materials to support this need, the Marshall County Parks and Recreation Department initiated a program to encourage public donations of these materials to their parks.

In establishing their "Christmas Tree Donation Program," several aspects were considered which would make the program attractive to the public. By offering the service of delivery, set-up of live trees in the home and pickup after the holidays, people were offered the necessary incentive to consider this type of donation program. Aside from this incentive, the purchase of their annual Christmas tree became a charitable donation and a tax deduction.

First staff coordinated the program with a local nursery. They arranged to have a selection of balled and burlapped evergreens available that corresponded with the county's list of landscape materials. After purchasers selected and paid for their firs, the nursery tagged the trees with their names, phone numbers, and addresses. In turn the county contacted purchasers and arranged a time and day for delivery. Efforts were made to coordinate deliveries to keep the county's expenses to a minimum.

As the trees were delivered to each home, county staff offered a typewritten sheet of suggestions for the care of the tree during the holidays. (See Figure 2.6.) They also set a date for pickup of the trees after the Christmas season.

FIGURE 2.6

Suggestions for Care of Donated Trees

Special Care Necessary for Your Evergreen While Inside

In order to increase the chances of survival for your Christmas evergreen donation, consider the following recommendations:

KEEP THE TREE AWAY FROM DIRECT HEAT SOURCES — Warm and dry air circulation hastens the drying-out process and makes the adjustment to the outdoors more difficult.

DECORATE WITH A MINIMUM OF LIGHTS — The heat generated by your decorations also hastens the drying-out process.

MAKE THE INSIDE STAY AS SHORT AS POSSIBLE — Chances for survival decrease the longer your evergreen stays indoors. The maximum length of time is ten days.

Following these suggestions and using common sense greatly increases your evergreen's chance of survival when it is replanted. Your donation can then be enjoyed for generations by park visitors.

During the period that the trees are in the homes, the county prepares the areas to which they will be transplanted. Often, however, it is necessary to "heal in" the trees until milder weather.

By establishing the "Landscaping Material Donation Program," Marshall County can also provide some valuable landscape materials at a minimum cost and, in doing so, involve people and foster a sense of contribution and pride in their parks' development.

CHRISTMAS TREE RECYCLING

After the holidays, Christmas trees change from things of traditional beauty to lifeless forms that are expensive for cities to collect and dispose of at landfills. This program represents an innovative and successful approach to dealing with an expensive and traditional maintenance problem. It capitalizes on the saying, "one person's garbage is another's treasure."

Christmas tree recycling has turned the trash into a treasure of mulch for Austin. The trees are brought to pickup points by citizens and then chipped and put to use as mulch. The Water and Wastewater Department also uses them in a sludge-composting experiment. As mulch they are of great value in promoting soil structure, preventing soil compaction, ameliorating soil temperature extremes, and conserving soil moisture. They also smell good and provide for the slow release of nitrogen. Since pine is slightly acid, it helps neutralize the very acid soil prevalent in Austin.

Late in 1985, cooperation between personnel in Austin's Parks and Recreation Department and the Public Works Recycling and Waste Reduction Division resulted in a program to recycle Christmas trees into woodchips for use as mulch in parks, and to begin a sludge-composting experiment with the Water and Wastewater Department. Co-sponsors were two community groups — Ecology Action Community Recycling, Inc. and Keep Austin Beautiful, Inc. — with additional cooperation from seven local disposal and tree companies. These private companies donated nearly four thousand dollars worth of tree transport and tree-chipping services, while volunteers from the two community groups manned the drop-off locations during the collection period.

The program was widely publicized. (See Figure 2.7.) Good publicity and the citizens' willingness to recycle were two reasons the program was such a success. A spokeman noted, "We found on the weekends during the holidays that there isn't much news, so our collection centers got lots of coverage."A lead editorial in the city's major newpaper captured the spirit of the program. (See Figure 2.8.)

The program is operated through the three weekends after Christmas. Over six thousand residents delivered ten thousand trees for recycling. Many brought in the trees of their neighbors to the seven designated sites. (The number was increased to twelve in 1986.) The recycling yielded two hundred cubic yards of wood chips and about fifteen percent of the trees sold on Christmas tree lots in the city were recycled.

Collection points set up in parks drew some people who had never been to those parks before. This program was more than a maintenance activity; it became a true recreation experience. Whole families arrived at chipping sites to watch their trees be processed. To the delight of their children, who were pleased to watch the chipper do its work, many lingered. Some partici-

FIGURE 2.7

Chrismas Tree Recycling Publicity Poster

Please Post

CHRISTMAS TREE RECYCLING

WHY?

*Provides compost and
mulch for City parks

*Reduces waste

*Saves money in collection
and disposal costs

*Extends landfill life

WHEN?

10am — 5pm
SATURDAY AND SUNDAY

DECEMBER 28th & 29th

JANUARY 4th & 5th

OVER 70,000 CHRISTMAS TREES WILL BE SOLD IN AUSTIN THIS YEAR . . .

INSTEAD OF JUST THROWING AWAY YOUR TREE AFTER CHRISTMAS,
BRING IT TO ONE OF THESE ATTENDED COLLECTION POINTS . . .

WHERE?

* Garrison Park - 6001 Manchaca
* Givens Recreation Center - 3811 E. 12th
* Mabel Davis Park - 3427 Parker Lane
* Northwest Recreation Center - 2913 Northland
* Zilker Park - by the Playscape
* Walnut Creek Park — 12138 N Lamar
* Highland Mall Farmers Market

SPONSORED BY THE PARKS AND RECREATION DEPARTMENT, THE PUBLIC WORKS DEPARTMENT,
ECOLOGY ACTION, KEEP AUSTIN BEAUTIFUL, TEXAS DISPOSAL SYSTEMS, BFI WASTE
SYSTEMS,LONGHORN DISPOSAL, TREE CLINIC, BARTLETT TREE EXPERTS, ANDTREES, INC.

Please note: Trees With tinsel and flocking <u>are</u> acceptable, <u>but be sure to remove
all other ornaments from tree</u> before recycling.

FOR INFORMATION CALL   THE TRASHBUSTER HOTLINE: 479-6753

pants commented on the innovative use of their trees and were happy to put an otherwise wasted resource to good use.

Cost savings for disposal and collection were estimated at 15,500 dollars. The chips produced were valued at about three thousand dollars in mulch, fertilizer, and water savings. Total Park and Recreation Department costs were estimated at 3,940 dollars. In addition to these direct benefits and costs, the city reduced the amount of material which went into its solid-waste landfill.

BUILDING SAND DUNES WITH CHRISTMAS TREES

The uninitiated imagine sand dunes as the hills that narrow the beach or challenge dune buggies. However, dunes are a critical ecological feature which provide storm protection, decrease erosion, offer aesthetic pleasure, and prevent the filling of lagoons which are valuable spawning areas.

Along the beaches of Brazoria County on the Texas gulf coast, the main purpose of dunes is to minimize beach erosion and offer protection to coastal settlements against hurricanes. About four hundred acres of the Texas gulf coast is eroded each year. Dunes serve as stockpiles of sand which, by wave action, help replenish the sand on the beach. Unfortunately, in many areas a combination of natural forces and direct and indirect ecological intrusions by man have destroyed dunes. The adverse impact on Brazoria County, Texas, of Hurricane Carla in 1973 and Hurricane Allen in 1980 provoked interest in restoring the dunes.

The main tool for the restoration project has been discarded Christmas trees, which have proven effective, inexpensive, and easy to use. The cities of Freeport, Clute, and Lake Jackson in Brazoria County deliver their annual pick-up of used Christmas trees to a location near the beach. It is less expensive for the city trucks to transport the trees to the coastal site for free disposal than to pay for them to be dumped at a disposal facility. Vendors and nurseries in the nearby Houston area have also been approached, and have agreed to provide unused Christmas trees for the program.

Volunteers drive wooden stakes into the sand and tie the trees to them in such a way that they catch the sand blown from the beach and pile it up in wind rows

FIGURE 2.8

Lead Editorial in the *Austin American Statesman*, December 14, 1986

"Recycling Trees a New Tradition for Austinites"

Christmas is a time for traditions. While most of our holiday traditions are rooted in family history, there comes a time when a new tradition gets established and gradually becomes a permanent part of the richness of the season. The recycling of Christmas trees is for many Austinites just such a tradition.

Last year over ten thousand Christmas trees in Austin were recycled into mulch and compost for use in city parks. These trees were brought in from homes, businesses, and schools all over town and dropped off at convenient locations in every sector of the city. The atmosphere at the drop-off points was festive. Goodwill abounded on the part of individuals and families who were bringing in their trees for recycling as well as on the part of many volunteers who helped unload the trees from car trunks and pick-up beds. It seems that putting something to good use — more than once, at that — is also good for the spirit.

Although many of us have not even bought our trees yet this year, now is the time to remember that after the excitement of Christmas is over, the dry undecorated tree in the living room or lobby doesn't have to be thrown out with the turkey carcass. Thanks to the efforts of the Public Works and Parks and Recreation Departments, the following tree-recycling locations will be open from 8:00 am to 5:00 pm on Saturday and Sunday, December 27-28, the following weekend, January 3-4, and Saturday, January 10.

Austin Community Gardens, Zargosa Park, Bartholo:new Park, Schroeter Park, Toney Burger Center, Garrison Park, Northwest Recreation Center, Stacy Park, Walnut Creek Park, and Zilker Park by the Playscape.

Volunteers are needed as support staff at all of these sites. If you and your family and friends have a few hours to spare and would like to help out on this new Austin tradition, contact Darlene Berghammer at the Parks and Recreation Department at 477-5041.

covering the trees. The trees are placed vertically in a trench that is one-and-a-half to two feet deep and six inches wide; the butt end is placed in the trench and sand is packed firmly around the butts and over some low branches to firmly anchor the trees. The trees form a vertical fence about three to five feet in height.

The rate at which sand accumulates will vary. In some locations dunes four feet high or more build up in a year, while in others this amount of growth will take several years. The dunes may eventually reach a height of twelve to fifteen feet, but this height will be influenced by the installation of additional sand fences, vegetation, or Christmas trees. Beyond this height, the wind's energy is unable to lift the sand, or else it is carried over the top of the dune and deposited on the back side. Maintaining this height requires a vigorous maintenance program of repairing and replanting weak spots and controlling traffic.

Volunteers from local 4-H Clubs are solicited to plant the discarded trees each January. After small dunes emerge, they must be stabilized with beach grasses. These grasses are salt resistant, their roots penetrate to the water table, and the plants themselves grow taller as the sand accumulates. Their extensive root system stabilizes the new dunes and helps them grow as they catch the wind-blown sand along the beach. Brazoria County sponsors a Baby Dunes Day on a Saturday in April to intitiate this planting. Typically, about two hundred volunteers come from 9 am to 1 pm to help transplant beach grass from established sand dunes to the new baby dunes formed around the discarded Christmas trees.

Volunteer team leaders are trained to demonstrate the proper techniques for transplanting the culm beach grass. All volunteers receive a free lunch, a baby dunes birth certificate, and a free T-shirt. The volunteers bring their own work gloves and digging tools. The event is sponsored by 7-Eleven stores and a local radio station.

It is important to erect signs explaining why the trees are there. Without signs, beachgoers use the trees for firewood, or destroy them because they consider them to be intrusive and unsightly on the beach.

The Brazoria County program has become an annual tradition and a community event that has operated for seven years. Over ten thousand trees have been "planted" on the beach in that period. Many dunes now exist where once there was only flat beach, and this restoration has been achieved with minimal expense. It has been estimated that the purchase cost of the sand which accumulated in the two-year period in 1985 and 1986 would have been over 117,000 dollars, exclusive of any transportation costs.

OPERATION PLANT RESCUE

The City of Houston and surrounding counties have experienced rapid growth during the past decade that has involved the development of thousands of acres. Natural plant resources succumbed to this development, as vast numbers of native plants were lost to the bulldozer. Operation Plant Rescue was launched as a non-profit organization in an effort to reduce this waste of resources. It is designed to retrieve desirable plant species that would otherwise be destroyed during the clearing process necessary for development.

This program to recycle landscaping was the idea of John Koros, who is a native Houstonian and director of the Mercer Arboretum and Botanic Gardens in Houston. Operation Plant Rescue consists of a team of horticulturalists, biologists, and volunteers who make themselves available, at no cost ordinarily, to developers and owners of tracts of land destined to be developed. The tracts are inventoried and desirable plants are relocated to enhance the aesthetics of public parks, arboretums, or school campuses.

The program's intent is to be selective, not to take everything. For example, only trees which are easily transplantable are selected. This generally means they must be up to four inches in diameter and twelve feet high. The developers are allowed to count the value of the materials as a charitable donation for tax purposes. In some cases private contractors have been persuaded to donate the use of their tree-moving equipment, while other developers have made a contribution sufficient to enable the group to rent the tree spade or other necessary equipment.

Houston's Park People organization, which is a strong citizens group dedicated to improving Houston area parks, adopted Operation Plant Rescue as one its ongoing park projects and provided the initial volunteer impetus. They have been joined by other Houston conservation groups and garden clubs. Developers have been responsive and thousands of acres have been made available to the program.

SOURCES:

Superintendent, Marshall County Parks and Recreation
Department
Box 523
Moundsville, WV 20041

The Christmas tree donation article written by Charles
Murray first appeared in *Park Maintenance and Grounds
Management*, September 1985, pp. 16-17.

Forestry Division, Parks and Recreation Department
Central Maintenance Complex
2525 South Lakeshore Blvd.
Austin, TX 78741

County Marine Extension Agent, Brazoria County
Route 2, 1800, C.R. #171
Angleton, TX 77515

Director, Brazoria County Parks
County Courthouse
Angleton, TX 77575

Director, Mercer Arboretum and Botanic Garden
22306 Aldine Westfield
Humble, TX 77338

The Park People
One Houston Center, #1502
1221 McKinney Avenue
Houston, TX 77002

13

Kids for Parks

For years, Anaheim parks suffered from the problems most often associated with having facilities located adjacent to schools. Primary among those problems was vandalism in the form of graffiti, litter, loitering, and driving on the turf.

The normal approach to dealing with youth vandalism is to either accept it as routine or to react with force by calling in the police department. Such a response is reactive and does not deal with the root of the problem, which lies in the personal values of the children involved in the misdeeds.

A program was instituted in the Anaheim Parks, Recreation, and Community Services Department to take a proactive approach to youth vandalism. Anaheim has many of its parks located adjacent to schools, and the idea of combining these two resources to achieve a common good grew out of a staff meeting. This program, entitled "Kids for Parks," has developed into a highly successful approach to stemming vandalism in parks and schools.

The KIDS FOR PARKS program was originally planned at the start of the new school year in 1982 by school and city officials. Parks Superintendent Chris Jarvi and Recreation Services Manager Marie Dixon organized the event in consultation with principal Loretta Wakefield and her faculty at Francis Scott Key School in Anaheim. They planned activities for the 260 students to assist in maintaining the park and enjoying related environmental education programs.

Activities planned include fourth graders repainting picnic tables, a sixth-grade class renovating the main park entrance sign, and kindergartens' planting calendulas to provide spring blossoms in the city's Modjeska Park. A different class each week picked up litter on the park and school grounds using bags supplied by the city parks division. Project objectives were:

1. To foster a relationship between youth and the parks and to develop a sense of stewardship

2. To increase opportunities for students to receive environmental education and nature appreciation

3. To develop a cooperative program between parks adjacent to schools in the City of Anaheim which will emphasize community involvement by students and increase their appreciation for the value of parks, trees, and environment

4. To inspire students at a young age to community service by involving them in a volunteer program.

To meet the objectives, children also participated in several educational components of the KIDS FOR PARKS program. One class studied the plants in Modjeska Park and conducted nature walks for other classes. An Arbor Day program, including tree-planting, was conducted by third graders. They gave a presentation on the history of the park, including the story of actress Ann Modjeska, a prominent early

Anaheim resident. In classes and in outdoor sessions, they studied park problems and learned how the park was designed, built, and operated. Finally, they learned about safety with ground maintenance equipment.

Recognition activities play an important role in the program. As classes participate in an activity each month of the school year, the park maintenance staff award them special certificates at the school's monthly citizenship assemblies. Staff also wore KIDS FOR PARKS badges during park projects to identify the program and develop the concept among the youngsters. The badges also served to identify the workers when crowds of other children were around.

News of all activities went to children's families in the school's weekly newsletter. Parents were also involved through a photo/slide program at parent-teacher association meetings.

Staff also included rewards in the program. The parks division treated the Key student body to a field trip to the city's Oak Canyon Nature Center to help show the contrast between Modjeska's cultivated environment and the natural surroundings in Anaheim's canyons. The program culminates each year with a school-wide picnic in the park conducted by the Anaheim Hilton and Towers and the city Parks Division.

A warm rapport soon developed between students and park maintenance staff. Park staff were introduced during the citizenship assemblies and worked closely with students during work projects. Instead of being adversaries, kids and park staff became friends. Students even began to seek out park personnel by name to ask questions or talk about their park.

KIDS FOR PARKS at Key School was a pilot program intended for repetition at many other school-park sites. The program centers on the third-grade level, and from the initial pilot school it has now been adopted by eleven schools. A multimedia slide presentation was developed to show the model effort to other schools, park maintenance personnel, and civic clubs who might be interested in becoming participants in the overall activities.

The KIDS FOR PARKS PROGRAM is designed to create a strong, positive feeling of stewardship in the students. It is hoped that, as they grow older and recall these experiences, that they will be less apt to create problems in their schools and parks. Some may be even more positively affected and adopt a strong sense of community service with the realization that the

quality of life in their community depends on their direct involvement in community programs.

As a result of the widespread interest aroused by the program, the Anaheim department developed a start-up kit to enable other agencies to initiate the program. The start-up kit is comprised of two components. They are an administrative packet and an educational packet for teachers and students. This comprehensive start-up kit provides all the information and material needed to initiate the program. Both packets are obtainable from the Anaheim department. The contents of each packet are outlined below in two fliers issued by the department.

ADMINISTRATIVE PACKET

The administrative packet is designed to provide you with the necessary forms and work to set up a KIDS FOR PARKS program in your community. It includes the following helpful items:

1. Ten-page program overview. This program overview was the award-winning application for the California Parks and Recreation Society's 1984 Award.

2. Annual planning timeline. The June-July timeline was designed to walk you through a school-year program.

3. Program budget.

— KIDS FOR PARKS proposed budget (expenditures). This budget is for ten schools. The program coordinator's pay, number of work hours, and bus transportation costs vary from community to community. Volunteers help offset costs greatly.
— Cost analysis. This format shows another way of looking at the program. The form was included in a successful grant application.

4. Successful corporate proposal for funding. This proposal was successful in securing a one-thousand-dollar annual cash donation from a local business which has asked not to be named. The business was interested in funding minority programs and the proposal reflects this slant. The name of the business

has been replaced by XXXX. This proposal was submitted after one meeting with the general manager by the program supervisor.

5. Teacher's program manual index. This table of contents lists the content areas of the teacher's program manual. In addition, a brief overview of four lessons is included with a partial sample of each lesson.

6. Park workers training packet.

— Introduction to park visit. Emphasis is on suggestions for park staff to use in preparing for park tour.

— Horace Mann Third Graders Visit La Palma Park (step-by-step park tour)

7. Park workers schedule.

— Horace Mann School at La Palma Park. Use this format when teachers take two consecutive days at the park.

— Thomas Jefferson School at Boysen Park. Use this format for a school with two classes in the program.

— John Marshall School at John Marshall Park. Use this format for a school with five classes participating in the program.

8. Program coordinator's administrative forms

— Inventory. Use this form to keep track of supplies needed to run the program.

— Participating schools. Use this form for follow-up calls to schools invited to participate in the program.

— Monthly participation hours. Keep track of all participation hours. This includes all non-work-related activities such as classroom lessons, park visits, field trips, environment hunts, and picnics.

— Monthly volunteer hours. Record all work-related activities as volunteer hours. The number of volunteers times the number of hours gives you the total time spent (volunteered) on the project.

— KIDS FOR PARKS. This is a sample form used by the program coordinator to submit monthly participation and volunteer hours for departmental needs.

— KIDS FOR PARKS reminder. The program coordinator uses this form to remind staff of park visits or work projects scheduled. In addition, a phone call is used as a follow-up.

— KIDS FOR PARKS orientation meeting. We learn by doing, and we continually find ways to improve the program. Try our suggestions when you set up the orientation meeting.

— School-year evaluation form. This evaluation was given to all third-grade teachers, and they responded with valuable input. The response to the 1984-1985 KIDS FOR PARKS program is attached.

9. Certificate of Appreciation. This two-color award is presented to each third-grade participant at the culmination of the school-year program in June.

10. KIDS FOR PARKS badge with instruction.

— Sample of an actual KIDS FOR PARKS badge.

— Sample of camera-ready artwork for badge.

— Green sheet that contains instructions for using KIDS FOR PARKS badge during the school year.

KIDS AND TEACHERS PACKET

The program coordinator for the City of Anaheim's KIDS FOR PARKS program uses the sample format below to implement the program with the school districts around the city. This format is easy to use and has received a positive response from educators involved in KIDS FOR PARKS

1. Seventy-page teacher's program manual. When a school commits itself to participate in the program,

a teacher's program manual is given to each participating teacher.

2. Twelve worksheets for students (camera ready)

__ Challenge Sheet
__ Colors, Colors, Colors (1)
__ Colors, Colors, Colors (2)
__ Is it Alive?
__ Math Story Problems (3.1)
__ Math Story Problems (3.2)
__ Metric Madness in Class
__ Metric Madness in the Park (1)
__ Metric Madness in the Park (2)
__ Recycling Worksheet with Bar Graph
__ Visiting Your Park (1)
__ Visiting Your Park (2)

Our department mimeos the worksheets to make the program more appealing. It also distributes the worksheets to all participating teachers. Teachers in our area are limited to the amount of paper used in the classroom; therefore our worksheets are appreciated. In your community you might want to contact a local business to see if they are willing to xerox the worksheets and teacher's program manual.

3. Teachers'/principals' orientation packet. The sample letters and information sheets were used by our department to contact potential participants and then to follow up with an orientation.

— Letter inviting principals to be a part of the KIDS FOR PARKS program. Follow up with a phone call.

— Letter inviting principals/teachers to an orientation meeting.

— Orientation meeting agenda to be used at the orientation meeting. Include items mentioned in the agenda to prepare a packet of information for all educators attending the orientation.

— KIDS FOR PARKS information sheet. This is a sample of our contact list and other pertinent information teachers need when they participate in the program.

— Schedule-of-events school-year form. Teachers fill out and return this form to the program coordinator for confirmation.

4. Sample permission slip for students to participate in KIDS FOR PARKS.

— Pink-copy (camera-ready) letter to parents. Whenever students leave school, parents must sign a permission slip. With this letter, parents sign for all events at one time.

— White-copy (camera ready) Spanish translation letter to parents.

5. Field-trip guidelines, a flier to send home to parents. Our city is fortunate to have Oak Canyon Nature Center. If your community doesn't have a nature center, state park, or National Forest, use other available facilities such as an arboretum, open-space area, or regional park. You can also contact local conservation groups to find out if they conduct field trips in your area.

6. KIDS FOR PARKS school-of-the-year contest. "Anaheim Beautiful" is a local organization that sponsors the KIDS FOR PARKS award in Anaheim. Based on the above criteria, one school is selected to receive the perpetual award plaque at the organization's luncheon in June. The principal and participating teachers are invited to accept the award. Check to see if your community has a group who would be willing to sponsor a contest for your program.

— Sample letter to principals/teachers inviting them to participate.

— Sample guidelines for procedure to participate in the contest.

— Yellow copy (camera-ready duplex) volunteer hours. Participants use this form to record all non-work-related activities relating to the KIDS FOR PARKS program.

— Pink copy (camera-ready duplex) participation hours. Participants use this form to record all non-work-related activities relating to the KIDS FOR PARKS program.

SOURCE:

KIDS FOR PARKS Program
Anaheim Parks, Recreation and Community Services Department
200 S. Anaheim Blvd.
Anaheim, CA 92805

Section 3

Partnerships with Business

The search for additional resources has caused recreation and park agencies to seek partnerships with the private sector. The emphasis here is not on seeking donations. Rather, agencies are concerned with offering corporations sound investment opportunities from which they will derive a satisfactory return while at the same time improving the range of services a public agency can offer to its constituents. Joint public-private capital development arrangements and contracting-out services are not commonplace. The five cases presented in the section describe less well-known strategies for facilitating partnerships with the private sector.

Case 14 describes the variety of approaches one agency used to comprehensively service the corporate sector. By recognizing that businesses constitute a market that must be served and offering direct programming to that market, recreation and park agencies are able to foster direct relationships, develop trust, understanding, and credibility, and establish the contacts crucial for corporate support.

Most agencies actively pursue sponsorship by the business community. However, for many reasons success is frequently elusive. Increasingly, agencies recognize that consistent success comes only if an effective system is implemented. Case 15 describes the very sophisticated and highly successful approach to sponsorship adopted by Jackson County.

Cause-related marketing is a way of melding business with social responsibility. It was pioneered by American Express, who found that civic pride is a powerful stimulant for the sale and use of the company's products and services. Case 16 illustrates that recreation services have been a primary beneficiary of this new type of partnership, and that its potential is exciting. Again the principle can be adapted to communities of all sizes and many types of businesses.

Case 17 describes the resources offered by the National Association for the Exchange of Industrial Resources (NAEIR). This is a non-profit association which acquires donated excess industrial products from many hundreds of companies and then redistributes them to its non-profit organization members. Case 18 presents two innovative approaches to reducing energy bills, both of which involve partnerships between a recreation and park agency and a private-sector supplier.

14

What Are You Doing for Your Corporate Constituency?

This case first appeared as an article co-authored by Leon Younger and the author in the May, 1983, issue of Parks and Recreation. Almost every community has the opportunity to develop a range of offerings targeted at the corporate sector. Serving corporations can both generate revenue and build substantial community and corporate support for the agency. This case describes the variety of approaches which one agency used to comprehensively serve the business market.

In the past, corporations have not been widely recognized as an appropriate market to be served by public recreation and park agencies. Traditionally, people tend to regard leisure services associated with the workplace as the exclusive domain of colleagues in the field of "industrial recreation." Unfortunately, such provision is exceptional; in most communities relatively few companies offer recreation for their employees.

It is likely that during the next few years, this corporate market will emerge as one of the field's most important client groups. Serving corporations enables recreation and park agencies to reach citizens who have never previously used their services and to create additional citizen support.

Agencies are frequently urged to solicit resources from the business community to at least partially off-set the declining availability of tax dollars. Indeed, President Reagan has suggested that business has a moral commitment to increase its voluntary contributions to public organizations in return for the substantial tax reductions they are accorded.

Although President Reagan wants business to respond to the reduced tax rates with increased private philanthropy, his policies have in fact reduced the incentive for business to donate. Reduced taxation levels mean that businesses now write off a smaller part of each donated tax dollar against their tax payments. The annual permissible write-off proportion has been raised from five percent to ten percent of pre-tax profits, but since less than one percent of businesses donated the five percent anyway, this increase is not likely to have a substantial effect upon donation incentives.

Given that the need for additional resources from the business community is greater than ever before and that donation incentives have been reduced, what can recreation and park agencies do to gain increased corporate support? One approach is to recognize that businesses constitute a market that must be reached. Through their property tax payments, corporations are likely to be substantial financial contributors to public recreation and park systems. If recreation and park agencies offer direct service and foster direct relationships, they are likely to develop trust, understanding, credibility, and contacts upon which corporate donations depend.

An example to consider is the Johnson County Park and Recreation District, which serves a suburb of the greater Kansas City area with a population of 217,000. Twenty-two cities, six school districts, and five additional city recreation and park departments are located in this county.

In 1979, the Bendix corporation asked the Johnson County Park and Recreation District for assistance. Bendix was providing recreation opportunities for its employees but had difficulty securing adequate facilities in which to participate with other groups. This initial approach led the district to realize that corporations were a potential market with a need for recreation services to be met.

Within three years, this corporate group had become the district's largest and fastest-growing market. The program grew so that fifteen thousand employees from eighty-four corporations enrolled as members of the corporate program that the county offers. Many of these employees signed up for more than one program, and their total number of participation days exceeded 450,000.

New enrollments in the county corporate program were accepted throughout the year to accommodate different corporate budget planning and decision periods. Once a corporation had enrolled, the district undertook two surveys. First, the corporation's plant was inspected to identify possible areas for conducting classes and programs at the work site. All spaces, including work areas, were inventoried and their potential recorded and stored in a computer.

Second, the district conducted a needs assessment. If company policy permitted, instruments were distributed through employee paychecks. The alternative was to leave them with the personnel officer, who distributed the surveys at the workplace.

Employees returned surveys to boxes located at convenient and prominent places in the plant. Typically, staff computed a thirty-three percent return rate. The survey consisted of a single sheet with questions on both sides. Survey instructions stated:

Recreation has been defined as "what anyone likes to do in his or her leisure time." In order that our recreation program will fully reflect your interest, this questionnaire offers you an opportunity to indicate those recreation activities in which you are interested — the things that you would like to do in your spare time. Although not all of these activities are now part of our program, a definite attempt will be made to add activities in which a substantial interest is expressed. If you have a favorite hobby or interest that is not listed, add it in the blanks provided.

The questionnaire listed a total of 120 recreation activities classified in five major categories: (1) sports activities; (2) social activities, sub-divided into (a) card and table games and (b) other social activities; (3) outing activities; (4) cultural activities, sub-divided into (a) theatricals, (b) out-of-town visits to concerts, opera, lectures, etc., (c) fine arts, (d) handicrafts, (e) movies in the plant, (f) music, and (g) other cultural activities; and (5) miscellaneous activities such as fashion shows and first-aid programs.

The forms were coded and analyzed by computer. The district identified activities that employees requested. Staff also delineated the interests of different groups. Experience had shown that senior management, middle management, shop-floor personnel, and secretaries, for example, preferred to recreate with members of the same group and did not want to mix with other groups.

The Johnson County Park and Recreation District served as a broker to bring together employee constituents desiring specified recreation services with the necessary facilities and qualified instructors. A recreation committee was established within each corporation to suggest service improvements to the district. Members of this committee were drawn from all segments of the work force and required to become active participants in the program. The district handled all employee registration for programs. Only those that had proven successful elsewhere in the county were offered. This decreased the risk of compromising program quality.

The county used four operational alternatives to provide programs and services to its corporate constituency. The preferred approach was to offer programs on site. The initial corporate facility inventory revealed those spaces in the plant or on the grounds that could serve as areas for fitness classes, instructional programs, leagues, and special events. However, in many instances in-house facilities were inadequate for accommodating all employee interests.

A second alternative was to offer corporate employee programs at public facilities. Johnson County's recreation division did not own any tax-supported recreation facilities, but it leased space on a short-term basis at seventy-nine locations in the county, mainly from the six school districts. The leasing policy had at least one advantage; because the agency was not tied to specific facilities, it could be flexible and better adapt its offerings to shifts in population and interest.

Only thirty percent of Johnson County households had children in the school systems. When school facilities were not being used, they served as recreational areas for some of those community members with no children. This way more households became receptive to additional tax support for area school systems.

School districts are reluctant to lease their facilities directly to a private corporation. Typically, they assign the business low priority in any competition for space, and charge substantially higher rates than those paid by public entities. Since school districts are very willing to lease facilities to the district, however, Johnson County was able to act as broker and make them available for corporate use. This partially explains the district's success in attracting six companies into its corporate program that had their own full- or part-time recreation personnel. (During times of troubled economy, management is often reluctant to justify a full-time position for recreational duties. The position is instead assigned to a staff member with additional public relations or personnel duties.) These companies were limited in what they could offer because of a restricted number of facilities. Participation in the district's corporate program enhanced the range of recreational opportunities that they were able to offer employees.

A third service approach was to integrate corporate programs with those offered to the general public. In all general class programs, leagues, or tournaments, the district reserved twenty-five percent of the places for its corporate constituents. Thus, in a class with a maximum enrollment of twenty, fifteen places were allocated to the general public and five to corporate employees. If either group did not use its entire allocation, the remaining spaces were offered to members of the other group on the waiting list. This provision made it possible to cater to employee interest groups that were too small to make it financially feasible to run programs at the plant site. Although this agenda was geared primarily to the general public, companies subsidized their employees' participation because they believed it was equitable to support *all* employee recreation interests and not only those that justified large programs.

A fourth alternative was to organize classes for employees at private facilities. Staff negotiated agreements with two bowling alleys, both county ice rinks, a tennis center, five racquetball clubs, and three fitness centers. This added a dimension to the district's relationship with the corporate sector. In essence, this approach to brokering services meant that Johnson County contracted with recreation businesses to provide services for the employees of other business.

Staff approached a commercial recreation business and asked if it would be interested in the district's recreation division contracting for non-prime time for lessons, short-term leagues, or free-play periods. The businesses benefited from receiving income at off-peak times that they would not otherwise have gotten and from introducing clients to their facility who later became regular users. In addition, businesses received considerable promotional exposure because the district advertised their locations when it advertised program offerings.

Program participants were able to sample recreational opportunities at a relatively low cost without any long-term membership commitment. For example, an annual subscription at a fitness club was likely to cost around three hundred dollars, while the district's class cost thirty dollars.

This "sampling" was viewed as a trial period. If participants wanted to join a fitness club, the club deducted thirty dollars from the three-hundred-dollar membership. The district benefited from using commercial facilities because it gained credibility by offering good facilities and good instructors.

Traditional recreation classes and program offerings built consistent credibility with corporations over a period of years. As a result, Johnson County was able to broaden its services. Staff developed an extensive trip program for the corporate constituency. Organizing employee excursions emerged as a major service. Trips that featured skiing, floating, rafting, fishing, hunting, and visits to football and baseball games proved most popular. Again, the district was a broker. Its staff found out what employees wanted, developed a package tailored to satisfy those wants, and then invited local travel agents to bid on the package or organize it in-house.

Overall, Johnson County staff found that companies have considerable dollars available for employee recreation. However, the district recommended that employees pay some of the costs rather that having the company assume full responsibility. If individual employees did not pay, they tended to be less committed to the program. Most companies offered to contribute half the cost and expected employees to pay the remaining half. Involvement of spouses and children occurred at the discretion of the company. The company's personnel or recreation officer was also responsible for collecting fees and paying invoices submitted by the district for activities selected by employees.

The corporate program operated as an enterprise fund and was self-sufficient. One district staff person was in charge of the entire corporate program. She had a cadre of fifty part-time supervisors or instructors with whom the recreation division contracted to deliver each of the services offered. Johnson County's invoice to the corporation was calculated on the basis of 130 percent of the direct cost of a program. (The thirty percent overhead cost was sufficient to cover all administrative and fixed costs of the corporate program.) The major promotional tool was the district's monthly corporate newsletter, which was mailed to senior management and employees enrolled in the program. Flyers and brochures broadened the advertising.

THE CORPORATE CHALLENGE

The Kansas City Corporate Challenge, which the county co-sponsored and initiated in 1980, was a natural evolution of this corporate program. It provided more rigorous competitive opportunities. Today it is jointly organized by the Jackson County and Johnson County Park and Recreation Departments. In 1986, fifty-eight companies had six thousand employees participating with each other in sixty activities over two long weekends. (See Table 3.1.) Preliminary in-house competitions, organized by corporate personnel officers, yielded representatives to the larger event. Jackson and Johnson County coordinated and arranged the facilities for these internal competitions.

TABLE 3.1

1986 Participating Companies in the Kansas City Corporate Challenge

American Stair Glide Corporation
AT&T Technologies
Baptist Health Services
Bendix Kansas City Division
Bethany Medical Center
Black & Veatch
Blue Cross & Blue Shield
Business Men's Assurance
Butler Manufacturing
Citi-Corp. Credit Services
Commerce Bank
Continental Healthcare Systems
Defense Mapping Agency
Deluxe Check Printers
Electronic Data Systems
Employers Reinsurance Corporation
Farmland Industries
Federal Reserve Bank of Kansas City
Hallmark Cards
Harmon Industries, Inc.
Home Box Office
Housing Authority of Kansas City, Missouri
Howard-Needles-Tammen & Bergendoff
JC Penney Catalog
Johnson County Employees
Kansas City Bulkmail Center
Kansas City Life Insurance
Kansas City Power & Light
KCSI/DST
Kansas City Star-Times
Lawyers Association of Kansas City
Leo Eisenburg & Company
Marine Corps Finance Center
Marion Laboratories
The Marley Company
Mercantile Bank & Trust
Missouri Public Service
Mobay Chemical Company
Owens-Illinois
Panhandle Eastern Pipeline
Payless Cashway, Inc.
Peterson Manufacturing
Proctor & Gamble
Shawnee Mission Post Office
Southwestern Bell
St. Luke's Hospital
United Missouri Bancshares, Inc.
United States Postal Service, Kansas City, Missouri

US Telecom
Waddell & Reed
Western Auto
W.W. Grainger
Yellow Freight Systems

Corporations take the Challenge seriously, recognizing its morale and team-oriented potential. Some of them record employee performances on video, which they show periodically in company dining rooms, during recruitment efforts, and at new-employee orientation sessions. The entry fee is 650 dollars per company; profits are donated to the Special Olympics and companies provide all volunteers. Jackson and Johnson Counties select officials and "game captains" who serve as coordinators for each of the sixty activities.

If a company develops its own facilities, it has to invest substantial capital dollars and cater only to the relatively small number of employees who can be accommodated by the facilities. Hence, from the companies' perspectives, the park and recreation district corporate program is the most cost-efficient approach to offering an extensive range of recreation opportunities to employees.

Employers are more and more committed to making recreation and sports activities available for employees. This is considered a sound investment because it contributes to employee well-being. Three factors have stimulated this investment in employee recreation: (1) it may attract new employees and help retain staff, (2) it may reduce absenteeism, sickness, and accidents, and (3) it may improve working relationships.

From the employee's perspective, the corporate program has four major attributes: First, most people like to engage in activities with others rather than by themselves. Reasons for not participating have included, "There's no one else to do it with," and "I don't know anyone else in the program, so I don't want to go." The corporate program ties into the existing social network at the workplace and increases the likelihood that familiar people will participate, too. Another dimension of this networking is the opportunity to establish contact with personnel in other corporations.

Second, whenever possible, the corporate program tries to provide opportunities at the work site that adjoin working hours. This helps employees limit travel time and makes involvement more appealing.

Third, information about the activities is relatively easy to find. Citizen awareness of public recreation opportunities is often low because communication with target groups is difficult. In contrast, in the corporate program it is relatively easy to contact employees directly and develop promotions specifically for them. The social-group network makes it easier for word-of-mouth communication to reach established opinion leaders.

Fourth, because all program offerings are guided by each corporation's advisory committee, they can be tailored to the wishes of each corporation's employees. Some companies, for example, prefer to use adapted rules rather than abide by generally accepted rules of a game.

Public recreation and park agencies frequently solicit support from the business community to offset to some degree the declining availability of tax dollars. Yet continued government cutbacks have led to increased competition for corporate giving. Servicing corporations through leisure-service brokerage opportunities establishes rapport and credibility with management. Seeking donations is thus likely to be easier.

NON-CORPORATE PROGRAMS

The success of the corporate program caused Johnson County Park and Recreation District staff to expand the concept to include apartment complexes, county clubs, hotels, day-care centers, and churches. These efforts had mixed success.

Five apartment or condominium complexes enrolled in the program as well. However, the effort to serve this group was not as vigorous as that committed to the main corporate program because the high turnover rate of apartment-complex managers was disruptive. In addition, they generally did not have a good communication channel, such as a monthly newsletter or magazine, through which to promote programs. Nevertheless, this was perceived as a market with considerable potential.

These complexes had recreational facilities, but complex managers were not trained to offer recreation programs or operate facilities. Johnson County offered lessons, for example, in swimming and tennis and created senior-citizen programs for residents. The district paid and trained all recreation personnel, which eliminated some of the liability risk from the complex area. In turn, complexes provided facilities at no charge to Johnson County because they added to their market appeal.

Additionally, the district was approached by a tennis club and asked to manage the club's tennis and pool complex. This involved maintaining the facilities, offering programs and lessons, and hiring all personnel.

There were not many hotels in Johnson County, but their number was increasing, so staff initiated a joint program. Four hotels agreed to participate, and the recreation division provided passes and a directory of programs and facilities that hotel staff distributed to guests upon request. If guests wished to participate in any of the district's general programs, the hotel supplied a pass that secured admission. Then the district redeemed the value of the pass from the hotel. In this manner, the hotel gained goodwill and did not have to install extensive, expensive recreation equipment and facilities to attract guests.

The program had only limited success for two reasons. First, when guests check in at a hotel in the evening, they are usually fatigued and prefer Home Box Office television in their rooms and bar facilities within the building. Also, while hotel managers viewed the district's program as a means of catering to those guests who requested additional recreational amenities, they did not actively promote programs that cut into the time and money that guests spent on their own bars, restaurants, etc. In addition, the seasonal nature of Johnson County's programs created problems for front-desk hotel staff. They found it difficult to keep up with the changes in schedule.

The district contracted with a number of day-care centers to provide recreation programs for their children. These programs were offered at public-school facilities, particularly aquatic areas leased to Johnson County during slack seasons. In addition, the district offered programs after school and over summer vacation for the same age groups.

Staff also initiated a pilot program with a church that had indoor recreation facilities and had been offering programs to its members. Traditionally organized by volunteers, these activities were inconsistent due to an uneven voluntary effort, and the church wanted to channel the labor of its congregation into other functions perceived to be more central to its mission. This was where the district stepped in, providing volleyball, a preschool program, and aerobics classes for church members.

CONCLUDING COMMENTS

Almost every community has the opportunity to develop a program for corporations or the other sectors mentioned above. Corporations have not been a traditional market target for public recreation and park agencies, but in times of financial difficulty a corporate program offers a very cost-efficient way of reaching substantial numbers of citizens. Serving this market offers a large return on efforts invested to citizens employed by those companies, to the corporations, and to the recreation and park agency.

SOURCE:

A version of this case study first appeared as an article written by John L. Crompton and Leon E. Younger in *Parks and Recreation*, May, 1983.

15

Developing a Comprehensive Sponsorship Program

This case describes the successful systematic process that Jackson County has instituted to solicit sponsorship for special events and programs. It involves identification of potential sponsor companies, their target markets, key decision-makers in each company, and the companies' budget cycles; the identification of agency staff and supporters who have personal contacts in these companies; and the establishment of personal links between agency staff and company personnel. A description of how sponsorship proposals are developed is included.

In 1986, the Jackson County Parks and Recreation Department, which is located in Missouri in the Kansas City area, scheduled over forty special events. When the list of these events was presented to the county's legislators at the start of the financial year as part of the department's total program, all the sponsoring corporations, businesses, service clubs, foundations, and individuals had signed contracts. (See Figure 3.1.) These events received no tax support from the county in terms of direct costs. Direct cash received from the sponsoring organizations exceeded 300,000 dollars, and in-kind support that they provided was estimated to be more than that amount. The department initiates and coordinates the events and does allocate a limited amount of time and staff to each, but sponsors underwrite all other expenses, or else they are met by participant fees, permits, or trade-outs. The

typical amount requested from sponsors is between one and ten thousand dollars. This amount varies according to the event, its location, the market and how well-established the event is.

FIGURE 3.1

1986 List of Special Events and Projects

Event/Project	Sponsor/Donor
Sport Show	Marine Dealers Association
Boat Show	Jacomo Sailing Club
	Jacomo Pontoon Club
Show Crazy '86	WHB Radio
Riverboat Cotillion	Kansas City Riverboat, Inc.
Missouri Town Planting Day	Friends of Missouri Town
Special Recreation's Day of Champions	Jerry's Sports Shop
1st Annual Brookside Fine Arts Fair	Merchants of Blue Springs
5th Annual Fishing Derby for Kids	*Kansas City Star*
Wellness Fair	Baptist Memorial Hospital
NTFL Tournament	Coors
Fort Osage Riverdays	Riverdays Committee
	Kansas City Power & Light

Mid-America Cerebral Palsy Games	Kansas City Sports Shop
Summer Spirit Beach Party	Dannon Yogurt
Ed Whitney Soccer Tournament	Coca Cola
	Kansas City Printing
Kidfest	Discovery Toys
	Kansas City Parent Magazine
Special Recreation Softball Showdown	Kansas City Baseball Club (Royals)
Senior's Old-Fashioned Picnic	Doubletree Hotel
	Kansas City Masterpiece Bar-B-Q
Heritage Programs & Museums Craft Show	Merchants Association of Independence
Special Spirit Festival	Pizza Hut
Missouri Town 1855 Independence Day Celebration	Velvet Cream Popcorn
	Friendship Baptist Church
	Gate's Bar-B-Q
	Newcomer and Sons
Fishing Tournament	Pro Bass Inc.
Sandtastic Saturday	Kansas City Chiefs
	Jones Stores
Bike Race	Merillac Center for Children
Kansas City Comets Soccer Clinic	Kansas City Comets
Kansas City Comets Coaches Clinic	Kansas City Comets
H20 Expo	KLSI Radio
	Miller Bee
	Swinkles
	Vess Company
Fort Osage Rendezvous	Stone Container Corporation
	KMBZ TV
Labor Day Soccer Tournament	Coke
Sr. Adult Golf Tournament	Area Hotels and Restaurants
Fort Osage Knap-In Traders Row	Tom's Produce, Inc.
	Strauser Hardware
Heritage Programs & Museums Antique Show	Merchants of Independence
Goin' Hog Wild - Sr. Hayride/Pig Roast	R. B. Rice Company
Special Recreation Chili Dinner	Bob's IGA
Special Recreation Haunted Mansion	Discovery Toys
Jacomo/Longview Cleanup Day	McDonald's
Children's Day at Missouri Town 1855	*Kansas City Parent Magazine*
	Children's Palace

Missouri Town 1855 Christmas Open House	Friends of Missouri Town
Longview Celebrity Golf Tournament	Many prize donors,including: Airlines, hotels, furriers, etc.
Educational Poster for Youth	Kansas City Southern Industries
4 Triathlons	US Sprint, Baptist Hospital, Menorah Hospital
Day of Champions	Kansas City Chiefs
River Days	Port Authority
Bike Tour	Coors
First-Grade Forestry	County Extension Service
Beautification Day	Wake Up to Missouri campaign.

Jackson County does not approach a corporation for charitable donations. Instead the department seeks funds from its promotions budget for projects that bring a return on an investment. This reflects a recognition that managers of a business have no right to give away the company's money in donations.

The department's managers view themselves as providing corporations or organizations with the opportunity to invest in product promotion or public relations through special events, trade-outs, or projects. They make every effort to match a prospect corporation's interests, products, and target markets with the nature or theme of an event and the socio-demographic make-up of the clientele likely to participate. In seeking sponsors or contributors, the key question staff must ask is, "What kinds of businesses can use this project or event, given the target market it is likely to draw, to improve their public visibility?"

The key to developing this extensive sponsorship program lies in the thorough, detailed, and systematic networking approach that the department has implemented. It is designed to assist staff members in initiating corporate contracts for services, manpower, and materials that offset the cost of county-sponsored programming. The intent is to encourage local corporations and service organizations to invest in park and recreation programs and services on a continuing basis; to secure corporate contacts for (1) annual programs, (2) special-event sponsorships, and (3) major capital projects. It also stimulates gift-giving for community programs in the form of service, manpower, materials, and supplies.

Networking and scheduling is computerized. It enables the department to scan corporate interests and characteristics, then quickly compile a list of prospective corporations or service organizations likely to sponsor or partially invest in a particular event or project. Thus the department can make the right contract with the right sponsoring organization at the right time.

RESEARCHING SPONSORSHIP CANDIDATES

All area businesses, professional and civic organizations, and social clubs deemed to be potential candidates for sponsorships or contributions were identified. Staff identify them through the Yellow Pages, local chamber-of-commerce business listings, libraries, and the *Kansas City Business Journal.*

Staff also made an effort to identify people in the community who have contacts at each of the companies on that list and who support Jackson County's park and recreation programs. All management staff also named contacts they themselves had at these businesses. Members of the thirty-four advisory interest groups (e.g., sailing clubs, soccer associations, historic groups) with whom the department works were also inventoried and their company contacts identified. Finally, staff shared the list with civic and political leaders in the community who support the department's programs.

The role of the contact person is to "open the door" and secure an interview for a Jackson County staff person with the key individual at each business who can make the sponsorship decision.

In addition to this community network, the department established a public relations advisory board comprised of people who are public relations professionals in radio, television, the press, sales, advertising, and graphics. These people are able to serve as "gatekeepers" because they have an extensive range of business contacts and can assist the department in accessing sponsors. This board provides a steady flow of information on corporations' promotional needs. They assist in analyzing which company may be the best target for sponsoring an event and which media are most likely to be interested in cosponsoring it or providing trade-outs.

A key resource in compiling this list is the *Contacts Influential Directory.* This directory is published in over thirty major metropolitan market areas by Contacts Influential Marketing Information Services. It provides a comprehensive, current listing of all area businesses, identifying their location, mailing address, phone number, type of business, number of employees, and the names and responsibilities of senior managers. Companies are further classified as one of three types: national headquartered locally, national with local branch offices, and locally owned.

The *Standard Directory of Advertisers* is also a valuable source of information. It contains an extensive inventory of the largest advertisers in the United States, their annual advertising budgets, the month which begins the cycle, and the media through which they advertise. In some cases the advertising budget is broken down by media. Many major companies headquartered in the Kansas City area are listed in this publication.

A new information source in which the department is considering investing is *DATEXT*, a data base-cum-software which costs between 9,600 and 20,000 dollars depending on the particular data bases needed and the amount of on-line connect time used. The complete package consists of a CD-ROM player; four CD-ROM disks covering over ten thousand public companies in the service, technological, industrial, and commercial sectors; and CD/Newsline, a direct link to the Dow Jones News/Retrieval data base that allows your computer to gather current news and quotes from that source. New, updated CD-ROMs are sent out to buyers monthly.

In addition to the type of information provided by the *Contacts Influential Directory*, the *DATEXT* data base contains a very comprehensive set of financial data consisting of fifty-seven different criteria such as return-on-equity, return-on-assets, net sales, net income, gross margin, income statements, balance sheets, stock reports, and investment reports. In addition, lists of subsidiary companies and an abstracted bibliography of recently published articles related to the company of interest are included. A list of corporate officers and their titles, ages, and salaries is contained on each company's profile. Each executive also has a separate data file that contains this informaion and a personal biography. The biography features such details as date and place of birth, educational background, marital status, family members, professional and social affiliations, and career history.

New companies moving into Jackson County have proved to be particularly responsive targets. Frequently, the chamber of commerce compiles a weekly list of such companies. These companies are often looking for vehicles that give them a positive image, rapid visibility, name recognition, and maybe even product-trial opportunities. They may be especially appropriate targets for a first-time event with which a company can be associated at the outset and grow with as the event develops in subsequent years.

COMPUTER FILES

A computer file, CORPNET, was created using the SMART Data Manager Software to store the information. Staff issued each company an account number of 0 through 6 using the following classification:

0 — <100 employees
1 — 101-250 employees
2 — 251-500 employees
3 — 501-1000 employees
4 — National Headquarters (regardless of size)
5 — >1000 employees
6 — Civic, social, and service organizations and churches

Each record contains the account number, the company name, address, phone number, contact person and title, type of company, product or service provided, advertising budget, budget cycle, advertising media, and space to record any contributions that a company has made. (See Figure 3.2.) Companies are added to the network as new contacts are made and new projects are explored.

FIGURE 3.2

The CORPNET File

| Account Type: | 4 |
| Prospect Corp.: | Jones Manufacturing |

Mailing Address:	P.O. Box 1000
Mailing City:	Kansas City
Mailing State:	MO
Mailing Zip:	64141
Location:	31st & Southwest Trafficway
Location City:	Kansas City
Location State:	MO
Location Zip:	64141
Telephone:	(816) 968-1234
I Contact/Title:	Frank Jones - Chief Executive Officer
II Contact/Title:	Bill East - President
Type of Company:	HEADQUARTERS building systems manufacturing
# of Employees:	500
Product/Service:	Engineering, manufacturing, marketing of building systems for non-residential construction and grain-storage bins and farm buildings. Underfloor electrical distribution systems, agricultural products and energy-management systems.
Budget Month:	October
Adv. Budget:	$3,000,000
Adv. Media:	Newspapers, consumer magazines, business publications, direct mail to consumers and business establishments, network and spot radio.
Contribution A:	
Date A:	00/00/00
Project A:	
Contribution B:	
Date B:	00/00/00
Project B:	
Contribution C:	
Date C:	00/00/00
Project C:	
Reason Declined:	

The budget cycle for each company's promotion budget is identified. Each week the computer prints out a list of corporations whose advertising budget cycle is due to begin in eight weeks' time. This eight-week lead period gives staff the time to reestablish contact with the corporation's decision makers and to prepare a sponsorship proposal for possible inclusion in their next year's advertising budget. Many times opportunities for sponsorship are missed because, although a corporation is interested, it cannot offer support because the project is not included in the current budget.

Each management person in the department is assigned to be the department's liaison with a number of businesses. They are responsible for identifying who controls the spending for advertising and establishing a relationship with him or her. In making these assignments, the department attempts to match the personalities and interests of each staff member with those of the corporation's decision-maker. Being liaison person with a corporation does not mean that a staff person is responsible for implementing the event that is sponsored. To avoid burn-out within the department, no staff person is permitted to directly implement more than three sponsored projects per year. This also ensures that special-projects expertise is widely spread throughout the staff.

A second file, FOLLOW-UP, maintains a record of all contacts made with prospective sponsors or contributors by phone, mail, or in person. Each record contains the company name, the person contacted, and the project with which the contact was concerned. Files are provided for the dates and explanations of four contacts, their decisions to accept or decline a proposition, and comments they make about the association that might be helpful at a later date. (See Figure 3.3.) In this file staff also keep a log of the companies to which a sponsor or contributor proposal was sent, the date it was mailed, and all follow-up contacts concerning that project. This type of system is valuable in preventing duplication; companies are not invited by different people to sponsor different events without internal coordination of these requests.

FIGURE 3.3

The FOLLOW-UP File

Company:	ABC Company
Contact:	Joe Smith, VP/Sec.
Project:	Missouri Town Educational Poster for Youth
Date:	07/09/86
Explain:	Mailed 1986 and 1987 Missouri Town 1855 Educational Poster Youth Sponsor Proposal
Date:	07/17/86
Explain:	Received letter asking to set up time for a presentation. Set meeting for August 1, 1986, 9:00 am
Date:	08/01/86
Explain:	Meeting with Mr. Smith and John Jones. Explained the restoration project and the poster concepts. They will be in touch with us after they make a decision.
Date:	09/01/86
Explain:	Mr. Smith phoned. ABC Company accepted our proposal.
Conclusion:	Contribution of $25,000 for poster project.
Comments:	

PROPOSALS/SPONSOR PACKAGES

Long before an event or the beginning of a special project (the time varies according to magnitude and type), staff compile a list of sponsorship needs. These are usually categorized under money, manpower, materials, and special services. The director and project coordinator then identify companies that appear to have matching interests and target markets that would be capable of supplying these needs. A list of target sponsors/contributors is compiled and a sponsor/contributor package carefully tailored to each company is developed. This package is incorporated into a proposal that explains the event or project undertaken and the commitment sought.

The proposal is limited to two pages and outlines the goals of the project, benefits to sponsors and the community, promotional plans, and other useful information pertaining to the project. If the sponsor expresses interest, details are discussed and agreed on in subsequent face-to-face visits. A sample proposal is presented in Appendix 1. Figure 3.4 lists some of the general benefits accruing to sponsors/donors. Each specific project has different benefits associated with it.

The director gives each sponsor a verbal commitment that the company will receive at least three times the value of their investment in media

---

FIGURE 3.4

Some of the Benefits Accruing to Sponsors for Investing Their Time, Materials, Manpower, Money, or Products

PSAs Promoting Event
    The department develops and submits PSAs to local newspapers and radio stations to promote events. This promotion works to maximize attendance at events and increase sponsor exposure. Established contacts with key media personnel ensure effective use of PSAs.

News Releases Acknowledging Contributions
    Contributions to the Parks and Recreation Department are publically acknowledged through newspaper articles, radio, and TV as appropriate.

Tax Deductions
    All donations, direct or through sponsorships, are tax deductible.

Recognition in Park Tabloid
    Sponsors and contributors are recognized in the Jackson County Parks and Recreation tabloid, which is distributed to 100,000 homes quarterly.
    Electronic Media Coverage of Events
    Many of the major projects and events receive television coverage that attracts attention to the sponsors.

Plaques Placed in Prominent Positions
    The department acknowledges donations by erecting plaques or placing signs in prominent positions. Examples include plaques in parks or on golf courses, or signs on donated vehicles or playground equipment.

Names in Brochures
    Sponsors of events are featured in brochures printed by the department to promote the event.

Sponsor Boards
    When appropriate, sponsor boards with color photos are produced for display in the sponsor's place of business and in the park building (pool, golf clubhouse, historic building, etc.)

Right to Promote Services at an Event
    Sponsors are given the right to promote their product or service at the event through signage, giveaways, premiums, novelties, coupons, or other methods agreed upon by the department.

---

publicity. The agency tracks all media mentions of the sponsor, assigns a dollar value to each reference based on the paid advertising rate, and includes this documentation in the post-event evaluation given to the sponsor. Surveys are conducted at sponsored events so the demographics of participants can be related back by both the agency and the company to the company's target market. This may also be useful for selling the event to another company with a similar target market in the future if the original sponsor withdraws.

The department can deliver celebrities such as local television newscasters or professional sports personalities to an event. This substantially increases the quantity of press coverage provided and enhances the quality of the event in the public's eyes.

If the company agrees to sponsor an event, standard binding contracts are signed that clearly document the expectations and responsibilities of both partners (See Appendix 2.) The contracts are drafted by the county attorney's office, reviewed by the Parks and Recreation Director, amended as necessary, and then presented to the county's legislators for their final approval. The department seeks not only to obtain monetary sponsorship, but also to involve the corporation's employees in assisting with it. The department's staff are given flexibility to negotiate for this cooperation. Someone from the company is appointed and expected to contribute to, the special-event project committee. Therefore the company is fully aware of the planning and costs that go into producing the event.

In addition, volunteer groups from the company may be involved in the project, e.g. at information booths, as on-site hosts, or in post-event pick-up and trash collection. This involvement by employees leads to a much greater sense of commitment by the company and often leads them to increase their investment by suggesting additional components for the event or up-grading existing components.

The chief executive officers of companies tend to change rather frequently, and such changes often lead to a review and perhaps termination of previous sponsor-ship arrangements. A new chief executive may seek changes in the company's image, and this may involve changing promotion strategies and advertising agencies so that existing sponsorships may no longer be compatible with the company's goals.

When a targeted sponsor rejects a sponsorship pro-posal, staff always make an effort to find out why. They ask themselves questions like, was the package wrong? Did we fail to deliver enough benefits? Was the return on the sponsor's projected investment inade-quate? Did we ask for too much of an investment? Did we misread the sponsor's target market? Did we send the wrong person? Was the presentation ineffec-tive?

It is essential to follow up and ascertain why the proposal was not accepted and if the company would be interested in working with the department in the future. This information is entered into the computer.

Experience in Jackson County suggests that there are three major reasons why targeted corporations reject sponsorship opportunities when the department feels confident of success. First and most common is the fundamental mistrust which some corporations have of a government agency. Most of a corporation's dealings with government are often perceived to be negative be-cause they tend to be associated with such items as propery evaluation, taxation, inspections, and zoning. This general negativism is hard to overcome if deci-sion-makers in the business are not acquainted with the park and recreation department's operations.

Second, sponsoring companies are required to insure the county against liability associated with a special event as well as insure themselves since the county is self-insured. Sometimes companies refuse to do this. Finally, there are political nuances. For example, if the county commission is predominantly Democratic and a corporation's chief executive is Republican, it may preclude that corporation from sponsoring a county event.

SOURCE:

Jackson County Parks and Recreation Department
22807 Woods Chapel Road
Blue Springs, Missouri 64015

APPENDIX 1

Sample Proposal Seeking Corporate Sponsorship

Introduction. The Jackson County Parks and Recreation Department has undertaken a project at Missouri Town 1855 to restore the original Colonel's House. The house has sat in a shell state for eighteen years and has been the centerpiece of the town's development since it was moved from Bates City, MO. The total number of dollars needed to restore the house is two hundred fifty thousand. The Jackson County Parks and Recreation Department has put in fifty thousand dollars to develop all architectural plans and specifications. This will ensure that the home is restored to its original state.

Jackson County Parks and Recreation has contracted with John Muller & Co. to assist us in the development of an educational poster that can be used as an educa-tional tool for the eighty thousand students and teachers who visit Missouri Town 1855 each year.

The colorful poster is unique in that there are one hun-dred questions relating to facts about life in 1855 that are presently portrayed at Missouri Town. Each student is provided with a poster and a pen. As they reach each question, they color the area directly below and the cor-rect answer to the question emerges from invisible ink, helping the student learn about Missouri Town and his heritage. This visual learning aid will be given to each student who comes through the town and is paid for by the group tour fee. All proceeds from the poster will be used in the restoration of the Colonel's House.

Sponsorships are needed to fund the poster. This pro-posal outlines the benefits of participating in the poster project.

1986 & 1987 Goals for the Missouri Town 1855 Educa-tional Poster for Youth

A. Create an awareness among the youth, teachers, and parents who visit Missouri Town each year of the heritage and history of what life was like in 1855 through a colorful educational poster.

B. Create a poster that generates positive public awareness for individual sponsors through pre- and post-poster publicity and on-site impressions.

C. Create a poster within a limited budget that returns the profits to the restoration of the Colonel's House to ensure future generations the opportunity to view what life was like in 1855.

D. Ensure attractive demographics that match a sponsor's targeted demographics in developing the poster.

Pre- and Post-Poster Publicity

The Jackson County Parks and Recreation Department will mail programs to approximately 10,000 teachers in the Kansas City area promoting the poster for fall educational school trips to Missouri Town.

Jackson County will host a press conference announcing the poster concept and a sponsor's participation in the development of the poster.

Jackson County will provide a promotional ad in the County Parks and Recreation tabloids that are distributed to 100,000 homes each season in Jackson County and surrounding counties for Fall 1986, Winter, Spring, Summer, and Fall 1987.

Jackson County will post the poster on activity bulletin boards in Jackson County schools.

Jackson County will promote the poster and sponsor at the Fall 1986 and 1987 Missouri Town Festival, a two-day celebration which annually draws 50,000 people.

Jackson County will submit to print media through PSA and written articles the concept and usage of the educational poster to these prominent publications:

Teachers' Magazines
KC Times
KC Star
USA Today
Raystown Post
KC Magazine
Corporate Report
Scholastic Magazines
Independence Examiner
Blue Springs Examiner
Lee's Summit Journal

Grandview Advocate
Children's magazines
Historic magazines
"Heritage Programs
 & Museums" newsletter

"Friends of Missouri
 Town" newsletter
*Kansas City Business
 Journal*

Jackson County will encourage electronic media coverage through special news reports inviting stations to come out to Missouri Town 1855 and look at the restoration project and the youth poster concept. This will include channels 9, 4, 5, 62, and 41.

Reports to Sponsors

Ensure the sponsor receives accurate demographic breakdowns during 1986 and 1987 of who received the poster by age, sex, race, and the area of the city in which they live. This will help to assure the sponsors that the posters were used as envisioned in the original plan and provide an account of both parents' and youths' reactions to the poster.

Benefits to the Community

The primary goal of the poster is to raise money for the Colonel's House through generous sponsor donations in development of the educational poster. The program will accomplish two things: demonstrate that history education can be fun and beneficial to students through the poster concept, and complete the Colonel's House, which will restore a major piece of the total Missouri Town Master Plan that the 150,000 visitors each year can appreciate.

APPENDIX 2

Cooperative Agreement

This Agreement made and entered into, by and between Jackson County, Missouri, a corporate body acting through its Chief Executive (hereinafter referred to as the "County") and Heartland Entertainment, Inc., a Missouri corporation located at 6114 Morningside Drive, Kansas City, Missouri 64133 (hereinafter referred to as "Heartland").

WITNESSETH:

WHEREAS, the County may contract with one or more individuals, municipalities, counties, and other organizations for the purpose of providing entertainment to the citizens of Jackson County; and

WHEREAS, Heartland proposes to produce THE LITTLE BLUE RIVER FESTIVAL, a festival of old-time music and special related events;

NOW THEREFORE, the parties hereto do mutually agree as follows:

1. *Services to be Performed.* Heartland will provide a music festival with related activities as more fully set out in Exhibit A, which is attached hereto and incorporated herein by reference. Said event shall be held on June 22, 23, and 24, 1985, on the Fleming Park grounds.

2. *Responsibilities of Heartland.* In addition to those responsibilities outlined in Exhibit A, Heartland covenants to:

a. provide on-site security for the event
b. provide bonded ticket handlers
c. provide all stage lighting and sound and all staging facilities for food and crafts displays
d. remove all festival-related items from park grounds within seven (7) days of the completion of the festival
e. provide pre-event forms for camping reservations at County-owned campsites
f. secure all necessary permits
g. provide County 15 days prior to festival a certificate evidencing the issuance of a general liability insurance policy protecting the parties from loss due to personal injury or death of participants and/or spectators and/or loss due to damage to property of others. Said public liability shall provide a limit on each accident or occurrence of not less than $1,000,000.00 Personal Injury and $1,000,000.00 Property Damage.
h. not permit garbage and other refuse to accumulate on park property during the festival, except in suitable garbage receptacles provided by the County.

3. *Financial Reporting.* Heartland will provide within 15 days a final ticket audit of the festival. Said report shall be submitted to the Manager of the Division of Finance, 415 East 12th Street, Kansas City, Missouri 64106.

4. *Rental Fee to County.* Heartland covenants to pay County the sum of $8,000.00 plus five percent of its gross ticket receipts for use of the site and for the services set out in paragraph 5.

5. *Services by the County.* The County shall provide the following services to Heartland

a. Clear site of all underbrush and small trees to a perimeter agreed upon by Heartland and County
b. Clear or clean up additional areas as agreed upon by Heartland and County
c. Provide adequate sanitation facilities (portable toilets), traffic control, trash receptacles, and trash removal at the end of each day
d. Provide for camping at normal designated County-owned camping sites, including normal security for sail camping sites. All fees from camping will be collected by and benefit the County

6. *Accountability and Records*. The County further reserves the right to examine and audit, during reasonable office hours, the books and records of Heartland pertaining to the finances and operations of the festival.

7. *Non-discrimination*. Heartland covenants to not discriminate on account of race, sex, religion, color, national origin, or age in the employment of any person or in admission to the festival and all related events.

8. *Option*. Heartland reserves the option to produce the festival at the designated site through 1988 with the option to renew for an additional five-year term. All terms of the agreement to be negotiated annually.

9. *No Conflict*. Heartland warrants that no officer or employee of the County, whether elected or appointed, shall in any manner whatsoever be interested in or receive any benefit from the profits or emoluments of this contract.

IN WITNESS WHEREOF, the County and Heartland have executed this Agreement this _____ day of _____, 1984.

JACKSON COUNTY, MISSOURI

By _____
                County Executive

HEARTLAND ENTERTAINMENT, INC.

APPROVED AS TO FORM:

_____
        County Counselor

_____

ATTEST:

_____
                Title

_____
    Clerk of the Legislature

EXHIBIT A

THE LITTLE BLUE RIVER FESTIVAL will feature a variety of continuous live musical performances and contests, plus workshops for the public on country dance, instrument-making, and performance technique on related instruments; from 2:00 pm to 8:30 pm on Friday, June 22, and from 10:00 am to 8:30 pm on Saturday, June 23, and from 10:00 am to 8:00 pm on Sunday, June 24.

The show producers will assign up to fifty spaces for music-oriented crafts; concessions for food and soft drinks; a limited number of commercial merchandisers, i.e. apparel, music (tapes and records); and instrument-makers.

Admission prices will be $6.00 for adults, $3.00 for children aged five to twelve, and free for children under five years of age. A ten-dollar weekend pass will be offered, too.

SITE AND SITE DEVELOPMENT

The Producer, in cooperation with Jackson County Parks and Recreation, designates the area of Fleming Park, now known as the Overflow Picnic Area, as the site for the festival, and has designated an appropriate site for a stage (amphitheater) location. Plans for a stage, which will serve as a first stage in this development, are attached.

The cleared area up to the second gate will serve as a parking area with the present Overflow Camping Area reserved for festival participants. Total usage of the area results in a contained, easily secured festival/special-event site. The easy access to primary roads (Highway 291), is noteworthy, as well as the proximity to existing park concessions and services.

ENTERTAINMENT, SPECIAL EVENTS, AND CHILDREN'S ACTIVITIES

THE LITTLE BLUE RIVER FESTIVAL is to be patterned after numerous successful events held annually in other parts of the county, including Vancouver, Philadelphia, and Winfield, Kansas. The old-time music theme, which includes country, bluegrass, gospel, and folk music, will feature headliners of this genre as well as professional and amateur talent from mid-America. In addition to scheduled performances, workshops and contests will be held both days.

CONCESSIONS

An area for food and soft drinks is planned, with adjacent park space for participants. The food available will be in keeping with the spirit and ambiance of the event. Chili- and barbecue-cooking competitions are planned, too.

CRAFTS BOOTHS

A limited number of booth spaces for handmade crafts will feature items in keeping with the music festival theme. Craftsmen will be invited to submit their proposed merchandise for jurying. Possible craft items include: musical instruments, music stands, camp stools, etc.

COMMERCIAL MERCHANDISE

Certain vendors appropriate to the festival theme will be allowed space within the festival, such as commercial instrument-makers, sheet-music salespeople, and tape, record, and western-apparel retailers. A festival shop might be developed that will feature memorabilia of the event.

16

CAUSE-RELATED MARKETING ®: Doing Well by Doing Good

CAUSE-RELATED MARKETING ® was pioneered by American Express. Every time somebody uses a company's product, the company makes a contribution to the cause it has adopted. This approach opens an entirely new channel of monetary support for park and recreation agencies and for non-profit arts and conservation organizations. It also harnesses the creative marketing talents of private companies and puts that skill to work improving awareness and interest levels of leisure projects or services.

Several examples have emerged of corporations linking with public or non-profit service agencies with the explicit objective of directly increasing sales of their product. This is termed "cause-related marketing" or "affinity-group marketing." It is a way of melding business with social responsibility.

American Express coined and copyrighted the phrase "cause-related marketing" to differentiate campaigns which tie charitable contributions directly to product promotions from standard corporate donations where dollars are given outright to a charitable cause. Every time somebody uses its products, the company makes a cash contribution to its non-profit partner. The non-profit partner receives not only the cash contribution, but also extensive publicity. The company's promotional effort typically includes an extensive advertising campaign that stresses the programs and community benefits delivered by the non-profit agency, together with ways in which the public can assist this organization.

This technique is particularly effective with affluent audiences. It is based on an appeal to Americans' social consciousness, the decline of the "me" generation, and an awareness that government is less willing or able to finance these causes than in the past. The rationale of American Express for using CAUSE-RELATED MARKETING ® is that local civic pride is a powerful stimulant to the sale and use of the company's products and services. At the same time, American Express gains the good will of a grateful community. In the words of their chairman, "cause-related marketing is our way of doing well by doing good."

American Express has been the most visible advocate of this approach. Since first adopting it on a test basis in four California cities in early 1981, the company has invested over thirty-one million dollars in cause campaigns over the past five years. During that period, sixty-four separate non-profit organizations received substantial direct donations based on the volume of American Express business transactions in their areas during set time periods. Eight million of the thirty-one invested consisted of direct donations to organizations. The remaining twenty-three million was spent on advertising for these programs.

Am Ex's chief executive officer states:

CAUSE-RELATED MARKETING ® is a registered servicemark of American Express and is used with permission.

CAUSE-RELATED MARKETING ® is not philanthropy. It is marketing in the public interest. Every organization must search out the fit between its own corporate activity and the public good. Business people miss this point entirely by thinking of corporate support only in terms of dollars.

The same principles used by American Express are applicable on a smaller scale to local businesses in all sizes of communities, and can be readily adopted by park and recreation agencies.

The surge of interest in CAUSE-RELATED MARKETING ® in the 1980s reflects the continuous search by companies to find a means of differentiating and distinguishing their product or service from those of competitors. It has been argued that a good cause helps shape a service's personality; "it can make one box of suds seem much more appealing than the next." Further, this approach is far less expensive for major corporations that a prime-time advertising campaign.

The company's chief executive officer states:

The program works. At first, we didn't know whether we'd found a new way to help business or just an interesting formula for giving money away. It's both. The increase in business we've seen in our cause-related markets proves the concept is as successful as any marketing program we've ever tried. We're doing good deeds, and we're also pleased with the commercial results.

Some advocates of CAUSE-RELATED MARKETING ® talk about the greater "bonding" with their brand that results when wholesalers, employees, and customers identify with the cause that is championed. Others have stated that retail chains are far more willing to adopt product promotions that are tied to a cause.

In addition to directly raising sales, companies also benefit from publicity and editorial acclaim that acknowledges their social responsibility. However, it is important to emphasize that in CAUSE-RELATED MARKETING ® this is only a secondary benefit and not of primary concern. The money for CAUSE-RELATED MARKETING ® comes from a company's marketing budget — not its philanthropic budget.

Each CAUSE-RELATED MARKETING ® program initiated by American Express begins with the announcement that the company will donate a small sum to the "cause" every time one of its clients in the area:

— uses the American Express card

— purchases American Express Travelers Cheques

— purchases a travel package of 500 dollars or more (excluding air fare) at an American Express vacation store

— applies for and receives a new American Express card.

Thus the size of donation to the selected cause depends on business done by the company in a specific geographic area during a set time period, typically three months.

But it is the program's most distinctive feature — a tailor-made advertising campaign that describes both the cause and the way American Express clients can help it — that most dramatically links the two. Most public or non-profit organizations can't afford either expert creative talent to write and design first-rate advertising or the money for placing ads in media that reach the proper audience. When a CAUSE-RELATED MARKETING ® program is implemented, the same talent and experience that go into American Express's other advertising efforts are harnessed to explain both the cause and the program to clients.

Besides generating a wealth of good will, cause-related promotions have had powerful catalytic effects. Local donations to each cause have increased, sometimes dramatically, even after the promotion ended. For example:

— The program resulted in a 25,000 dollar increase in ticket revenues for the San Jose Symphony. The symphony also received 107,000 dollars in *additional* corporate grants as a direct result of American Express involvement.

— Several prominent Pittsburgh business leaders who first heard of the organization through the American Express campaign are now serving on the board of the Pittsburgh Center for the Arts.

— With its four-million-dollar nationwide ad campaign, the Statue of Liberty CAUSE-RELATED

MARKETING ® program alerted millions of Americans to the need for restoration at a time when fund raising had just gotten underway. An official of the Statue of Liberty-Ellis Island Foundation said of the program, "It gave us a great boost at a time when we needed to be brought to the attention of the American public."

EXAMPLES OF CAUSE-RELATED MARKETING ® PROGRAMS

Many different types of organizations have benefited from the American Express program. Among them:

— three art museums

— a museum of science and industry

— three theater companies and one circus

— seven symphony orchestras and four operas

— five ballet companies

— four conservation efforts and a major municipal zoo

— four groups working to save historic monuments and buildings

— a community sports association and nine Olympic teams

— "umbrella" arts organizations and community outreach programs in nine cities.

The CAUSE-RELATED MARKETING ® program that American Express established with the Chicago Lincoln Park Zoo illustrates their approach. The Lincoln Park Zoo is owned and operated by the Chicago Park District. It is also supported by the Lincoln Park Zoological Society, a non-profit organization that provides funds and services to enhance the zoo beyond the park district budget.

American Express selected the zoo to approach because it had widespread name recognition, was the oldest, most-visited zoo in the country, had positive connotations in Chicago, and a visitor profile consistent with the Am Ex target market. The company agreed to make a small cash contribution to the zoo's

renovation program every time American Express services were used in twelve counties in the Chicago area. Terms of the commitment were as follows:

— one cent for each purchase charged to the American Express card

— one dollar for each approved American Express application

— fifteen cents for each purchase of American Express Travelers Cheques

— five dollars for each travel package of five hundred dollars or more (excluding air fare) purchased at an American Express Vacation Store.

This arrangement was widely promoted.

The zoo received 152,000 dollars in cash from the arrangement. However, perhaps more importantly, American Express invested heavily in an advertising program in the Chicago area promoting the arrangement and giving the zoo considerable exposure. The company ran television, radio, and print advertising explaining the program and describing the zoo's unique features, animals, and current needs. Point-of-sale advertising was displayed in restaurants, hotels, retail shops, and department stores.

The zoo's own promotion budget was minimal, and this program created a level of awareness in the community about what was going on at the zoo that could not otherwise have been achieved.

The approach is particularly effective if other businesses also cooperate in the effort. For example, American Express mounted a statewide program to fund research that would prevent beach erosion near North Carolina's historic Cape Hatteras Lighthouse. Among the reasons for the program's outstanding results were that a commuter airline connecting the Tarheel State's key cities contributed free space on its ticket schedules for a reprint of the ad and that all the state's tourist information counters displayed containers of American Express card applications. An executive of American Express, commenting on the success of the whole CAUSE-RELATED MARKETING ® program, stated:

One of the most gratifying aspects of the whole program was the way our business partners rallied around.

Banks that were selling other brands of travelers checks began to prefer ours. Restaurants and retailers that never accepted any cards began accepting the American Express card. And hundreds of these businesses in many markets not only displayed point-of-purchase material but often participated by making marketing donations of their own.

The restoration of the Statue of Liberty offered American Express a similar opportunity. This was their first cause-related program that involved the entire country rather than specified cities or regions. For a three-month period, the company contributed a penny to the restoration every time one of its credit cards was used during the last quarter of 1983. The project generated 1.7 million dollars for the Statue and a substantial increase in American Express card use.

When the campaign was initially conceived, the company projected an eighteen percent increase in credit-card transactions during that period. In fact, card use jumped seventy-eight percent and applications increased by forty-five percent. A telephone survey of cardholders commissioned by the company revealed that those questioned had a high awareness of the widely advertised promotion. A substantial number also said that they had indeed used their card more often to help this good cause.

Other examples of successful cause-related campaigns are numerous. For instance, in 1985 the Dallas Symphony Orchestra was looking for funds to help support a European tour, and found the money through a cause-related promotion with American Airlines. Coincidentally, the airline was introducing service between Dallas and London at about the time the symphony was looking for support. The airline offered to donate five dollars for every passenger who flew the new route. Within six months, they had raised 100,000 dollars for the symphony. In return, American was named the official airline of the Dallas Symphony Orchestra and was promoted in brochures sent to the up-market symphony supporters — many of whom were likely to be frequent flyers.

Companies are also beginning to produce products with names that solidify the relationship to the cause with which they tie in. For example, the Scott Paper Company has introduced a range of seven "Helping Hand" paper products. Every time a consumer purchases one of them, Scott donates five cents to a group of six charitable organizations involved with helping

children. Consumers are not very brand loyal when it comes to paper products, but this way the company appeals to the consumer's social conscience to achieve product loyalty.

The magnitude of the benefit to a corporation involved in CAUSE-RELATED MARKETING ® was again illustrated by the link-up between General Foods and MADD (Mothers Against Drunk Driving). General Foods sponsored a March Across America promotion by placing forty-seven million coupons for its Tang drink in newspapers across the county. The company pledged to contribute ten cents to MADD for every coupon that was redeemed up to 100,000 dollars. As a result of this tie-in, a thirteen percent positive movement in the Tang brand was tracked. As a company spokesman noted,

> There was nothing else going on with the brand, so it was a very clean test of the program. In addition, the program had the added benefit of 315 million impressions via press and broadcast reports and trade support for end-aisle displays, features, and cooperative advertisements which was 166 percent above normal.

A growing number of partnerships are emerging between banks who issue credit cards and non-profit organizations. Again the banks are seeking to capitalize on the good will of people for the social-cause groups with which they identify. For example, between June and August in 1986, twenty thousand of the 374,000 members of the Sierra Club signed up for Visa cards that the environmental group is now offering. The card, which features a Sierra Club logo, is issued by a subsidiary bank of Chase Manhatten Corporation. Every time someone uses the card, the Sierra Club receives a donation from the bank that ranges from one-half of one percent to five percent of the amount charged. The Club anticipates receiving twenty to forty dollars a year from each card holder, which means that twenty thousand card holders will generate 400,000 to 800,000 dollars a year.

By tapping people's loyalty to causes in this way, banks have an opportunity to encourage card-switching and increase their market share. The cost to the banks is relatively small since these payments reflect a small portion of what they earn from annual fees and the interest they charge card holders. It is also a small part of the percentage of each transaction — which ranges from 1.5 to six percent — that they charge their participating merchants.

According to many bank officials, these "donation-linked" credit cards may transform the credit-card market, and are likely to bring millions of dollars to non-profit organizations. Promoters of these cards challenge consumers to answer the question, "Why use a bank card that just gives money to the bank, when you can use one that gives money to a group you support?"

Credit-card marketing services are paid by banks to do research on organizations' memberships and then help sign up members. The cards are illustrated with the non-profit organization's logo and an appropriate inscription or illustration. For example, the Sierra Club's card includes a quote from John Muir: "When we try to pick out anything by itself, we find it hitched to everything else in the universe."

Not all such CAUSE-RELATED MARKETING ® programs are successful in improving company sales. For example, American Express developed a campaign called Project Hometown America. This project addressed the problems of drug abuse and homelessness, but failed to improve American Express sales. Refusing to hide behind vague statements about the project's publicity value, a company spokesman noted that the program had raised four million dollars for local social programs throughout the country. But the incremental increase in use of the American Express card and new card holders was marginal, so the program had to be judged a flop in terms of marketing. The real winners were the media and the ad agencies, who shared sixteen million dollars in ad spending for Project Hometown.

At a more local level, American Express raised ten thousand dollars in 1985 for the Broward County, Florida, public library by offering to donate fifty cents each time someone used their card at Fort Lauderdale's Galleria Shopping Mall. Each time a store in the mall forwarded a new credit-card application, the company contributed two dollars. This campaign increased credit-card use.

The potential for using the principle of CAUSE-RELATED MARKETING ® in the context of parks was illustrated by the link-up between the First National Bank of Denver and the Platte River Development Committee. First National is one of Denver's leading banks, and the agreement committed the bank to pay for planting a tree on the South Platte River corridor in the name of each depositor who put two

hundred dollars or more in a new or existing account during a given time period. The program was advertised extensively, giving substantial exposure to the South Platte River reclamation project. It raised thirty thousand dollars for the project.

Similarly, American Express donated five cents to the San Francisco Arts Festival every time customers used their card and two dollars for each new card member signed. The company exceeded its marketing goals because the program greatly stimulated card use. The Festival received a contribution of over 100,000 dollars.

CONCLUDING COMMENTS

CAUSE-RELATED MARKETING ® opens an entirely new channel of monetary support for parks and recreation agencies and for non-profit arts and conservation agencies. At the same time, and perhaps more importantly, it also harnesses the creative marketing talents of private companies and puts that skill to work improving awareness levels and heightening interest in leisure pursuits.

To this point, most of these projects have arisen from the initiative of the private company. For example, in the case of American Express, they hire consultants who visit each city anonymously and scan the cultural scene. They talk to community arts leaders, get important data on various groups such as planning calendars and financial statements, and evaluate specific projects. The consultants then recommend to the company the arts group to benefit from the program. Given the potential pay-offs in a community for both businesses and highly visible park, recreation, or cultural projects, it is surely appropriate for recreation and park agencies to be proactive in packaging such arrangements and soliciting private partners with whom to cement CAUSE-RELATED MARKETING ® relationships.

SOURCES:

American Express Travel Related Services, American Express Tower, World Financial Center, New York. 1986.

Bragdon, Frances J., "CAUSE-RELATED MARKETING ®: Case to Not Leave Home without It," *Fund Raising Management*, March, 1985, pp. 42-48, 67.

Editorial, "Music to a Symphony's Ears." *Personnel Journal* 64(6): June, 1985, p. 27.

Gottlieb, Martin. "Cashing in on a Higher Cause." *New York Times*, July 6, 1986, Section 3, p. F-6.

Higgins, Kevin T., "CAUSE-RELATED MARKETING ®: Does It Pass the Bottom-Line Tests?" *Marketing News*, May 9, 1986, Vol. 20, No. 10, pp. 1, 18.

Hunt, Avery, "Strategic Philanthropy," *Across the Board* 23(7), July/August, 1986, p.23.

Whitney, Barbara, "Zoo Society Finds Corporate Partnership Easy to Change," *Fund Raising Management,* March, 1985, pp. 48-50.

Yarrow, Andrew L., "New Allies: Credit Cards and Causes," *New York Times*, February 7, 1987.

17

Getting Something for Almost Nothing: The National Association for the Exchange of Industrial Resources

The National Association for the Exchange of Industrial Resources is a non-profit association which solicits donations of excess materials from hundreds of corporations. It then distributes these materials among the non-profit organizations that constitute its membership. This enables such organizations to acquire valuable materials at nominal cost.

Many recreation and park agencies are moving away from being direct providers of recreation and cultural services toward being catalysts or facilitators for non-profit organizations who deliver these services. These non-profit organizations may find the National Association for the Exchange of Industrial Resources (NAEIR) to be a useful resource. NAEIR is a non-profit association which matches new, excess industrial products to the needs of educational and non-profit organizations.

Consider the following situation:

People who make widgets in the world of business and industry are always having problems. John Doe orders 4,015 size 3 1/2 purple widgets. The Able Corporation develops and makes all 4,015 of them, and then Mr. Doe cancels his order. No one else

likes (or needs) size 3 1/2 purple widgets, even if they are cheap. So what's a corporation to do? Or say the standard green widgets have been updated this year, and nobody will buy the old ones anymore because the super-new modern ones are selling for less money. What happens to all those perfectly nice (but one-year-behind-the-times) old green widgets? Isn't there *somebody* who could take them off the company's hands and still make good use of them?

It is these kinds of situations which NAEIR seeks out. The Able Corporation can donate all its size 3 1/2 purple widgets and all those green widgets and any other products sitting around not making anybody any money to NAEIR. Corporations discard millions of dollars of excess inventory each year that non-profit organizations would appreciate having.

EVOLUTION OF NAEIR

NAEIR was founded in January, 1977, by Norbert C. Smith, who is the association's president. Smith first got involved with gifts-in-kind programs in the early 1970s while working as a charitable gifts consultant for several major corporations. As a consultant, he learned that industry had millions of dollars worth of new, useful but excess merchandise. Often, that material was sold to jobbers at a fraction of its worth or was scrapped. Smith saw the need for an organization that would collect those products from industry, then distribute them to non-profit organizations.

NAEIR started with a one-story, twelve thousand-square-foot structure as its first warehouse. Ten years and several moves later, its national distribution center is a 450,000 square-foot building in Galesburg, Illinois that serves both administration and warehousing operations. This one-floor, ten-acre structure was donated to the association. A team of 107 employees staff the office and warehouse, and a computerized control system keeps track of inventory. This system tracks all donated material from the time it is received until it is reported to members through the association's gift catalogs and shipped to them in response to their requests.

ACQUISITION AND DISTRIBUTION OF MERCHANDISE

Any tax-exempt 501(c)(iii) non-profit organization may join NAEIR for an annual membership fee of 395 dollars a year. On the average, each member receives approximately five thousand dollars worth of free merchandise annually. In 1986, forty-three million dollars worth of merchandise was donated to NAEIR to distribute to its 6,500 non-profit-organization members. Members get a quarterly gift catalog from which they request items. They pay only shipping costs and a small handling charge that does not exceed twenty-five dollars; the merchandise itself is free. NAEIR does not accept government surplus, reconditioned, or used items, and all products must be new.

Corporate interest in this gifts-in-kind program was stimulated by a 1979 clarification of Section 170(e)(3) of the Tax Reform Act of 1976. This clarification gave corporations more of an incentive to donate because it allowed donors to deduct the cost of their merchandise plus half the difference between their cost and their selling price, not to exceed twice the cost. For example, if a company purchased or manufactured an item for a dollar and sold it for two dollars, they took a deduction of a dollar and a half. However, if their markup was greater than three times the cost of

the product, they were still limited to a deduction of twice the item's cost.

Under these conditions, it made economic sense for manufacturers, wholesalers, and distributors to donate their slow-moving or excess inventory rather than throw it away or sell it to surplus distributors for practically nothing. By increasing companies' awareness of this ruling, NAEIR considerably expanded its list of donors. (See Figure 3.5.)

Although this was a stimulus and provided momentum for NAEIR's brokering service, changes in the 1987 tax law are not expected to have a major adverse impact since link-ups and a rapport have by now been established with a large number of companies.

Most corporations give to NAEIR because it is convenient. Rather than dealing with a multitude of non-profit groups, a company can send everything to one central warehouse, cutting down considerably on paperwork, shipping, and follow-up. Most donors don't want personal contact with the member organizations receiving their goods. They only want assurance that the items went to a worthy cause, and are pleased to let NAEIR handle the details.

Currently, NAEIR has about five hundred "very active" corporate donors who range in size from large Fortune 500 concerns such as 3M, Gillette, and Westinghouse, to small businesses. In addition, there are approximately 2,500 "less active" or occasional givers. Donors are required to pay the costs associated with shipping their merchandise from their facility to NAEIR's national distribution center in Galesburg, Illinois. However, the shipping costs are also tax-deductible since the IRS considers them to be part of the contribution. Donations are most plentiful in the last two months of the calendar year, when thirty-five percent of incoming goods are received as businesses start thinking about end-of-year tax requirements.

The donor companies contribute a wide range of products. Typical catalog items include:

— Office supplies
— Computer supplies
— Books
— Hand and power tools
— Sporting goods
— Janitorial and maintenance supplies
— Electrical and plumbing fixtures
— Arts and crafts

FIGURE 3.5

NAEIR Advertisement

Donate your surplus inventory and I will give your company an <u>above cost</u> tax deduction!

Do non-productive, excess inventories have you saying uncle? Slow moving inventories clutter up the financial statement as well as the warehouse. The government has established Section 170(e) (3) of the Internal Revenue Code to encourage businesses to donate excess materials that can be used by schools and other selected non-profit groups. Donors may take a tax deduction up to 100% above the material cost.

All materials donated to NAEIR are distributed FREE to its more than 6,500 qualified members, including schools, universities, hospitals, day care centers, and other non-profit organizations. With one shipping point and its ten years of experience, NAEIR greatly simplifies such donations. Eliminate excess inventories. Help educational and other non-profit organizations. Enjoy a significant tax benefit.

Call or write NAEIR's Director of Donations for complete information.

naeir

National Association for the Exchange of Industrial Resources

A Non-Profit Organization
560 McClure St., P.O. Box 8076, Galesburg, IL 61402 309-343-0704

— Children's activity items
— Wallcoverings
— Lighting fixtures
— Lubricants and vehicle parts
— Abrasives
— Electronics
— Furniture
— Laboratory equipment

The association's 1987 winter catalog (see Figure 3.6) consists of over six hundred 11-x-16-inch pages that list over 7,500 different types of items. Each item is described in detail, and in many cases pictures of the merchandise are included.

Merchandise is distributed to member organizations on the basis of need, not first-come-first-served. Staff make efforts to allocate each member the same dollar value of merchandise. Since more members often seek a particular item than the association can accommodate, a computerized allocation process is used to select who gets what. Typically a member requests a large number of items from each of the quarterly catalogs, and the computer program then allocates the items to be sent. It also calculates their value with the intent of ensuring that each member organization gets a similar purchase price of merchandise each quarter.

A summary of the benefits that NAEIR offers to its member organizations is presented in Figure 3.7. The association provides a guarantee that eliminates any risk to new members. NAEIR's president states,

If after the first year the value of the material received as a new NAEIR member was not worth at least twice the cost of the annual dues, we will either give you a second year's membership free or refund your dues.

FIGURE 3.6

NAEIR 1987 Winter Catalog

FIGURE 3.7

NAEIR Benefits Summary

BENEFITS TO MEMBERS

- **NAEIR** members receive useful materials on a regular basis. They do not have to wait for sporadic gifts from a donor. Our large gift catalogs are issued quarterly, and we urge every member to send in their requests. The best part is that all material is FREE!

- **NAEIR** members can choose from a wide variety of merchandise. No matter how large their school — or how small — every NAEIR member can find useful material and equipment in our catalogs. Members will find items for their offices, maintenance departments, buildings and grounds, laboratories, shops and classrooms.

- **NAEIR** members don't have to worry about asking for donations. As a member, all you have to do is fill out your requests from the quarterly catalogs. NAEIR's full-time Donor Relations Department solicits gifts from corporations large and small across the United States. Using statistics and suggestions from our members, we seek out the kinds of supplies and equipment schools want and need.

- **NAEIR** members receive only new merchandise. When you become a member of NAEIR, you will never receive surplus or used materials. We accept and distribute only NEW items.

- **NAEIR** members are treated equally, no matter their size, location, or status. Our specially designed computer allocation program assigns the same dollar value to each member so that everyone is treated fairly. Small schools have an opportunity to receive FREE merchandise as do large ones. If they take full advantage of our program, members average $4,200 in merchandise in a year. However, institutions are allowed multiple memberships. Individual schools within a large district or different departments within a college or university often have their own membership.

- **NAEIR** members are eligible to participate in the Association's unique Grab Bag Section. Four times a year, they may come to the National Distribution Center in Galesburg, Illinois, and pick up FREE merchandise — in addition to what they receive from the quarterly gift catalogs. The gymnasium-sized Grab Bag Section has a huge variety of materials, ranging from office supplies and vehicle parts to building materials and furniture. And there is no cash register; those items are all FREE! One cartload from NAEIR's Grab Bag can more than offset the cost of annual membership. Members come from all over the country to participate in Grab Bag.

- **NAEIR** members are under no risk at all their first year because NAEIR gives all new members a MONEY BACK GUARANTEE. If, after the first year, the value of the material received as a NAEIR member was not worth at least twice the cost of the annual dues, NAEIR will either give a second year's membership at no cost or cheerfully refund your dues.

SOURCES:

Chapman, Becky, "NAEIR: A Storehouse of Corporate Gifts, *The Grantsmanship Center News*, January/February, 1984.

NAEIR, Department ER
560 McClure Street
P.O. Box 8076
Galesburg, Illinois 61402.

18

Energy Economy Partnerships

The two cases presented here describe innovative approaches to reducing energy bills. The innovative dimension of the first case was the lease-purchase arrangement used to acquire equipment. This agreement structured lease payments so they reflected a proportion of the energy savings which accrued. No capital payments were required for the equipment and no payments were made if energy savings were not forthcoming. The second case discusses how an agency substantially reduced its energy costs by becoming an officially recognized cogenerator of electricity.

SHARED ENERGY SAVINGS LEASE AGREEMENT

The St. Louis County Park and Recreation Department in Missouri requested proposals for equipment to reduce energy costs at three ice rinks that they operated. The successful bidder was Sachs Energy Management Systems (SEMS). Following specifications provided by the county, the company installed a fully integrated, automated "turnkey" energy-monitoring and control system.

The innovative part of this arrangement was its financing. The total cost of the system for each rink was approximately fifty thousand dollars. SEMS leased the equipment to the county for sixty months, after which ownership reverts to the county. All expenses and costs incurred for installing and maintaining the equipment were paid for by SEMS. The county's

base payments are determined by savings that accrued from equipment use. The county agreed to pay SEMS a monthly sum equal to a percentage of the county's energy savings generated by the equipment and calculated in accordance with the schedule of percentages shown in Figure 3.8.

FIGURE 3.8

Lease Payments Based Upon Energy Savings

First Year of Operation Following Starting Date
  80% to SEMS, 20% to County

Second Year of Operation Following Starting Date
  80% to SEMS, 20% to County

Third Year of Operation Following Starting Date
  60% to SEMS, 40% to County

Fourth Year of Operation Following Startup Date
  60% to SEMS, 40% to County

Fifth Year of Operation Following Startup Date
  60% to SEMS, 40% to County

Sixth Year of Operation Following Startup Date
  0% to SEMS, 100% to County

Before the department could assess the total savings attributable to the SEMS equipment, there had to be agreement on a figure that represented the existing energy output. This base figure was determined by averaging the energy output of each facility for the three previous years. Figure 3.9 shows the average kilowatt hours for one of the ice rinks.

Provisions were included in the contract to account for such refinements as changes in occupancy hours or comfort conditions in the buildings; deviation in the number of heating and cooling days compared to those used in calculating the base average figure (Figure 3.9); and deviation from the temperature set points agreed on by SEMS and the department.

FIGURE 3.9

Calculation of a Base-Year Average at One Facility Against Which Utility Cost Savings Are Measured

	'81/'82	'82/'83	'83/'84	(BASE YEAR) AVERAGE
SEPTEMBER	60,160	73,520	103,840	79,173
OCTOBER	273,040	236,560	282,080	263,893
NOVEMBER	331,040	305,520	332,320	322,960
DECEMBER	378,960	312,400	367,600	352,987
JANUARY	346,960	361,840	306,240	338,347
FEBRUARY	320,160	232,160	314,960	289,093
MARCH	99,920	169,920	234,080	169,973
APRIL	105,680	117,360	75,920	99,653
MAY	53,360	57,840	61,360	57,520
JUNE	85,920	84,880	58,240	76,347
JULY	80,000	103,280	57,280	80,187
AUGUST	83,360	109,440	63,440	85,413
TOTALS	2,218,560	2,164,720	2,257,360	2,213,547

Data of energy use are in kilowatt hours.

COGENERATION OF ELECTRICITY

The Rancho Simi Recreation and Park District in California installed a cogeneration system that substantially reduced electrical costs. Cogeneration is any system whereby a user of electricity also becomes a provider of electricity along with the power company.

A gas company is by law required to sell gas to an agency that generates its own electricity at the same price it charges the electric company from which the agency buys its power. In addition, if an agency produces more power than it can use, it has the option of selling it to the power company, which is obliged to buy it.

In the Rancho Simi case, cogeneration is a system whereby natural gas is used as a fuel for an engine that has a heat exchange and an electric generator attached to it. The burning of the gas makes heat to warm the water of the district's fifty-meter Olympic swimming pool, while the operation of the engine turns a generator of electricity.

The district has installed two generators, each of which produces sixty kilowatts, to light three softball diamonds, four tennis courts, a snack bar, the pool, and running-water pumps at the pool and a 2.5-acre artificial stream and lagoon. Future lighting load will include an additional four tennis courts, two basketball courts, and a practice soccer field. This will use up the excess energy-producing capacity; hence the district does not run the system to sell electricity to Southern California Edison. Such an operation would waste the excess heat and would not be cost-effective.

The cost of installing two engines and generators was 110,000 dollars, but break-even was projected to occur within two years. The volume of natural gas use increased, but the cost per therm for gas dropped from $0.719 to $0.420. At the latter rate, the gas bill was substantially reduced even though the volume of use increased. The electricity bill for pool heating and park lighting was essentially eliminated except for infrequent occasions when usage exceeds the power generated.

Operation and maintenance costs for cogeneration are about 11,500 dollars annually. A comparison of annual costs before and after installation is shown in Figure 3.10.

FIGURE 3.10

A Comparison of the Annual Cost Before and After Installation of a Cogeneration System

	Before Cogeneration	After Cogeneration
So Cal. Gas Company 69,849 therms	$ 50,200	—
86,231 therms	—	$ 36,200
So. Cal. Edison (electricity)	56,300	-0-
Cogeneration O&M Costs	—	11,500
Insurance	—	800
Total Annual Cost	$106,500	$ 48,500
Annual Net Savings After Cogeneration Installation		$58,000

An agency interested in pursuing cogeneration should contact their local gas company for information and possible engineering and consulting grants. It is also helpful to talk with representatives at the power company. They can provide copies of contracts that must be executed to become a recognized cogenerator. They also have some options for power buy-back if it exceeds the agency's needs, and can give some cogenerator-equipment-supplier referrals. Some of these equipment suppliers are capable of providing a computer print-out of costs, break-even, and annual operating savings over several years.

SOURCES:

Superintendent of Recreation and Cultural Services
St. Louis County Department of Parks and Recreation
41 South Central Avenue
Clayton, Missouri 63105

Revenue Production Administrator
Rancho Simi Recreation and Park District
1692 Sycamore Drive
Simi Valley, California 93065

Section 4

Innovative Financing for Capital Projects

The four cases in this section describe public methods of financing capital projects which have not been widely adopted. Tax increment financing and the real-estate transfer tax are described in Cases 19 and 20. They can both be interpreted as user pay funding mechanisms that are likely to be more acceptable politically than traditional general-obligation bonds backed by general property or sales taxes.

Cases 21 and 22 detail a number of recreation and park projects that have been funded by revenue bonds. Traditionally, professionals in this field have not widely used these bonds. However, as user prices rise, revenue bonds are increasingly likely to become a feasible alternative.

19

Developing Facilities with Tax Increment Financing

A majority of states have passed enabling legislation permitting tax-increment financing, but it remains unfamiliar to many park and recreation administrators. This case describes such a financing mechanism and the situations in which it can be used appropriately. Examples of how it has been implemented to develop park and recreation facilities are provided, along with potential abuses.

Tax-increment financing (TIF) has recently received an increased amount of attention from local and state governments, but the mechanism is not new. It was first introduced in 1952 in California, where it was termed tax allocation financing. Tax increment financing is now used by government entities in most states. During the period between 1952 and 1975, seventeen states enacted the necessary legislation. However, TIF use grew most rapidly from 1976 to 1980, when an additional twenty states authorized it.

Although state enabling legislation has to be passed before TIF can be used, it is essentially a local development finance tool. It acknowledges that urban blight or decay exists in cities, and recognizes that this often results in an uneven city tax base. As blight occurs, the tax base in that part of the city decreases, but the cost of providing necessary city services to such areas often increases. Taxpayers in economically healthy jurisdictions are required to make up the resulting shortfall in revenue with higher property taxes.

Recognizing the adverse impact of blighted areas on the tax base, many local governments have turned to TIF as a tool that may help arrest urban decay.

WHAT IS TAX INCREMENT FINANCING?

Local jurisdictions can use TIF by preparing and adopting a redevelopment plan for a specified area. Such a plan serves as a management tool as well as the legal guide for implementing development. Any amendment to it must be passed via ordinance by the governing body of the local jurisdiction. After determining that the plan is economically feasible, local government proceeds by creating a new separate entity, or designating an existing one, to operate a special redevelopment district.

The TIF enabling laws passed by states typically authorize local units of government to recover costs from tax increment funds established to collect property taxes generated by redevelopment projects. A variety of methods are available for financing public improvements in this district. These include revenue bonds, general obligation bonds, the general fund, and pay-as-you-go-financing as long as tax increments realized in the zone from year to year are used to repay the debt. Huddleson (1982) notes that many states have also authorized mechanisms such as industrial bonds as financing mechanisms in these districts.

In addition to this set of relatively traditional approaches, governments may issue increment bonds in redevelopment districts to provide a source of funding for public improvements. Tax increment bonds differ from general obligation bonds in that they are secured only by projected increases in revenues from the development — not by the full faith and credit of the city. Repayment is contingent upon increases in the taxable value of the property in the district.

These bonds are usually exempt from consideration in assessments of a city's taxing power, general credit, and debt limits. However, tax-increment bonds do require evidence of financial viability before they can be sold in the bond market.

Because these kinds of bonds are considered riskier than the general-obligation variety, they are likely to carry higher interest rates, which inflates the cost of a project. Yet in some situations there may be no other way to launch redevelopment. In many states jurisdictions cannot issue general obligation bonds for amounts greater than the total assessment of property in their jurisdiction (DePalma, 1986). Cities that have reached that limit are unable to undertake widespread improvements using general-obligation bonds. A further difficulty is trying to convince an entire community to pay for improvements in just a small area. If the majority of taxpayers live in viable areas of a jurisdiction and see no benefit in upgrading older areas that are run down, they are unlikely to support the use of general-obligation bonds for this purpose.

The distinctive feature of TIF districts is that they rely on property taxes created directly by revitalization projects in the district, projects that pay for redevelopment costs incurred by the public. The tax base of the property in the designated area is frozen at its current level before redevelopment. All entities that have taxing authority agree to this freeze — cities, counties, and school districts, for example. (Remember that only the tax base is frozen, not the tax rate.)

Since rejuvenation of the district is likely to increase the value of their assets, landowners and residents have every reason to support the district's establishment. Other jurisdictions like school districts, cities, and counties do not lose revenue by agreeing to freeze assessed property values because without rejuvenation this assessed value would decrease over time. In the short term, rejuvenation activity makes it less likely that these jurisdictions will lose any of their tax base. In the long run, they are likely to gain substantially

since most states require bond repayment within thirty years. Once bonds have been retired, increments flowing into the special fund are phased out, the special district is dissolved, and all property taxes go to local taxing agencies. As project redevelopment occurs, property values are likely to increase because of the improvements created by the invested capital.

While state laws vary, all include a provision that enables each of the taxing jurisdictions to continue receiving that share of the taxes they had collected in the past from the frozen tax base. (See Figure 4.1A.) Each taxing jurisdiction first applies its tax rate to the frozen value, then to the new property value. The difference between the two is the tax-revenue increment available that year for repaying capital debts accumulated by the project. (See Figure 4.1B.) These incremental dollars go to the special district that issued the bonds. As assessed valuation in the district increases above the frozen tax base level, greater increments become available for retiring the redevelopment district's debts.

The TIF mechanism has to be carefully and clearly explained to residents because it is easily misunderstood. There is a tendency to confuse the increment in name with an additional tax, and this misunderstanding may stimulate opposition to TIF.

Because a TIF redevelopment project must generate its own funding to repay bond debts, projected tax increment cash flows are of crucial importance. Mitchell (1977) points out that it is advantageous to have substantial early development that results in larger tax increments. For this reason, it is common practice to sign a contract with a developer guaranteeing commitment to a major project that upgrades the district before issuing TIF. Such a commitment accelerates the progress of the project, resolves cash-flow problems, decreases the period for which the tax base is frozen, and assures prospective TIF bond investors that their investment will yield the anticipated return.

Decisions to buy TIF bonds are heavily influenced by the strength of any written agreement between the redevelopment agency and participating developers. If detailed agreements specifying proposed improvements, their value, and a development timetable do not exist, the agency has less of a chance of selling the bonds. Agencies must be careful to ensure that the tax increment materializes; otherwise they will default on the bonds. While the city is not legally responsible for any losses to bond investors, such losses are likely

FIGURE 4.1A

Frozen Tax Base

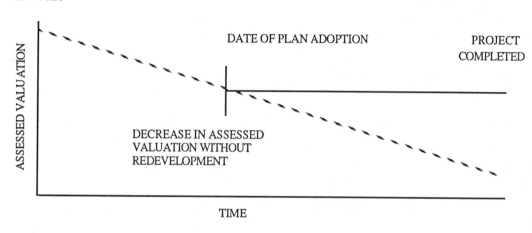

FIGURE 4.1B

Increased Assessed Valuation

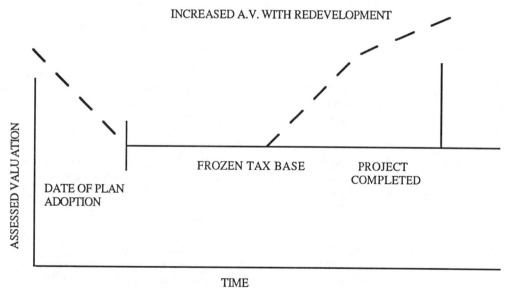

Source:R. Mitchell, "Tax Increment Financing," *Journal of Housing,*1977, 5. 227.

to make it more difficult to sell similar bonds in the future.

To make bonds more attractive to investors, some jurisdictions reduce the risk by obtaining an insurance policy or making provisions to levy special assessments on property in the district's area if the expected incremental tax increase does not materialize. These provisions are the option of the jurisdiction, and vary depending on state enabling legislation.

An alternative to these strategies for making bonds more attractive is to use general-obligation bonds in the first phase of a project, then replace them with tax-increment financing bonds after revenue begins to flow.

Redevelopment increases revenue not only from property taxes, but from sales taxes and business licenses. Because the latter sources are not part of the tax increment, local government receives benefits directly and can fund other public services.

Typically after a special district has been designated, the local government negotiates the relocation of people or property and signs contracts for demolition, clearance work, the removal of old infrastructure, and the installation of new public improvements and amenities.

Annual disclosure reports between each TIF district and a city are required in most states. The city's governing body must submit an annual report documenting the current status of the redevelopment effort to the chief executive officer of each taxing unit involved in the TIF district.

USING TAX-INCREMENT FINANCING FOR DEVELOPING PARK AND RECREATION FACILITIES

Tax-increment financing has not been widely used for funding park and recreation facilities. There appears to be relatively little awareness of this mechanism among park and recreation administrators. Professionals have focused most recent concern in the field on finding ways to meet operational rather than capital costs. However, in some jurisdictions sources of funds for capital development are becoming as much of a concern as those for operational costs. With tax increment financing, taxpayers in a district finance the costs of recreation and park facilities through increases in their property taxes. TIF bonds serviced by the tax

increments can be used to finance these facilities, a method seen by some as more equitable and often easier for elected officials to support than asking all the city's citizens to finance renewal in a specific district.

The *City of Minneapolis* has made extensive use of TIF through the Minneapolis Community Development Agency. To date, they have created twenty TIF areas, including the Loring Park district, a forty-three-acre, nine-block site. Loring Park is a residential neighborhood convenient to the central business portion of the city. Over a period of eight to ten years, approximately two thousand new rental and condominium apartments and townhouses have been developed here. The Loring Greenway, completed in 1980, and an extension of the Nicollet Mall finished in 1981 provide a pedestrian walkway that connects downtown Minneapolis with the Loring Park District (Minneapolis Community Development Agency, 1984).

Prior to bonds issued in 1973, the assessed value of the Loring Park district was 6,572,748 dollars, while the 1983/1984 value was 43,964,449 dollars. A public investment of thirty-seven million dollars has been projected to generate two hundred million in private investments. The district returns nearly five million dollars in real-estate taxes annually, whereas before 1973 it returned less than 900,000 dollars a year.

Also located in the district is a 44-million dollar hotel/merchandise mart complex consisting of a 540-room Hyatt Regency Hotel, a five-level merchandise mart, and an athletic club (Minneapolis Community Agency, 1984). This development contributes to Minneapolis' effort to attract convention trade.

The Nicollet Lake district was established in 1975 and consists of an eight-block area. This zone was intended to recreate a healthy commercial area. Developments constructed since the zone was created include the Minneapolis Institute of the Arts Complex.

Bonds for the city center district were issued in 1977. The current assessed valuation rate is 53,311,000 dollars — up from 9,214,147 dollars in 1977. This district is located in downtown Minneapolis. It was created to redevelop commercial properties, expand retail and office space, and strengthen Hennepin Avenue as a regional entertainment center.

The Hubert H. Humphrey Metrodome is located in the Industry Square redevelopment tax-increment district. Sited on the eastern edge of the downtown area, this zone encompasses 223 acres. The Minneapolis

Parks Board is also involved in the planning of the Mills district planning area of Industry Square adjacent to the Mississippi River (Minneapolis Community Development Agency, 1984).

In the *City of Portland*, Oregon, TIF has been used as seed money to finance the downtown business area and its nearby waterfront (US Department of the Interior, 1979). In contrast to Minneapolis, where TIF districts are primarily small areas, Portland has focused its TIF on developing a single large area. The Portland Downtown Development Commission is the city's designated urban renewal and development agency. It is responsible for implementing the downtown waterfront urban-renewal plans that involve three hundred acres on the west bank of the Willamette River, including a thirty-five-acre, one-and-a-half-mile-long linear park.

Prior to 1972, when the city council adopted the downtown plan, Portland had already begun revitalization of an area near the waterfront through the traditional urban-renewal approach. Included was a civic auditorium, pedestrian mall, and new office and housing development, along with a noted fountain designed by Lawrence Halprin. The success of these projects and the subsequent tax revenue generated created a positive atmosphere for more extensive redevelopment and encouraged the city to submit proposals for the nearby Willamette waterfront.

Two plans, the Downtown Waterfront Urban-Renewal Plan and the Waterfront Park Plan, were adopted by the city council in 1974. In 1976 the Waterfront Urban-Renewal district sold ten million dollars worth of tax increment bonds and another fifteen million in 1978. Funds generated from the sale of these two bond issues financed the first two phases of the Waterfront Park, which involved preservation and improvement efforts in two abutting historic districts.

When the districts were established in 1974, their assessed valuation was a hundred million dollars, but by 1984 the assessed valuation had increased to four hundred million dollars. Waterfront Park has a mile-long esplanade on the riverfront that is currently becoming further extended with plazas, extensive open grassy areas, pension and condominium projects under construction, a recently completed public marina, and a large center for restaurants, retailers, entertainment, special events, and dance performances.

In addition to its waterfront project, Portland also used one million dollars of TIF as seed money to con-

struct the eight-million-dollar Pioneer Square. This is a central public square with fountains, seats, and a pleasant environment whose upkeep is the responsibility of the parks department.

The *City of Corpus Christi,* Texas, designated the bayfront area of the city as a TIF zone. The project plan created for the zone envisages seventy specific public-improvement projects undertaken there from 1983 through 2002. Their cost in 1983 dollars is estimated at ninety million dollars. Of this amount, 15.8 million is earmarked for marina and shoreline improvements, 2.9 million for park renovation, 2.3 million for landscaping, and ten million for a new 12,000-seat arena.

The project plan included an assessment of how much of the ninety million dollars could be raised from tax increment funds. In 1982 the zone generated almost three million in property taxes. The amount produced from the tax-increment base, or "frozen" base, will continue to be allocated and paid over to the collection units that levy taxes in the zone, based on their respective tax-rate shares. Before the area was designated, contractual agreements were negotiated with each of the other taxing entities. These agreements enabled them to share part of the tax increments in some instances.

Since it is impossible to predict what development will occur beyond what is already committed or considered firm, the project plan offered two separate levels of likely tax increment production: low-range and moderate-range.

The low-range projection was based only on the value of private developments that were either definitely committed or under construction. It is estimated that thirteen million dollars in tax increments would be accumulated from these new developments over the twenty-year period. However, the maximum yield of 750,000 dollars per year would not be possible until 1987. It would then remain at this level for the remainder of the twenty-year period.

This projection reflects the usual "front-end" lag affecting most tax-increment projects. In other words, increments do not begin to show up until the tax-producing developments are on the ground and fully taxable. Among the thirteen million dollars worth of public improvements that can be financed based on this projection, 5.125 million is to go for marina and shoreline improvements and two million is to go for parks.

The moderate range projection included projects that, while not yet contracted, were considered highly probable. This estimate anticipated that thirty million would accrue in tax increments over the twenty-year period in addition to the thirteen million projected on the low-range assessment. The maximum yield of 2.5 million would first emerge in the sixth year. Among the expenditures the city would make with this additional money would be 6.45 million for the marina and shoreline, ten million for the 12,000-seat arena, 500,000 dollars for park renovation, and 300,000 for landscaping.

The project plan suggests that both the low- and moderate-range projections may prove conservative given the growth potential of Corpus Christi. It points out that initial success usually enhances the overall development climate, thus producing a "spin-off" or exponential effect. Many cities have had this experience with the tax-increment financing tool.

An important part of the Corpus Christi strategy is to finance improvements from the cash flow generated by tax increments rather than from tax increment bonds. Utilizing this approach, substantial earnings will increase because high funding costs will be eliminated.

Once annual increment yields build up, the city is in a position to maintain a steady level of capital improvement investments within the tax increment zone. There is also the added flexibility at this point of utilizing tax-increment bond financing should the need arise. Bonds issued at this time could be easily marketed and placed at comparatively favorable rates because the increment base will already have been established. The city maintains the flexibility to issue revenue bonds based on future tax incremental payments should future review of the project plan and its priorities make it necessary to shorten the time it takes to install improvements.

The strategy of financing improvements from cash flow generated by tax increments rather than from tax-increment bonds is more tenuous since it assumes that all agencies that initially commit themselves to the TIF project will sustain their enthusiasm for it. A change in political philosophy or an unanticipated financial emergency may cause a participating agency to withdraw its commitment and use the cash flow to resolve its immediate problems. If bonds are issued, it is much more difficult for such an agency to abrogate its commitment since the bonds must be repaid.

SOME POTENTIAL ABUSES OF TAX INCREMENT FINANCING

In his 1981 study, Huddleston identified three major abuses of the TIF method. First, agencies often over-commit land. Of the TIF districts in Wisconsin that he reviewed, forty percent indicated that at least twenty-five percent of their development land was vacant. He found that many Wisconsin cities devoted over twenty percent of their land area to TIF districts. The inclusion of such a large proportion of the tax base in a TIF district often results in increased city taxes because TIF monies cannot be assigned to operational budgets, and only taxes derived from the frozen tax base in the TIF district are available for operational purposes.

A second abuse identified by Huddleston was the considerable license taken by some cities in defining TIF zones. They often tenuously linked declining areas with growth areas by using a connecting road between a blighted and a booming district. This reduces the financial risk of the TIF zone by enabling it to capture tax increments that may not be attributed to public investment in the blighted areas financed by TIF.

Similarly, some cities created redevelopment districts in situations where development would have occurred without TIF funds. They tended to focus on the amount of revenue that could be generated if the district were created anew instead of redeveloped from a blighted area as intended by enabling legislation. Such liberal interpretations of TIF districts may lead to accusations by outside developers that their competitors within these areas have the unfair advantage of benefiting from an injection of public funds.

The potential for abuse increases when voter approval to establish a TIF district is not required by a state's enabling legislation. Since officials of the TIF district are appointed and not elected, citizens may feel they have little control over decisions to use TIF or to invest in these districts.

CONCLUDING COMMENTS

In the past, many cities have relied on federal and state programs like community-development block grants and urban development action grants as major supplementary sources of capital funds. However, such intergovernmental transfers are generally declining. Local agencies must now initiate innovative mechanisms for funding capital as well as operational costs. Initially, the use of TIF was limited in many jurisdictions to providing local matching funds for federal or state grants, but in recent years as these funds have declined it has been adopted as a primary method of financing for local development.

The use of TIF affords local government units the opportunity to work with the private sector to encourage development and facilitate a public/private partnership with the strengths of both so that all will benefit. The public sector can assist the private sector in developing urban areas by securing lower-cost financing through TIF bonds, providing costly infrastructure prior to development, or by providing public amenities like parks and recreation facilities that will enhance the attractiveness of a blighted area for private developers.

The local political climate strongly influences any decision to use TIF. Traditionally, cities have borne the costs of development alone while other taxing jurisdictions have shared in the benefits. Complaints often arise from counties, school districts, and other taxing agencies that do not at first comprehend how they will benefit from a TIF district, and perceive it as a threat to their revenue base. For example, school districts may complain that the cost of providing services increases as redevelopment occurs. Because of the frozen tax base, they are unable to respond to the increased service demands. However, the school district does have the power to raise the tax rate in order to increase revenue. In addition, some states have addressed this problem by writing enabling legislation that permits the return of partial revenues from the tax increment to school districts instead of directing it all to the TIF fund.

The size and scope of TIF districts varies widely. However, the 1986 federal tax-code revision places more restrictions on the use of tax-increment financing bonds. One of the most significant changes is limiting their use to districts of at least one hundred acres.

This is likely to reduce the number of TIF districts that are established in the future.

TIF provides a source of funding that can inject amenities like recreation and park facilities into deteriorating urban areas. The infusion of such investments is intended to stop the deterioration, attract private investment into the area, and revitalize the district so that it once again becomes a vibrant part of the city. The important ingredient is that the physical environment is upgraded by these infused amenities or attractions in such a way that people again become attracted to the area.

Parks and recreation administrators have generally not considered TIF as a tool, but it appears to have tremendous potential for upgrading park and recreation facilities in deteriorating urban areas.

SOURCES:

DePalma, Anthony, "An Innovative Path to Recovery," *The New York Times*, November 9, 1986, Section 8, p.2.

Huddleston, J.R., "Variation in Development and Subsidies under Tax Increment Financing," *Land Economics*, 1981, 57.373-84.

Huddleston, J.R., "A Comparison of State Tax Increment Financing Laws," *State Government*, 1982, 55.29-33.

Minneapolis Community Development Agency, "City of Minneapolis Tax Increment Projects Summary Report," 1984, July 30.

Mitchell, R., "Tax Increment Financing." *Journal of Housing*, 1977, 34.226-29.

US Department of the Interior, *Improving Your Waterfront: A Practical Guide*, December, 1979.

20

The Real-Estate Transfer Tax: An Alternative Source of Acquisition and Development Funds

Decreases in federal funding and increases in demands for recreation opportunities have forced many public recreation and park providers at the state and local level to seek alternative sources of funding. This case explores the potential of expanding the real-estate transfer tax as a source of acquisition and development funds. A number of jurisdictions at both the state and local level in the United States have adopted such a tax and found the generated funds to be a relatively reliable source of capital for park and recreation agencies.

A real-estate transfer tax, sometimes called a documentary stamp tax, is one imposed on transfers of real property within a taxing authority's jurisdiction. It is levied when property is sold, granted, assigned, transferred, or otherwise conveyed from one person to another.

The most visible examples of its use in the parks and recreation field have occurred in Maryland and Florida. The philosophical justification for using a real-estate transfer tax for park acquisition and development is well-expressed by the commission that initially recommended its implementation in Maryland in 1968:

The idea behind the transfer tax is that the person who buys a home or other property for private use has hastened the decline in available open space land. By paying a tax at the rate of one-half of one percent of the property purchase price, that same person would help to support the buying of land which could be used and enjoyed by the general public. (Maryland DNR, 1979, n.p.)

This principle is akin to that which underpins the justification for mandatory dedication and impact fees, but whereas such mechanisms are confined to local urban jurisdictions, the real-estate transfer tax can also be used at the state level.

The real-estate transfer tax has a long history in the United States and has been widely adopted by other countries. For example, in the United Kingdom, it is levied by central government at the rate of one percent on houses costing more than 45,000 dollars.

First introduced at the federal level in the Federal Revenue Act of 1921, this tax was repealed soon after. Then it was reinstated by the Federal Revenue Act of 1932 and remained in effect with periodic amendments until it was again repealed in 1965. This Act required that:

on each deed, instrument, or writing by which any lands, tenements, or other realty sold shall be granted, assigned, transferred, or otherwise conveyed to, or vested in, the purchaser or purchasers, or any other person or persons, by his or their direction, when the consideration or value of the interest or property conveyed (exclusive of the value of any lien or encumbrance remaining thereon at the time of the sale) exceeds $100, a tax at the rate of 55 cents for each $500 or fractional part thereof (US Code, 1964).

A prime philosophical argument supporting repeal of this tax at the federal level was that real-estate taxes should be the exclusive prerogative of local and state governments, and should not be imposed by the federal government. When legislators repealed the federal tax, its revenue potential was predictably recognized by a number of state and local governments who subsequently adopted it.

In recent years, there has been some debate over whether the real-estate transfer tax is an excise tax or a property tax. The distinction is important since in some states it may determine whether or not municipalities have the constitutional authority to impose it either under their prerogative as home-rule cities or under the specific terms of their particular municipal charters. The complex legal arguments involved in this issue are summarized by Bauer (1981).

The real-estate transfer tax is currently being used at the state level for park acquisition purposes in Maryland and Florida, as well as by a number of municipalities. The characteristics of these programs are discussed in the following sections.

THE STATE OF MARYLAND

In 1968 it was apparent that the State of Maryland was experiencing a substantial increase in population and thus a deficiency in the amount of recreation area required to accommodate the needs of this new population. It was observed that the number of people being turned away at many state parks would at times equal the number of those who could be accommodated (Maryland DNR, 1979).

In the state legislative session of 1968, a legislative commission was appointed to consider creating a program to expedite the purchase and development of outdoor recreation lands. The resolution sponsoring the commission's appointment declared that "valuable recreation areas are rapidly being converted to other

uses and lost forever as recreation spaces." It also observed that land values "are increasing at an alarming rate of 10 percent annually."

The commission recommended that the state undertake a "crash program" of land acquisition during the next five years to erase an estimated deficit on open-space lands of about fifty thousand acres. To pay for these improvements, they proposed a 150-million-dollar program, with 107 million of that amount to be provided by the sale of general-obligation bonds and the remainder by state revenues from a transfer tax on land sales (Maryland DNR, 1979).

When the commission's recommendations were introduced into the legislature, opposition was forthcoming from two sources. First, real-estate developers and brokers objected because they felt that the transfer tax would add to the costs of buying and selling property and thus make such transactions more difficult. Second, some representatives of local government voiced opposition because if the state imposed the transfer tax, it would be intruding into an area of taxation already imposed by several local jurisdictions.

The bill survived these objections and became law in 1969, although the program's bond authorization was reduced from 107 million to sixty million dollars. The original legislation limited the program's use to the acquisition of land. However, in 1971 the legislature amended it so they could also use a portion of the funds for development.

Program Open Space is funded with current revenues from the real-estate transfer tax. On every real-estate transaction in Maryland, a tax of one-half of one percent is imposed. The rapid economic growth in the state has ensured substantial activity in the real-estate market since the program was launched, ensuring its success. Between 1969 and 1982, the transfer tax generated over 271 million dollars. The state used this money to acquire over 100,000 acres for state parks, forests, natural-environment areas, natural-resource management areas, and wildlife-management areas.

The success of the real-estate transfer tax in raising revenue caused Governor Hughes to suggest in 1984 that the legislation be amended to permanently transfer eighteen million dollars from the dedicated fund to the state's general fund. This suggestion resulted from the forty-two million dollars generated by the tax in 1983, which reflected a boom in real-estate activity that year. However, opponents pointed out that this was an extraordinary year, and that the usual figure was between twenty and twenty-eight million dollars. The governor's proposal was defeated because its adoption would have meant the effective demise of Program Open Space except in years of unusually high real-estate activity (Hooton, 1984).

THE STATE OF FLORIDA

In 1963, the State of Florida established the Land Acquisition Trust Fund (LATF) to provide for expansion of the state-park system and to assist local government in acquiring and developing park and recreation areas. (This is not a real "trust" fund since the term only means that the fund is earmarked.) The fund was financed by a sales tax on recreational equipment.

In 1968 the fund's revenue source was changed. The state repealed the recreational equipment sales tax because it was unpopular with some manufacturers. It was replaced by an excise tax on legal documents that derives about ninety percent of its revenues from real-estate transactions. The tax on real-estate transactions is based on the value of the property involved in the transaction. It is currently assessed at the rate of 4.5 dollars per one thousand dollars of assessed valuation (*Florida Tax Handbook*, 1983).

In fiscal year 1984-85, this tax generated over three hundred million dollars. However, only 13.3 percent of this sum is dedicated to the LATF. The state divided the remaining amount to allot 79.5 percent to the General Revenue Fund and 7.2 percent to the Water Management Lands Trust Fund. Between 1972 and 1983, the documentary stamp tax generated over 170 million dollars for the LATF. By law, the LATF is set aside exclusively for recreational use.

IMPLEMENTATION BY LOCAL JURISDICTIONS

In addition to the two states that have implemented a real-estate transfer tax to finance park acquisition and development, it has also been adopted by a number of cities. This section describes its use in Seattle, Washington; a number of Colorado cities; Nantucket, Massachusetts; and San Jose, California.

Seattle, Washington. In 1982, Seattle passed an ordinance that imposed an excise tax on the sale of real estate at the rate of one-quarter of one percent of the selling price. The proceeds from this tax are deposited in the city's Cumulative Reserve Fund for municipal capital improvements.

The city has designated this fund for construction or renovation of buildings and for acquiring property. Five agencies in the city are eligible for these funds. They are the Parks and Recreation Department, Seattle Center (the old World's Fair area), the Library Board, the Seattle Engineering Department, and the Department of Administrative Services, which manages all the municipal buildings except the Parks and Recreation and utility buildings (Seattle Ordinance 110674, 1982). The Parks and Recreation Department has received about 3.5 million dollars per year from this fund for major capital improvements and repair (Girtsch, 1985).

Colorado Cities. The search for new sources of income has led a number of Colorado home-rule municipalities to adopt real-estate transfer taxes. The towns of Avon, Breckenridge, Crested Butte, Gypsum, and Vail, and the cities of Aspen and Rifle have enacted ordinances imposing a tax on most transfers of real property (Bauer, 1981).

The amount of the tax varies. In Vail, Rifle, and Breckenridge, it is set at one percent of the selling price, in Aspen at .5 percent. In Crested Butte the tax rate is based on the length of time the property has been owned, ranging from five percent for less than a year to .5 percent for more than five but less than ten years. No tax is paid if the property has been owned for ten years or more.

In several of these cities, parks and recreation is designated as a major beneficiary of the revenues generated. For example, in Vail they are used exclusively to acquire property for parks, recreation, or open space. In Aspen, the funds are designated for reconstruction and maintenance of the Wheeler Opera House and support of the visual and performing arts. In Crested Butte, the money may be used for public-improvement projects that include parks, recreation, and open space.

Nantucket, Massachusetts. Nantucket Island protects about one third of its 31,000 acres through various government agencies and the Nantucket Conservation Foundation. However, several years ago residents feared that the island's increasing popularity would threaten its rustic atmosphere. The number of building permits had accelerated, and property values had risen at fifteen percent a year (Guenther, 1985).

In 1983 residents embraced the idea of establishing a land bank for preserving additional land. In 1985 Nantucket issued ten million dollars' worth of revenue bonds to finance acquisition of beaches and moors threatened by development. These bonds are to be redeemed by a two percent transfer tax on real-estate transactions, which means that most current Nantucket residents will not contribute to the cost of purchasing the land. Instead, the bulk of the expense will be borne by people moving onto the island and reducing the amount of open space. This tax received widespread support from real-estate brokers and home builders who recognized that it would help preserve the island's attractiveness.

San Jose, California. San Jose's real-property conveyance tax is imposed at a rate of $3.30 per thousand dollars on all real-property transfers within the city. The tax yielded 38 million dollars in the five fiscal years from 1980 through 1985. Officials have designated park projects to receive sixty-four percent of the revenue, which was twenty-five million dollars during this time period. Over ninety percent of the tax funds must be spent for capital improvements (City of San Jose, 1985).

MECHANICS OF IMPLEMENTING THE TAX

At the time title ownership of property is transferred, the responsible party must report to the taxing authority the consideration paid for the transfer, the names of the parties, and the location of the property. Specific legislation or ordinance determines whether responsibility for tax payment lies with the seller, the purchaser, or both. For example, in the Colorado cities of Avon, Aspen, and Breckenridge, the purchaser is responsible; in Crested Butte and Gypsum, the seller is responsible; in Vail and Rifle, both the seller and the purchaser are responsible.

The agency designated to collect the taxes has to be reimbursed from these funds to cover costs of collection. In Florida, sixty-seven state tax assessors collect and remit taxes monthly to the Florida Department of Revenue for certification into the LATF. As compensation, they retain one percent of the proceeds of the taxes collected to defray collection costs.

CONCLUDING COMMENTS

The real-estate transfer tax is a relatively reliable source of revenue, particularly in those areas where the population is growing and an active real-estate market exists. It is an appropriate source of revenue for park acquisition and construction since land development often decreases recreation opportunities at the same time it creates a need for more recreation areas. In this respect, its conceptual justification appears to be strong and similar to that which underpins mandatory dedication and impact fees. However, there are two important distinctions. First, mandatory dedication is imposed only on initial property development, whereas a real-estate transfer tax is imposed on each occasion that the property changes ownership. Second, mandatory dedication usually applies only to residential dwellings while a real-estate transfer tax is usually imposed on all types of property transactions.

The rationale for imposing the on-going real-estate transfer tax rather than the one-time mandatory dedication or impact fee is that recreation and park properties deteriorate with use and need periodic renovation even when they are well-maintained. Mandatory dedication and impact fees do not provide the on-going source of funds necessary for such renovations.

There is a conceptual justification for making the tax the responsibility of either the buyer or the seller. The seller, as a current resident, has enjoyed access to the facilities and contributed to their depreciation. Thus the selling household should contribute to restoring them before they leave. The buyer enjoys immediate access to established recreation and park facilities, but has made no capital contribution to them. This "freeloading" is eliminated if the buyer has to contribute through a real-estate transfer tax.

There is also an important political consideration here. If the tax is made the buyer's responsibility then most of the burden does not fall on current residents but rather on newcomers. This is particularly likely to occur in areas of rapid growth.

In some instances both state and local agencies impose a real-estate transfer tax. This occurs, for example, in Metropolitan Dade County in Florida, where the county uses the tax to finance a loan program for the purchase and rehabilitation of homes for low- and moderate-income people, while the State of Florida levies its own real-estate transfer tax to fund the LATF (Lucoff, 1983).

Using real-estate transfer taxes incorporates an inherently attractive financial balancing mechanism. The private real-estate market is substantially influenced by prevailing economic conditions. Because the real-estate transfer tax is tied to that market, the amount of revenue it generates also depends on economic conditions in the area. However, downturns in the economy do not necessarily reduce its purchasing power, even though the amount of available funds decline as real-estate market activity slows. This is because the cost of acquiring park land is likely to be lower in periods of slow real-estate activity, particularly since a public agency is likely to purchase in cash. Therefore less revenue is needed to purchase the desired land. Conversely, when the real-estate market is active, the tax generates more revenue, a necessity since land prices are also likely to be higher.

In a growing number of jurisdictions, the real-estate transfer tax provides a valuable source of funds for park acquisition and development. In view of anticipated reductions in traditional funding sources, it seems likely that many other jurisdictions will explore the potential of this revenue source in the future.

SOURCES:

Bauer, J. Albert, *The Colorado Lawyer* (real-estate law newsletter), December, 1981, pp. 3093-3098.

City of Seattle Ordinance 110674, 1982.

Florida Senate Finance, Taxation, and Claims Committee, *Florida Tax Handbook*, 1983, p. 45.

Girtch, C.M., Director of Operations, Seattle Department of Parks and Recreation, letter to the author, August 30, 1985.

Guenther, Robert, "Nantucket Races Developers to Preserve Its Open Spaces," *Wall Street Journal*, March 27, 1985, p. 33.

Hooton, Tom, "Perils Seen to Program Open Space," *Baltimore Sun*, March 4, 1984, Section C.

Lucoff, Morton, "Dade Raises Deed Tax to Assist Home Buyers," *Miami News*, September 20, 1983, p. 4A.

Maryland Department of Natural Resources, *Program Open Space: Ten Year Report 1969-1979*, unpublished manuscript.

Task Force on Urban Services and Construction and Conveyance Task, City of San Jose, final report to San Jose City Council, February, 1983.

US Code Title 26, Internal Revenue Code, Chapter 34: Documentary Stamp Taxes; Section 4301: Conveyances, 1964.

21

Funding Outdoor
Athletic Field Facilities
with Revenue Bonds

Revenue bonds have long been recognized as a potential source of capital funding, but have been used only rarely by public recreation agencies. Traditionally, managers have pointed out that few public recreation facilities generate sufficient income to cover operational expenses and to redeem revenue bonds. However, examples in recent years in Johnson County, Kansas, and Johnson County, Missouri, have demonstrated that agencies can successfully use revenue bonds to finance athletic facilities. Five revenue-bond-funded facilities from these two agencies are described here.

DEVELOPING A SOFTBALL COMPLEX (1)

In 1979, Johnson County, Kansas, used revenue bonds to develop an eighty-acre seven-field softball complex, with three additional multi-purpose fields for soccer and flag and touch football, all irrigated, and a two-and-a-half-acre lake for fishing and ice-skating, jogging trail, playground area, concession stand, restroom area, picnic shelters, and parking lot. A Land and Water Conservation Grant of 246,000 dollars was matched with 260,000 of revenue bonds to develop the complex. The county already owned the land, but they had no capital money with which to develop it. They would not back the bonds with a cross-pledge of tax revenues, so the revenue bonds had to be sold at full risk on the commercial market.

The Johnson County Softball Players Association was approached. They contacted their forty-five hundred members, who agreed to pay a surcharge of five dollars per player to provide the funds needed to repay the revenue bonds. This surcharge was in addition to the normal fee paid to Johnson County that covers all operating, maintenance, utility, minor-improvement, and overhead costs. The athletic associations were pleased to cooperate since it meant they would have additional facilities available for their use. In the spring of 1979, over 240 softball teams were turned away by the district, and a thousand were turned away in the total Kansas metropolitan area due to a lack of facilities. This was evidence of a substantial demand for new ballfields.

The bonds were redeemable from the revenues received from players and teams playing in the softball and soccer leagues and tournaments scheduled through Johnson County. Figure 4.2 illustrates that revenues from this source were projected on a yearly average of 1.95 times the necessary income to cover the average yearly principal and interest payments required, along with operation and maintenance costs. This income was derived from the approximately six thousand players (three thousand in each of two seasons) whom the county projected were likely to use the facility. A second source of security was unencumbered recreational fees derived from other recreational programs scheduled through the Johnson County Park and

FIGURE 4.2

Financial Feasibility of Revenue Bonds

YEAR	# ANNUAL SEASONAL SOFTBALL TEAMS	# ANNUAL SEASONAL SOCCER & FOOTBALL TEAMS	TOTAL TEAMS	TEAM ANNUAL SPECIAL ASSESSMENT MAINTENANCE FEE	TOTAL (1) GROSS REVENUE	ANNUAL (1) FACILITY MAINTENANCE EXPENSES	AVAILABLE FOR DEBT SERVICE	BOND ISSUANCE(2) DEBT SERVICE	ANNUAL DEBT COVERAGE
1980	470	77	547	$ 84	$ 45,948	$ 5,000	$ 40,948	$ —	—
1981	800	77	877	85	74,545	15,000	59,545	31,212.50	1.90
1982	800	77	877	86	75,422	16,500	58,922	30,387.50	1.93
1983	800	77	877	87	76,299	18,150	58,149	29,562.50	1.96
1984	800	77	877	88	77,176	19,965	57,211	28,737.50	1.99
1985	800	77	877	102	89,454	21,961	67,493	27,912.50	2.41
1986	800	77	877	103	90,331	24,157	66,174	32,112.50	2.06
1987	800	77	877	103	90,331	26,572	63,759	30,912.50	2.06
1988	800	77	877	103	90,331	29,229	61,102	29,712.50	2.05
1989	800	77	877	103	90,331	32,151	58,180	33,512.50	1.73
1990	800	77	877	111	97,734	35,366	62,368	31,912.50	1.95
1991	800	77	877	111	97,734	38,902	58,832	30,312.50	1.94
1992	800	77	877	111	97,734	42,792	54,942	33,662.50	1.63
1993	800	77	877	111	97,734	47,071	50,663	31,600.00	1.60
1994	800	77	877	111	97,734	51,778	45,956	29,537.50	1.55
1995	800	77	877	111	97,734	56,955	40,779	32,475.00	2.27*
							$905,020	$463,562.50	

AVERAGE ANNUAL DEBT COVERAGE   1.95

(1) Total gross revenues and annual facility maintenance expenses increase in annual team assessment to cover anticipated increases in annual costs.
(2) Actual debt service.
* Coverage for 1995 includes $33,000 in Bond Reserve.

Recreation District. Since these had historically exceeded 100,000 dollars, this latter provision enabled the bonds to be rated AA instead of A.

The surcharge was imposed for one year before the county sold the bonds in order to demonstrate to the banks that the scheme was feasible. In that year, officials collected 36,000 dollars from the five-dollar surcharge. This convinced a consortium of local banks to buy the bonds, which had a fifteen-year pay-back period at eight to 8.25 percent interest. The park and recreation district agreed to place the 36,000 dollars in a special reserve account as an additional source of security to the lending banks. This amount exceeded the highest yearly payment for interest and principal (Figure 4.3) and was meant to be used only to prevent default of payment of principal and interest on the bond.

After six years of operation, the complex has proved to be a financial and recreational success. After

FIGURE 4.3

Interest Rates and Payback Schedule of Revenue Bonds

START DATE: 4/1/80

$260,000.00

Date	Principal	Coupon Rate	Interest	Payment	Annual Payment
11/1/80			$12,891.67	$12,891.67	$12,891.67
5/1/81	$10,000	8.5	11,050.00	21,050.00	
11/1/81			10,625.00	10,625.00	31,675.00
5/1/82	10,000	8.5	10,625.00	20,625.00	
11/1/82			10,200.00	10,200.00	30,825.00
5/1/83	10,000	8.5	10,200.00	20,200.00	
11/1/83			9,775.00	9,775.00	29,975.00
5/1/84	10,000	8.5	9,775.00	19,775.00	
11/1/84			9,350.00	9,350.00	29,125.00
5/1/85	10,000	8.5	9,350.00	19,350.00	
11/1/85			8,925.00	8,925.00	28,275.00
5/1/86	15,000	8.5	8,925.00	23,925.00	
11/1/86			8,287.50	8,287.50	32,212.50
5/1/87	15,000	8.5	8,287.50	23,287.50	
11/1/87			7,650.00	7,650.00	30,937.50
5/1/88	15,000	8.5	7,650.00	22,650.00	
11/1/88			7,012.50	7,012.50	29,662.50
5/1/89	20,000	8.5	7,012.50	27,012.50	
11/1/89			6,162.50	6,162.50	33,175.00
5/1/90	20,000	8.5	6,162.50	26,162.50	
11/1/90			5,312.50	5,312.50	31,475.00
5/1/91	20,000	8.5	5,312.50	25,312.50	
11/1/91			4,462.50	4,462.50	29,775.00
5/1/92	25,000	8.5	4,462.50	29,462.50	
11/1/92			3,400.00	3,400.00	32,862.50
5/1/93	25,000	8.5	3,400.00	28,400.00	
11/1/93			2,337.50	2,337.50	30,737.50
5/1/94	25,000	8.5	2,337.50	27,337.50	
11/1/94			1,275.00	1,275.00	28,612.50
5/1/95	30,000	8.5	1,275.00	31,275.00	31,275.00
TOTALS	$260,000		$213,491.67		$473,491.67

making all bond payments and paying all operating and overhead expenses, a 100,000-dollar surplus remained in this fund at the end of this period. The county reinvested it to produce further capital improvements in the project. After the feasibility of financing this complex had proven successful, banks were more willing to purchase revenue bonds and support other such projects.

DEVELOPING A FOOTBALL AND SOCCER COMPLEX

The Johnson County Football and Cheerleading Club, whose programs service 2,500 young people, had been using facilities that the Johnson County Park and Recreation District leased from the YMCA for them. These areas were in very poor condition, and when the YMCA indicated that they required a higher lease fee, the district investigated the feasibility of constructing its own complex.

In addition to the Football and Cheerleading Club, the Soccer Association, Community College, Johnson County Park and Recreation Adult Touch Football and Soccer teams, and Shawnee Mission School District all expressed interest in using a sports-field complex.

The district issued bonds to the value of 225,000 dollars to pay for the project. These bonds enabled a nine-field unit, called the Heritage Sports Complex, to be developed on land that the park district already owned. The complex was developed to a high standard with irrigation so it could be extensively used. The district invested 196,000 dollars in grading, fencing, gates, irrigation, and seeding the area before issuing these bonds. The bond money was allocated for a concession and equipment building (98,000 dollars), parking lot (75,000 dollars), sewage (10,000 dollars), bond reserve (32,000 dollars), and costs of bonds (10,000 dollars). The amount included for bond reserve was equal to the estimated annual debt service.

The Football and Cheerleading Club was the primary beneficiary since their members would be providing most of the revenue. They agreed in writing to raise their fees to cover their share of the principal and interest payments on the bonds. However, because football season is so short, soccer teams could use the fields at other times during the year.

Principal and interest payments on the bonds were payable over a fifteen-year period from revenues the dis-

trict derived from players and teams playing in the softball leagues, flag football and soccer teams scheduled through the Johnson County Park and Recreation District, and unencumbered recreational fees derived from other recreation programs, including revenue from concessions, gate fees, coaches' fees, clinics and tournaments. (See Figure 4.4.) Revenue from the sources shown in Figure 4.4 was projected to cover the average yearly debt service on the bonds and operations and maintenance costs by more than three times. (The payback schedule on the bonds is shown in Figure 4.5.) The bonds did not constitute a general obligation of the district, and the taxing power of the district was not pledged to the payment of the bonds as to either principal or interest.

JOINT DEVELOPMENT OF PLAYING FIELDS WITH A SCHOOL DISTRICT

Jackson County Parks and Recreation Department in Missouri entered into an agreement with the Fort Osage School District to jointly develop playing fields. The school district had a large campus where elementary, junior high, and high schools were located, along with a vocational technical college. A site of twenty-two acres was adjacent to this campus. The school district contributed the land to the project and the county paid for the development of facilities.

The project consisted of four soccer fields, three softball fields, one baseball field, a running trail, jogging trail, concessions building, and parking area. The cost was 360,000 dollars. The school district uses the facilities in the daytime and the county on evenings and weekends.

In the six months that constitute their season, soccer and softball players did not generate enough revenue to redeem the bonds. The school district allowed the county to use the gymnasia in all four campus buildings on evenings and weekends. They agreed to forego the normal rent of seventeen dollars per hour for use of each of these facilities. However, this cost was still passed through to the participants. The surplus revenue from operating the gymnasia, most of it the result of the school district foregoing their rent, was dedicated to repaying the revenue bonds for the playing fields. This additional source of revenue, when added to that likely to accrue from the use of the fields, made the project feasible.

FIGURE 4.4

Projected Facility Use, Maintenance, and Revenue for Proposed Sports Complex

Year	Total Annual Youth Football Player Fees Available	Total Annual Youth Cheer-leading Fees Available	Total Youth Coaches Fees Available	Total Annual Youth Sponsor Fees Available	Total Annual Youth Football Gate Fees	Total Youth Soccer Assoc Fees Available	Total Youth Soccer Cheerleading & Football JCCC	Total Clinic Fees Available From Youth Soccer & Football JCCC	Total School Usage Available 512 & Fees	Total Annual Adlt Soccer & Football Fees Available	Total Annual Concession Fees	Total Gross Revenue	Annual Program & Facility Maintenance Debt Service	Avail-able for Debt Service This Issue	Debt Service This Issue	Debt Service Coverage This Issue
1984	49,000	18,000	1,250	4,875	12,500	29,600	8,500		25,600	20,000	38,000	123,625	91,400	32,225	No Bond Prmt.	2.75
1985	51,800	20,400	1,500	5,200	13,125	29,600	8,500	59,000	25,600	20,000	68,250	302,975	191,150	111,825	40,625	2.75
1986	51,800	20,400	1,500	5,200	13,725	29,600	8,500	59,000	25,600	20,000	69,950	305,325	195,925	109,400	32,000	3.41
1987	54,600	22,800	1,750	5,525	14,470	36,000	8,925	62,000	30,370	22,000	71,700	330,140	215,520	114,620	31,000	3.69
1988	54,600	22,800	1,750	5,525	15,190	36,000	8,925	62,000	30,370	22,000	73,490	332,650	220,910	111,740	30,000	3.72
1989	54,600	22,800	1,750	5,525	15,950	36,000	8,925	62,000	30,370	22,000	75,330	335,250	226,430	108,820	29,000	3.75
1990	57,400	25,200	2,000	5,850	16,750	39,600	9,375	65,000	35,440	24,200	77,220	356,035	242,550	113,485	28,000	4.05
1991	57,400	25,200	2,000	5,850	17,590	39,600	9,375	65,000	35,440	24,200	79,150	360,805	250,663	110,140	32,000	3.44
1992	57,400	25,200	2,000	5,850	18,465	39,600	9,375	65,000	35,440	24,200	81,120	363,650	256,930	106,720	30,500	3.49
1993	57,400	25,200	2,000	5,850	19,388	39,600	9,375	65,000	35,440	24,200	83,152	366,555	263,350	103,205	30,000	3.55
1994	60,200	27,600	2,250	6,175	20,350	43,200	9,845	68,000	40,810	26,620	85,230	390,280	284,420	105,860	29,000	3.55
1995	60,200	27,600	2,250	6,175	21,370	43,200	9,845	68,000	40,810	26,620	87,360	393,430	291,530	101,900	27,500	3.84
1996	60,200	27,600	2,250	6,175	22,440	43,200	9,845	68,000	40,810	26,620	89,540	396,680	298,820	97,800	31,000	3.28
1997	63,000	30,000	2,500	6,500	23,560	46,800	10,345	71,000	46,460	29,280	91,780	421,245	322,725	98,520	29,000	3.37
1998	63,000	30,000	2,500	6,500	24,740	46,800	10,345	71,000	46,480	29,280	94,070	424,715	330,790	93,925	27,000	3.64
1999	63,000	30,000	2,500	6,500	25,975	46,800	10,345	71,000	46,480	29,280	96,425	428,305	339,059	89,246	27,500	3.24
														$1,609,431	$454,125	

1. Total estimated gross revenues and annual facility maintenance expenses increase in fees to cover anticipated increases in annual operation and maintenance costs.

2. Actual debt service is based on assumed debt-service schedule page.

3. Average revenues available for debt service divided by average available for bond debt-service provide an estimated coverage of 3.54.

4. Estimated projections are based on historic trends projected by district staff.

FIGURE 4.5

Estimated Debt Service for the Revenue Bonds

Fifteen Years $225,000

DATE	PRINCIPAL	INTEREST RATE %	INTEREST	PERIOD TOTAL	ANNUAL TOTAL
5/1/85			$23,000.00	$23,000.00	
11/1/85	$ 5,000.00	10.000	11,500.00	16,500.00	$39,500.00
5/1/86			11,250.00	11,250.00	
11/1/86	10,000.00	10.000	11,250.00	21,250.00	32,500.00
5/1/87			10,750.00	10,750.00	
11/1/87	10,000.00	10.000	10,750.00	20,750.00	31,500.00
5/1/88			10,250.00	10,250.00	
11/1/88	10,000.00	10.000	10,250.00	20,250.00	30,500.00
5/1/89			9,750.00	9,750.00	
11/1/89	10,000.00	10.000	9,750.00	19,750.00	29,500.00
5/1/90			9,250.00	9,250.00	
11/1/90	10,000.00	10.000	9,250.00	19,250.00	28,500.00
5/1/91			8,750.00	8,750.00	
11/1/91	15,000.00	10.000	8,750.00	23,750.00	32,500.00
5/1/92			8,000.00	8,000.00	
11/1/92	15,000.00	10.000	8,000.00	23,000.00	31,000.00
5/1/93			7,250.00	7,250.00	
11/1/93	15,000.00	10.000	7,250.00	22,250.00	29,500.00
5/1/94			6,500.00	6,500.00	
11/1/94	15,000.00	10.000	6,500.00	21,500.00	28,000.00
5/1/95			5,750.00	5,750.00	
11/1/95	20,000.00	10.000	5,750.00	25,750.00	31,500.00
5/1/96			4,750.00	4,750.00	
11/1/96	20,000.00	10.000	4,750.00	24,750.00	29,500.00
5/1/97			3,750.00	3,750.00	
11/1/97	25,000.00	10.000	3,750.00	28,750.00	32,500.00
5/1/98			2,500.00	2,500.00	
11/1/98	25,000.00	10.000	2,500.00	27,500.00	30,000.00
5/1/99			1,250.00	1,250.00	
11/1/99	25,000.00	10.000	1,250.00	26,250.00	27,500.00

DEVELOPMENT OF A RANGE OF OUTDOOR RECREATION FACILITIES

Jackson County in Missouri is issuing seven million dollars worth of revenue bonds to develop a golf course, a marina, an equestrian center, and a playing field complex incorporating eight soccer fields and thirteen softball fields. An enterprise fund was established to operate and finance these facilities. Local banks purchased the bonds. The revenue to finance operation costs and bond repayment will be forthcoming from three sources: users of the facilities, other recreation activities not used to service other revenue projects, and the *interest* from tax dollars in the general fund. It would be illegal in Jackson County to use tax dollars themselves for this project without voter approval.

This funding mechanism prevents the county from having to ask voters at a referendum to authorize GO Bonds for these projects. In Jackson County, General Obligation Bonds require a two-thirds majority for approval, and since these facilities serve relatively small interest segments, it is unlikely they would be authorized.

The county owns the land and the stadium in which the Kansas City Chiefs professional football and the Royals baseball teams play. The Chiefs and Royals pay rent for the facility to the county, which has established a separate non-profit corporation to handle these funds. The county is able to pledge these funds to redeem the revenue bonds if the revenues from the three sources identified above are inadequate. This cross-pledge provides additional security to the bond purchasers that there will be adequate revenues to redeem the bonds.

DEVELOPING A SOFTBALL COMPLEX (2)

Jackson County already owns the land for this project. On the site the South Suburban Girls Softball Association currently operates seven softball fields. These fields have been developed piecemeal by the association over a long period and are not high-quality.

The department is replacing these seven fields with a five-field star complex that would be high-quality. In addition, it proposes to build a four-field soccer center. The department's enterprise fund would borrow the money from the county's general fund. The load would be interest-free and repayable over a fifteen-year period. The cost of the project is estimated at 400,000 dollars for the five softball fields and 200,000 dollars for the four soccer fields. The fields will be paid for by a surcharge on the players.

SOURCES:

Jackson County Parks and Recreation Department,
22807 Woods Chapel Road
Blue Springs, Missouri 64015

Johnson County Park and Recreation District
6501 Antioch Road
Shawnee Mission, Kansas 66202

22

Funding Recreation and Park Facilities with Revenue Bonds and Lease-Participation Certificates

Conventional wisdom would dismiss any suggestion that facilities such as a public park and an indoor sports center could be financed with revenue bonds. Rarely do such facilities generate sufficient income to match their operating expenses, and it would appear ludicrous to suggest that their income is adequate to meet costs of facility development in addition to operating expenses. However, the two case studies discussed here refute this conventional wisdom. They are also good examples of entrepreneurial imagination and ability.

The first case describes how a river authority with no power to tax for recreation successfully developed and then operated a two-hundred-acre park. The authority owned the land, but issued 880,000 dollars worth of revenue bonds to develop the park and construct facilities in it. The second case illustrates the important role of lease participation certificates, which are conceptually similar to revenue bonds enabling an agency to construct and operate an indoor sports complex without the use of tax funds.

DEVELOPING A PARK WITH REVENUE BONDS

The Guadalupe-Blanco River Authority (GBRA) is a non-taxing political subdivision of the State of Texas. Enabling legislation does not give it the power to tax. Nevertheless, in 1980 GBRA developed Coleto Creek Regional Park. This park consists of 190 acres that lies on the southwest shore of the 3,100-acre Coleto Creek Reservoir near the city of Victoria, Texas.

A traditional type of park similar to many small state parks, Coleto Creek is financed very differently. Because GBRA has no tax support for any of its operations, it must raise enough revenue from the sale of water, sewage-treatment service, electric power, land leases, and recreation use charges to meet debt service, operation, and maintenance costs for each of its operations.

The capital cost of the Coleto Creek park, including an administration building for the reservoir, is approximately 1.1 million dollars. Land acquisition costs are not part of this figure since the land was required to operate the reservoir and would have been acquired even if it were not considered for recreation development. A Land and Water Conservation Fund grant of 231,000 dollars was obtained, but most of the financing came from the 880,000 dollars worth of revenue bonds bought at 6 3/4 percent interest by Victoria (Texas) Bank and Trust Company. The local bank bought these revenue bonds on the basis of fifteen-year revenue and cost projections developed by GBRA.

Facilities developed in the Coleto Creek park include a headquarters complex, basic support facilities, and a great deal of recreation equipment for picnicking, camping, and boat-launching.

The headquarters complex consists of an administration building, maintenance shop, and adjacent equipment yard. Also included are basic sanitary facilities such as a water well, ground storage tank, chlorination equipment, and a septic tank and drainfield. The headquarters complex serves both reservoir and park operations.

Basic support facilities consist of access roads, parking lots, an electrical distribution system, and several restroom buildings with septic systems. One of the restroom buildings includes space for a small concession stand. Also included are appurtenances such as signs, fences, and security lighting. The authority has also constructed a sewage dump station for recreation vehicles.

As recreational facilities, the authority has provided a number of multi-use campsites with water and electrical connections and a day-use area with picnic tables and a multi-lane boat ramp. In 1985, after the park had operated successfully for four years, the park authority added a two-hundred-foot lighted fishing pier and eighteen additional picnic sites, and expanded an existing day-use parking lot. Total cost for these additions was 100,000 dollars, half of which was obtained through a grant from the Land and Water Conservation Fund. The authority borrowed the remaining money from the GBRA general fund at an annual interest rate of seven percent.

SOURCES OF INCOME

The operating budget for the first five years identifies six major sources of revenue. (See Figure 4.6.) The primary source of income is from entrance and user charges. However, budget figures indicate that the revenues from this source fall short of operating expenses. Hence, to reach break-even point *and* to ac-

crue the additional revenue needed to service the bonds, other funding sources had to be sought.

A second major source of revenue accrues from lease funds. In addition to the two-hundred-acre park site, GBRA owns 2,500 acres of land around the reservoir, which it had to acquire. GBRA leases this land, and the rate schedule for the lease program is graduated on the basis of use intensity. Under the terms of the lease, fees increase as use does.

Typically, private developers try to take advantage of water attractions and build "homes on the water" after an authority has constructed a reservoir. This creates additional pollution and control problems for the river authority while offering landowners and developers substantial profit opportunities. A lease fee increases when owners subdivide property. Therefore, as land use around a reservoir becomes more intense over time, the amount of income from this source similarly increases.

As part of its park development, GBRA included a headquarters building that serves as an entrance station for the park, a control headquarters for the reservoir, and additional office space for the authority's general staff. Rentals of office space and equipment by the general division of GBRA contribute substantially to total operating revenues.

Surface damages income is revenue received from granting rights for oil explorations, while miscellaneous revenues primarily mean income from concession sales.

Figure 4.6 shows a healthy net-operating revenue surplus — part of which is used to retire the bonds. No principal was scheduled to be retired during the first two years. As terminal-revenue bonds, they do not have to be returned to the bank until the end of the fifteen-year period. This provides some internal latitude, and means that high and low revenue years caused by changes in climatic or energy conditions can be balanced out over the retirement period.

If, in the early years while demand was gradually building, the project had had difficulty meeting interest payments on the bonds, then staff made provisions to borrow funds internally from the General Division of GBRA to pay the debt. Although interest (currently seven percent) would have had to be paid on these funds to the General Division, this internal lender of

FIGURE 4.6

Operations Budget Summary 1982-1986

OPERATING REVENUES	1982	1983	1984	1985	1986
Recreation Fees	$125,300	$162,768	$177,271	$194,799	$183,394
Lease Revenues	31,773	41,135	39,474	45,766	43,589
Equipment/Building Rent	69,739	77,816	74,471	64,843	62,406
Surface Damages	73,129	13,869	27,890	6,000	11,632
Interest Income		707	1,122	2,686	13,090
Miscellaneous Revenues (A)	14,330	2,009	3,748	1,200	1,713
TOTAL OPERATING REVENUES	314,978	298,719	325,540	312,068	315,824
TOTAL OPERATING EXPENSES	171,101	193,271	199,390	223,097	194,086
NET OPERATING REVENUES	$143,877	$105,448	$126,150	$ 89,511	$121,739

last resort was an important influence on the bank's decision to purchase the revenue bonds.

DEVELOPING A SPORTS COMPLEX WITH LEASE PARTICIPATION CERTIFICATES

The Jackson County Parks and Recreation Department near Kansas City, Missouri, has integrated the techniques for lease participation financing, lease-purchase, time-sharing, and a cooperation-and-use agreement to finance the construction and operation of the sixty-thousand-square-foot Longview Sports Complex.

The department entered into a cooperation-and-use agreement with the Junior College District of Metropolitan Kansas City, under which it sold ten acres of their Longview Community College Campus to the county for one dollar. The department agreed to develop a modern sports complex on the site and grant time and space in the complex to the district for an agreed-upon annual user charge until financing for the facility is complete. At that time the two entities will become joint owners of the complex.

The department will also lease space and time to other entities and conduct its own programs in the complex. Figure 4.7 contains a list of the amenities included in the athletic complex.

FIGURE 4.7

Longview Sports Complex Facilities

MAIN AREA
— Regulation Basketball Court
(optimum size 94 x 50')
— Three 3/4-Length Basketball Courts
(optimum size 75 x 50')
— Three Regulation Volleyball Courts
(optimum size 60 x 30')
— Retracted Bleacher Seating
— Scoreboards
— Skylights

(3) MULTI-PURPOSE CLASSROOMS (40 x 40')
— Dance (wooden floor in one room)
— Aerobics (padded surface in one room)

FIGURE 4.7 (CONTINUED)

— Wrestling
— Day-Care Facility
— Martial Arts Area

CONCESSION RESTAURANT
— Located for Viewing
— Indoor/Outdoor Patio

GENERAL OFFICE (15 x 40')
— Staff Offices
— Registration Area
— Facility Director's Office

STORAGE ROOM (15 x 15')
— Janitorial Supplies
— Equipment Storage

GYMNASTICS ROOM
— Tumbling Area
— Gymnastic Equipment

MEN'S AND WOMEN'S LOCKER/SHOWER FACILITY
(50 x 60')
— Lockers
— Showers
— Restrooms

TRAINING ROOM
— Sauna
— Steam Room
— Whirlpool

WEIGHT ROOM
— Line Weights
— Nautilus
— Exercise Equipment

50-METER INDOOR POOL
— Diving Tank (separate)
— 8-Lane Pool
— Therapeutic Pool (seperate)

6 RACQUETBALL/HANDBALL COURTS
— Glass Rear Wall

WELLNESS CENTER (5000 square feet)

The department financed the sports complex with lease-participation certificates issued by the Jackson County Public Facilities Authority, a "63-20" not-for-profit corporation established by the county as a financing vehicle. In the state of Missouri, the Hancock Amendment requires a two-thirds majority vote to pass a referendum that approves financing for any project that increases taxes or charges user fees. The county was able to bypass this referendum requirement by establishing a non-profit corporation under the terms of Internal Revenue Service ruling 63-20. Such a non-profit corporation may hold title to a project, secure financing, and later return title to the county. Since the debt is issued "on behalf of" the county, the land purchased from the Junior College District for one dollar was conveyed by the county to the 63-20 corporation.

As a passive entity serving only as a financial vehicle, the non-profit corporation constructed, installed and leased the facility to the county. A corporate trustee assigned under a trust indenture with the corporation sold certificates of lease participation. Proceeds were disbursed to the department, as the non-profit corporation's agent, to pay the costs of developing the sports complex.

The Public Facility Authority holds title to the sports complex and leases it to the department under an annual renewable lease agreement with an option to purchase. The department makes lease payments out of revenues from the operation of the complex directly to the trustee for the account of the corporation. The trustee then makes principal and interest payments on the certificates. (See Figure 4.8 for a graphic depiction of this financing structure.)

These lease-participation certificates are essentially the same as revenue bonds; however, unlike revenue bonds no public referendum is needed to issue them in Jackson County. Issuance of the certificates does not obligate the county to levy any form of taxation or to make any appropriation for their payment, and the Public Facilities Authority has no taxing power. The prospectus for the lease-participation certificates clearly specifies the county's limited obligations, stating that payments made by the county under the lease are payable solely from: (1) user fees from the facility, less cost of operation and maintenance, (2) "Amounts which may but are not required to be appropriated annually by the County," and (3) interest from temporary investment of the certificate proceeds, and proceeds from insurance and condemnation awards. The prospectus also states that "there can be no assurance that the County will appropriate funds

FIGURE 4.8

Financing Structure for the Longview Sports Complex

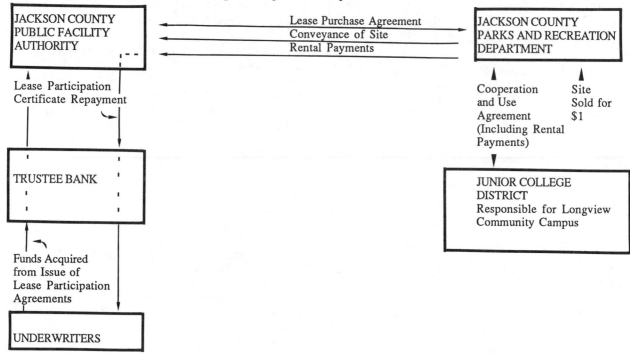

to make rental payments or renew the lease after the initial term or any renewal term on the lease."

Under the lease agreement, the department may elect to purchase the facility or not to renew the lease and surrender possession of the facility to the corporation at the end of any lease term. The corporation has granted a first mortgage on the facility to the trustee for the benefit of the certificate owners in the event that the department fails to renew the lease. In this case, the complex and the land on which it sits would be sold and the proceeds applied to the principal and interest due on all of the certificates to the certificate owners.

The total cost of the project is approximately four million dollars. The certificates are projected to be fully redeemable in twenty years with annual lease payments of around 350,000 dollars. When they have been paid, the Public Facilities Authority transfers the facility's unencumbered fee title to the department.

The cooperation-and-use agreement between the county and the college district then requires the department to convey to the district legal title to a one-half interest in the complex.

Under the cooperation-and-use agreement, the college district has priority time in the building from 8:00 am to 4:00 pm on weekdays during regular fall and spring semesters for student classes and programs. It is also committed to paying a dollar amount of at least 100,000 dollars a year for this building-use time. Jackson County has priority in prime-time scheduling from 4:00 to 11:00 pm weekdays, all day on Saturdays and Sundays, and exclusive all-day use from May 15 through August 15.

The college district will provide security at the facility. The department will maintain insurance coverage for the facility and general accident and public liability insurance for bodily injury. The district and the department will equally share the cost of design and specifications for the building, its utilities and maintenance. Any profits made by the facility will be put into a contingency fund until it reaches 500,000 dollars to be used for improvements. Disbursement of any profits exceeding the first 500,000 dollars will be mutually agreed upon.

Expected operating expenses of approximately 589,000 dollars and an annual lease payment of 350,000 dollars requires the complex to produce revenue in the range of a million dollars a year. The department plans to produce this revenue through subleasing, timesharing, general programming, sports leagues, memberships, a pro shop, and concessions as well as the 100,000-dollar annual college-use fee. The college also agreed to pay fifty percent of any operating loss associated with the project.

The department has preleased space in the complex to a well-known local hospital that plans to establish a wellness program on campus, and the college has assumed supervisory responsibility for the operation of a day-care center that has leased space in the complex. The college had previously identified a need for this facility since many students are older and need a service for their children while they attend classes. In addition to rent, the department receives a percentage of the gross revenues from these leases as an administrative fee for promotion and other benefits it provides.

Several large area corporations have also signed five-year time-sharing agreements with the department by which they lease time in the building for their own corporate recreation programs. The complex will house many of the department's recreational classes, programs, and leagues that are currently being conducted in buildings or on fields leased or obtained through trade-out agreements. Individual, family, and corporate memberships will be sold both for use of all facilities and amenities and for specific activities. Concessions will operate in two lounge areas to sell food and beverages — including beer and wine. Estimated expenditures and expected revenue are shown in Figures 4.9 and 4.10.

FIGURE 4.9

**Longview Sports Complex
(Estimated Projections)**

JUSTIFICATION OF EXPENDITURES
Operational Budget $588,945.00

Lease Payment   350,000.00
$938,945.00

ESTIMATION OF REVENUE
Corporate Memberships	$ 85,500.00
Memberships	307,500.00
General Programming	247,536.00
Corporate Leagues	32,160.00
Clinics	15,000.00
Rental	31,500.00
Preschool Lease	70,000.00
Wellness Center Lease (5,000 sq. ft. x $12)	60,000.00
Concessions	125,000.00
Pro Shop	35,000.00
Sponsorships/Advertising	20,000.00
Longview Community College Lease	100,000.00
	$1,129,196.00

FIGURE 4.10

**Longview Sports Complex
(Justification of Expenditures)**

100% Capacity

6 am to 11 pm — Seven (7) Days EXPENDITURES

I. SALARIES

*Center Manager	$ 22,000.00
*Center Assistant Manager	16,600.00
Center League Supervisors (Part Time)	22,920.00
*Secretary	10,400.00
*Custodian	10,088.00
Lifeguards/Pool Manager	51,200.00
*Concessionaires	9,450.00
Scorekeepers	17,220.00
Instructors (Swimming, Gymnastics, Fitness, Aerobics)	10,752.00
*Desk Management (2)	24,010.00
FICA (.07)	13,625.00
	$208,265.00

II. CONTRACTUAL SERVICES:

Officials	$159,360.00
Coaches' Clinics and Certification	10,000.00

FIGURE 4.10 (CONTINUED)

Printing and Binding/Publicity and Promotion	10,000.00
*Insurance (Property)	12,000.00
Postage	4,000.00
*Service to Maintain Building & Grounds	15,000.00
*Brochure Cost	2,000.00
Advertising	6,000.00
Instructors (Dance, Martial Arts, Classes, Racquetball/Handball, Clinics)	4,320.00
	$222,680.00

III. COMMODITIES

Concession Supplies	$65,000.00
Office Supplies	3,000.00
Recreational Supplies	2,500.00
*Chemicals (Pool)	8,000.00
*=Utilities (Gas, Water, Electricity)	75,000.00
Classroom Materials and Supplies	1,000.00
Awards	3,500.00
	$158,000.00

TOTAL EXPENDITURES	$588,945.00

*Fixed Cost

The complex will offer a place for socializing, fitness, competition, health, and learning. It will also supply a much-needed facility to both the college and the department at no financial risk to either, enhancing the image of the department and attracting members by offering "country-club class" in a public facility.

When this concept was presented to the county legislature, members received it so well that they authorized construction of a duplicate center at another location on the east side of the county. A similar format was negotiated with two school districts in the area, along with several interested corporations. The financial institutions that supported the Longview Center indicated that they were willing to back the duplicate center, which will again be funded by lease-participation certificates.

SOURCES:

Jackson County Parks and Recreation Department
22807 Woods Chapel Road
Blue Springs, Missouri 64015

Operations Manager, Guadalupe — Blanco River Authority
PO Box 271
Seguin, Texas 78156

Section 5

Improved Communication and Response to Citizens

The first two cases in this section offer specific mechanisms for improving responsiveness to an agency's constituents. Case 23 describes the sophisticated computerized process used by Jackson County for registration in its recreation classes. As an alternative to the government directly delivering services to target groups, some economists have advocated for many years that giving target-market vouchers would be a more effective and efficient use of tax dollars. Vouchers are provided by government, and the target market can use them to purchase the service of their choice from authorized suppliers. Suppliers then redeem the vouchers for cash from the government agency that issued them. Case 24 describes and analyzes the experience of city officials who used vouchers to deliver recreation services.

Cases 25 and 26 consist of articles by a bank manager and a hotel manager who are both concerned with developing a corporate culture focused on customers. The bank manager uses Disney World as his model, while the hotel manager deals with the Plaza Hotel in New York City. The principles and techniques they discuss in these sectors of the leisure industry are equally applicable to public recreation agencies.

The single most important reason that residents do not make better use of public recreation and park services is probably that they are not aware of them. Cases 27 and 28 describe two uncommon but effective promotional tools. Case 27 suggests that recent technological improvements in radio broadcasting and receiving have made low-power radio broadcasts a viable vehicle for promotion. These systems are relatively inexpensive to buy, and require minimal technical expertise to install and operate.

The Gus and Goldie animated characters created by the El Paso Aquatics staff to promote learn-to-swim programs have proven extraordinarily successful as vehicles for communicating with children. In Case 28 their success is explained by the same underlying principles that account for the popularity of Ronald MacDonald. The case describes these principles and suggests that animated characters are a good way for recreation agencies to enhance the effectiveness and efficiency of their communication efforts.

Consistent investment in staff development, recognition, and incentives, is central to improving an agency's vigor and influence. Case 29 offers four suggestions for enhancing staff productivity in these ways, and describes how they have been implemented.

23

Computerized Registration for Recreation Classes

The registration process for recreation classes described here has won national awards and recognition. It is client-oriented, comprehensive, and systematic.

The registration process developed by Jackson County has won several national awards for innovation. The computer software cost about thirty thousand dollars. The hardware investment was approximately 45,000 dollars.

The process begins with a quarterly recreation tabloid that lists the activities the agency will offer during each of its four seasons. Staff start planning the tabloid twelve weeks prior to its distribution. All information is arranged in a uniform format, printed, and distributed to fifty thousand households in Jackson County through direct mail. The agency also offers the tabloid at numerous community facilities and retail establishments. Particular care is given to code and class numbers since these provide check systems for the computer that guarantee correct participant records. Class descriptions are presented in the tabloid as shown below:

SWIM AND STAY FIT
Adults, 16 years and over
Eight weeks, $35

The American Red Cross Swim and Stay Fit Program is designed to increase the fitness of the average swimmer. Swimmers chart their distance in miles, and American Red Cross certificates are issued to those who achieve 10, 20, and 50 miles. Log your miles with the pool staff each time you swim. Registrants must be able to swim 200 yards.

Code	Days	Starts	Time	Location
63-5000-1321	M-T-W-Th	June 16	6:30-8:30am	YWCA-D
63-5000-1322	M-T-W-Th	June 16	11:30-1:30pm	YWCA-D
63-5000-1323	M-T-W-Th	June 16	4:30-6:00pm	YWCA-D

BASIC CANOEING CLASS
Six-hour course: $15 per person (senior adults $12)
Minimum age: 12 years, unless registering with a parent
Location: Jacomo Marina (Lake Jacomo)

This six-hour course covers personal water safety, instruction, and practice in basic strokes and maneuvers, terminology, and discussion of river-floating applications.

Code	Days	Starts	Time	No.Lessons
63-7012-0101	MON.	July 7	6:00-8:00pm	3
63-7012-0102	MON.	August 8	6:00-8:00pm	3

FIGURE 5.1

Jackson County Parks and Recreation Activity Roster for Season 3

Date: 12/08/86

DIV	CLASS	PROGRAM DESCRIPTION INSTRUCTOR	DAYS	START TIME	TERM LENGTH	MIN	MAX FEE	ENR REMARKS	RFN	YTD REV
63	50030406	YOGA	TH	061986 19:00	8 SESS 01:00	8	10 $27.00	0 AGE 15 & OVER	0	0.00
63	50030803	PLATINUM GYM CIRCUIT TRAINING	T,TH,S	062986 00:00	16 WKS 00:00	1	100 56.00	5 AGE 14 & OVER	0	246.40
63	50030905	INTRO TO WOMEN'S BODY BUILDING	T,TH,S	062986 00:00	16 WKS 00:00	1	100 56.00	0 AGE 14 & OVER	0	0.00
63	50031005	INTRO TO MEN'S BODY BUILDING	T,TH,S	072986 00.00	16 WKS 00:00	1	100 56.00	3 AGE 14 & OVER	0	159.60
63	50032405	BEGINNING EXERCISE	M&W	061686 19:30	16 SESS 01:00	6	12 34.00	0 AGE 18 & OVER		30.00
63	50082690	LACY'S REDGATE FAMILY MEMBERSHIP (JANE SMITH)		000000 00:00		1	999 126.00	4 OLD 126/NEW 151	0	499.00
63	50090110	SUMMER SOFTBALL LEAGUE- MEN'S C (JOHN DOE)	WED	052186 00:00	10 WKS 00:00	4	8 260.00	8	0	2080.50
63	50090122	SUMMER SOFTBALL LEAGUE- MEN'S D (JOHN DOE)	SUN	051886 00:00	10 WKS 00:00	4	8 260.00	8	0	2600.00
63	50082696	LACY'S REDGATE SWIM TEAM (JANE SMITH)		000000 00:00	00:00	1	999 25.00	0 MEM25/NONMEM35	0	0.00
63	50082694	LACY'S REDGATE INDIVIDUAL MEMBERSHIP (JANE SMITH)		000000 00:00	00:00	1	999 63.00	1 OLD 63/NEW 73	0	73.00
63	50070101	LACY'S CONCESSIONS AQUATICS	S-M	010186 00:00	00:00	1	999	4	0	4033.90 0.00

After compiling the information published in the tabloid, staff enter it into the computer. This data includes season (1-winter, 2-spring, 3-summer, 4-fall), division number, class code number, program name, days the class is held, starting date and time of the class, term length, minimum number required to hold the class, maximum number allowed, cost of the program, age level of participants, days the class is held, number of participants enrolled, number of available spaces, and amount of fees collected for each class. (See Figure 5.1.)

Registration for all classes and activities is a three-stage process. Staff give highest priority to those who mail in the registration forms provided in the tabloid. These are accepted immediately upon distribution of the informational material that promotes the activities. The second highest priority is given to those who phone in their registration and confirm it with a credit-card number. Telephone registration is not permitted until three weeks after the tabloid is mailed out, so those registering by mail have priority status. Staff charge a one-dollar handling fee for credit-card registrations, and the computerized record system enables personnel answering the phone to instantly check the status of a particular program. Finally, lowest priority is given to those who walk in and register; these applicants are accepted during the last three days of the registration period after phone-ins are over.

The percentage of registrants who use the mail, telephone, and walk-in services is approximately seventy, twenty, and ten percent respectively. Most people are paid on the last day of a month, so the registration period embraces at least the first two weeks of a month since that is when most money is available. Class fees must accompany all applications whether made in person or by mail. This priority order effectively prevents people from wasting their time waiting in line.

Registration periods for new classes deliberately overlap existing classes so instructors can sell the next season's activities to their clientele. Participant information, including name, address, phone number, and form of payment is entered into the computer. Staff can then print out this information by class for the instructors.

Computer overhead and operating costs are covered by one dollar added to each participant's class fee. Registration is the key to the success of the entire recreation program. This system is geared to offer potential participants maximum convenience. If it is inefficient, then it conveys a negative first impression of the agency's competence. No monetary refunds are given if people do not attend classes after registering. The following statement clarifies this rule on the registration form:

No refunds will be made except when classes are filled or cancelled by the recreation department and on request when day, time or location changes by the department prohibit attendance. As revenues from class fees must offset leadership, equipment, and facility costs, and as commitments for these services must be made prior to the start of a class, no other refunds will be made.

People who do not get into the class of their choice are called immediately and given alternative choices or offered a refund. Those who have registered for classes in the past are mailed class schedules and registration forms before these items become available to the general public. This makes them feel they are valued clients. The computer keeps track of people who have not participated in any of the agency's programs for over a year, and staff mail follow-ups encouraging these people to return. Staff also use mail and phone follow-ups to find out why they have not participated recently.

After the computer produces print-outs of registrants, the number of people who are new to Jackson County's programs are starred so instructors are aware of them and can make a special effort to welcome them. The computer not only prints out names, but name tags. These tags help class members get acquainted and comfortable on the first day. A neighborhood-designated class roster is also given to every class member to encourage carpooling.

After each of the four registration seasons, staff print out an alphabetical listing of participants sorted by zip code and zones set by the department. This helps determine where participants interested in a particular class live and the time they are willing to travel to participate. Such information aids in planning facility locations for various classes and enables staff to calculate the proportion of residents and non-residents who register for activities.

SOURCE:

Jackson County Parks and Recreation Department
22807 Woods Chapel Road
Blue Springs, Missouri 64015

24

Recreation Vouchers:
A Case Study of
How to Increase
Responsiveness to Citizens

This case, written by the author of this book, was first published in Public Administration Review, *November-December, 1983. The principle behind vouchers is explained, along with their use in other fields. An in-depth description of the city of South Barwon's recreation-voucher program shows the expectations, lessons, and limitations of their six-year operation.*

The basic idea of vouchers is to give resources to citizens so they can purchase the services of their choice from authorized suppliers. In their classic form, which was described by Milton Friedman over a quarter of a century ago, vouchers are offered to citizens by a government agency.[1] Citizens exchange the vouchers for services delivered by their preferred supplier. The provider of the services then returns them to the agency and receives cash for the vouchers acquired. The fundamental principle here is that potential users can have vouchers subsidize them directly, rather than allocating that same amount of subsidy to a service or facility or to an agency that operates that service or facility.

Efforts are continually being made to increase the responsiveness of local government to citizen needs and demands. There has been a continuing interest in how local governments can best incorporate citizen participation, attitudes, and preferences into delivery decisions to ensure that resources are responsively prioritized. Traditional approaches have often proven disappointing to staff who are trying to recruit participants. Accordingly, more recent approaches have offered more sophisticated techniques to determine what local government services the citizens of a particular community want to increase, retain, decrease, or terminate. Prominent among these techniques has been survey research.[2]

Vouchers may lead to more comprehensive and accurate citizen input than surveys because they enable citizens to vote for preferences with the equivalent of dollars. Each citizen has a direct, executive, and continuing voice in shaping public policy by his or her "vote" of vouchers.[3] Vouchers can be viewed as the ultimate in citizen participation:

> The voucher system in fact is able to bypass some of the most intractable problems inherent in most approaches to citizen participation. Difficult questions such as "who are the citizens, what is the public interest, and how can citizens' interests be represented?" can be largely avoided under a voucher system. With this system, each individual citizen can determine his or her own interest, and attempt to pursue it.[4]

Vouchers give citizens choice and control of service delivery while retaining the financial responsibility of government.

Medicare, the Food Stamp program, and the GI Bill are all examples of voucher systems administered by the federal government. For example, under the terms of the GI Bill, ex-military personnel receive a resource allocation for their education. These individuals select where to spend this allocation from among a wide range of authorized tertiary educational institutions. The US government then reimburses the educational institution, making the allocation in effect a voucher.

At the local level, voucher schemes have been proposed for public-housing programs, for allocating revenue-sharing funds from the State and Local Fiscal Assistance Act, for delivering recreation services, and for stimulating more responsiveness from cultural organizations.[5] The most extensive discussion of voucher use at the local level, however, has focused on their potential for use in the public schools. Education vouchers suggest a way of increasing influence of parents on educational decisions. In this context, vouchers are exchanged for services. Children or their parents select the schools they wish to attend. Those schools with programs that attract many children receive most vouchers and thus substantial financial resources. In contrast, those schools that attract few children are financially penalized because they receive fewer resources.

Early work by Jencks and his associates at the Center for the Study of Public Policy encouraged the federal Office of Economic Opportunity to sponsor an experimental educational voucher program.[6] The intent was to fund several experiments, but because of widespread opposition, primarily from education professionals, the experiment was ultimately confined to a single location, Alum Rock School District in San Jose, California, for a period of three years commencing in 1972.

The Alum Rock experiment was restricted in scope and was not a true open-market voucher scheme; however, vouchers equal in value to the per-student education cost were distributed to parents, who were then permitted to select the school and programs of their choice. It appears that some positive results emerged from the experiment.[7] They included: (1) the emergence of a more innovative and flexible curriculum in most schools; (2) an increase in the ability of teachers and administrators to select and design their work settings; (3) the development of new program alternatives; and

(4) accelerated decentralization of administrative authority to local school principals.

Despite the considerable intellectual debate which has taken place in the education field, the only other empirical test of a voucher scheme reported in the literature was another short-lived experiment in Salt Lake City from 1973 to 1978.[8]

There has been a paucity of chances to observe the advantages and limitations of vouchers in an operational context at the local level in any field. Thus, when an extended field experiment is conducted, careful scrutiny is necessary so lessons can be learned. This is the purpose of describing a recreation voucher scheme here — including how it operates and what the local government that introduced it expects, along with lessons, limitations, implications, and future directions.

CONTEXT

The city of South Barwon, population forty thousand, has operated a recreation-voucher program for the past six years. It is one of six municipalities that comprise urban Geelong, which has a combined population of approximately 150,000. Geelong is about fifty miles from Melbourne, the second largest city in Australia.

The city of South Barwon currently budgets 570,000 dollars for recreation and park services, which constitutes seventeen percent of its total tax revenues.[9] Of this total, seventy thousand covers its recreation-voucher scheme and 500,000 is allocated to recreation and park services in the traditional manner. City officials introduced the recreation-voucher scheme in 1976. It is important to note that funding for the program was not supplied by the existing budget but consisted of supplementary funds added to it.

All recognized private, non-profit, community recreation organizations in South Barwon that do not receive any services from the 500,000-dollar appropriation are eligible to receive funds from the voucher program. Organizations may use these funds for either capital or operating purposes since the City Council places no restriction on their use. Recipients of voucher funds are required to indicate the benefits that accrued from using these funds. The city then considers these responses and rules upon each organization's annual application for inclusion in the voucher scheme.

The South Barwon experience is not a "pure" voucher scheme. The literature suggests, however, that attempts

to introduce a pure voucher scheme that would fully replace traditional approaches to funding public recreation
services are likely to be frustrated and lie outside the
range of political feasibility.[10] The transformation
from traditional approaches to vouchers is likely to appear too conceptually radical and pragmatically disruptive for acceptance by public agencies.

OPERATION OF THE SCHEME[11]

Guidelines for administering the voucher scheme in
South Barwon are shown in Figure 5.2. Each taxpayer
receives his or her tax bill, a recreation voucher, and a
list of recreational organizations that have been
approved by the council to receive grants. The current
value of each voucher is four dollars and fifty cents.

FIGURE 5.2

City of South Barwon Guidelines for Recreation-Voucher Grants

1. All clubs and organizations must be first approved by
   Council before being eligible to receive a grant.

2. To qualify, clubs must be non-commercial, recreational and/or sporting organizations operating, or
   about to operate, within the City of South Barwon
   and, if outside the City of South Barwon, must not
   duplicate recreational services offered by any club or
   sporting organization within the City of South Barwon.

3. Recreation vouchers are valid in the municipal year of
   issue only.

4. Canvassing of support for the return of vouchers from
   the general taxpaying community will not be permitted and could cause Council to immediately
   disqualify that club from receiving further grants.

5. Vouchers must be returned to the city offices with tax
   payments. The name of the chosen club must be
   clearly designated on the voucher.

6. Clubs must submit an application each year for registration to qualify for a further grant. These applications must be accompanied by details of current of-
   ficebearers, etc. as requested.

7. The payment of the grant will be forwarded to the
   club's address as shown on the application for registration unless written notification is given to the
   contrary.

8. Vouchers are not transferable.

9. Vouchers not directly assigned by ratepayers will not
   be redeemed.

10. Vouchers assigned to non-approved clubs or clubs
    that do not qualify will not be redeemed.

11. The identity of taxpayers designating vouchers for
    any particular club will be retained by Council as
    confidential information. However, the total number
    of vouchers received by any club may be publicized.

12. Where the amount of vouchers allocated by taxpayers
    in any year is less than the funds set aside by Coun-
    cil for this purpose, the balance of funds will not be
    distributed among the clubs receiving grants.

13. Council reserves the right to withhold payment of a
    grant to a club.

14. Approval of a club as an organization qualified to
    receive a grant under one year does not necessarily
    pre-qualify that club for subsequent years.

15. Where a club based outside the municipality qualifies
    for a grant, this may be withdrawn in writing by
    council when a club with similar activities com-
    mences operation within the municipality and be-
    comes qualified.

16. Organizations that are presently provided for or op-
    erated with substantial Council support, such as li-
    braries or elderly citizens clubs and the like, do not
    qualify for a grant.

17. Political or religious organizations and the like do
    not qualify for a grant. However, *bona fide* recre-
    ational clubs that are part of such organizations may
    be approved by Council.

In order to reduce attempts at forgery, vouchers are
printed with the city crest and in such a way that they
are not easily duplicated. The actual value of the
vouchers is superimposed in an effort to clearly communicate their value to the taxpayer. (See Figure 5.3.)

Two separate organizations may be nominated on each voucher, but the full amount may be committed to only one organization. A voucher is issued for each taxable property in the city, so owners of more than one property receive a corresponding number of vouchers. By completing one and returning it to the city, a taxpayer is effectively saying, "Take $4.50 of my tax payment and give it to the recreation body x," or "Split it up into two lots of $2.25 each for recreation organizations y and z."

Each returned voucher is numbered and taxpayers are required to include their name, address, signature, and tax-assessment number. This information authenticates the vouchers and further safeguards against possible forgery. The individual taxpayer's nominated organization(s) remains confidential. Finally, the city distributes the taxpayers' "votes" to the organizations in the form of checks for the value of the total vouchers allocated to each group.

ADMISSION PROCEDURES

Any genuinely non-profit community recreation groups are eligible for admission to the scheme. The organization simply submits an application to the city each year. This application requires information relating to the location of the organization, its activities, and its membership fees. One person on the city staff serves as liaison for the voucher program and makes recommendations to the council on eligibility.

The 150 organizations declared eligible in 1981-1982 are shown in Figure 5.4. Of these 150 entities, eighty-six are specialized recreation groups situated outside city limits and fourteen are community-service organizations

FIGURE 5.3

Sample Recreation Voucher

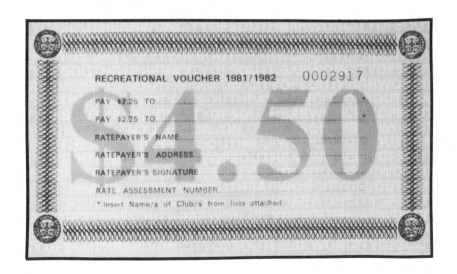

FIGURE 5.4

Organizations Eligible for the Voucher Program, 1981-1982

RECREATIONAL VOUCHER SYSTEM — The following list consists of approved clubs under the Recreational Voucher System:

ANGLING
Kardinia Angling Club
Torquay Motor Yacht & Angling Club

ARCHERY
South Barwon Archers

ASTRONOMY
Astronomical Society of Geelong

ATHLETICS
Grovedale Little Athletics Club
South Barwon Amateur Athletic Club
St. Bernard's Little Athletics Club

BADMINTON
Belmont Uniting Church Badminton Club
Grovedale Uniting Ladies Badminton Club
St. Bernard's Badminton Club

BASEBALL
East Belmont "Saints" Baseball Club
Grovedale "All Stars" Baseball Club

BOATING
Indented Head Boat Club

BOWLING
Barwon Heads Bowling Club
Belmont Bowling Club
Geelong Bowling Club
Geelong & District Carpet Bowls Association
Highton Bowls Club
Torquay Bowls Club

CAMERA/FILM
Geelong Amateur Movie Club
Geelong Camera Club
Geelong Cine Society

COAST GUARD
Coast Watch Radio
Flotilla 8 Australian Volunteer Coast Guard
Flotilla 9 Australian Volunteer Coast Guard

CRICKET
Alexander Thompson Cricket Club
Barwon Heads Cricket Club
Belmont Church of England Cricket Club
Belmont Church of Christ Cricket Club
Belmont Uniting Cricket Club
East Belmont Cricket Club
Geelong Football Umpires Cricket Club
Grovedale Cricket Club
Highton Cricket Club
St. Luke's Cricket Club
South Barwon Cricket Club

CROQUET
Belmont Croquet Club

CYCLING
Barwon Eagles BMX Club

DOGS
Geelong German Shepherd and Obedience Dog Club

EQUESTRIAN
Geelong Dressage Club
Barwon Pony Club

FIRE BRIGADES
Barwon Heads Urban Fire Brigade
Belmont Urban Fire Brigade
Connewarre Rural Fire Brigade
Grovedale Fire Brigade
Highton Urban Fire Brigade
Torquay Urban & Rural Fire Brigade

FLYING
Barwon Heads Model Aero Club
Geelong Aero Club
Grovedale Aero Club

FOOTBALL
Barwon Football Club
Barwon Heads Football Club
Grovedale Football Club
St. Augustine's Football Club
Torquay Football & Cricket Club

GEMOLOGY
Geelong Gem & Mineral Club

GO-CARTS
Geelong Kart Club

GOLF
Barwon Grove Golf Club
Barwon Heads Golf Club

GUIDES/BROWNIES
1st Barwon Heads Girl Guides
Belmont Local Association of Girl Guides and Brownies
Grovedale District Girl Guides and Brownies
Highton Girl Guides Local Association

HISTORICAL SOCIETIES
Geelong Historical Society

HOCKEY CLUBS
Barwon Boys Hockey Association
Geelong Hockey Club

HORTICULTURE
Geelong Garden Club
Society for Growing Australian Plants (Geelong Group)
Torquay Garden Club

MOTOR CAR CLUBS
Geelong Four Wheel Drive Club
MG Car Club (Geelong)
Morris 850 Car Club
Western District Car Club, Inc.
Western District Historical Vehicle Club

MOTORCYCLE CLUBS
Sporting Motorcycle Club

NATURALISTS
Geelong Field Naturalists Club

NETBALL
Barwon Heads Netball Club
Belmont Uniting Netball Club
Grovedale Netball Club
YWCA Southern Suburbs Netball Association

ORIENTEERING
Geelong Orienteering Club

ROWING
Barwon Rowing Club
Corio Bay Rowing Club

SAILING
Barwon Heads Sailing Association
Torquay Sailing Club

SCOUTS/CUBS
2nd Belmont Scout Group

3rd Belmont Scout Group
4th Belmont Scout Group
1st City of South Barwon Scout Group
1st Grovedale Scout Group
2nd Grovedale Scout Group
1st Torquay Scout Group Committee
Nindethana Park 1st & 3rd Highton Scouts

SHOOTING
Geelong Pistol Club
Geelong Rifle Club
Geelong Small Bore Rifle Club
Geelong Branch Victorian Field & Game Association

SOCCER
Barwon City Soccer Club

SOFTBALL
All Stars Softball Club

SURF LIFE SAVING CLUBS
Bancoora Surf Life Saving Club
13th Beach Surf Life Saving Club
Torquay Surf Life Saving Club

SWIMMING
Geelong Amateur Swimming Club
Geelong Sub-Aqua Club

TABLE TENNIS
Geelong Table Tennis Association

TENNIS
Alexander Thomson Tennis Club
Barwon Heads Tennis Club
Belmont Uniting Tennis Club
Connewarre Tennis Club
Geelong Lawn Tennis Club
Grovedale Tennis Club
Highton Tennis Club
St. Bernard's Tennis Club
St. Cuthbert's Tennis Club
St. Luke's Highton Uniting Tennis Club
St. Paul's Lutheran Tennis Club
St. Stephen's Anglican Tennis Club
Torquay Tennis Club

THEATRE/DRAMA
Geelong Repertory Society
Geelong Regional Youth Concert Band
Mill Community Theatre Company

WALKING
Geelong Bushwalking Club

WATERSKIING
Geelong Waterski Club

YOUTH CLUBS
Belmont Community Youth Club
Belmont Drop-in Centre
St. Stephen's Youth Club
Geelong & District YMCA Youth Clubs (South Barwon Branch)
— Basketball
— Girls Olympic Gymnastics
— Holiday Programs
— Indoor Soccer
— Indoor Hockey
— Little Athletics
— Little League Football
— Little League Soccer
— Roller Hockey
— Rollerskating
— Schools' Physical Education Program
— Toddlers Gym

MISCELLANEOUS CLUBS
Combined Pensioners Association, Belmont/Highton
Combined Pensioners Association, Barwon Heads
Geelong Ceramic Group
Geelong Professional Cross-Country Club
Social Organization for the Handicapped
Young Women's Christian Association of Geelong

who offer recreational services as part of their overall mission.

Groups from outside the city limits are permitted to participate in the scheme, reflecting its officials' belief that regional organizations are worthy of support if they provide services to city residents. This attitude recognizes that some specialized activities may not be available within the city's boundaries. However, for an internal organization to qualify, there must be no providers of similar services within the city.

Application forms that document eligibility are required from each group by September of each year. This provides time to adjudicate applications and print a list of those approved for inclusion with the tax bills that are mailed out in December. Payment of tax bills is due by the following April, which is also the deadline for return of the vouchers. The city mails checks to the selected organizations in June, together with application forms for the following year.

Administrative expenses associated with administering the scheme are surprisingly low. Approximately three hundred staff hours were required to distribute and collate vouchers in 1982. Additional personnel and supply costs were limited to printing vouchers and application forms, postage, recording lists of organizations and vouchers received, check processing, considering groups for approval, and handling correspondence related to this task.

EXPECTATIONS OF THE VOUCHER SCHEME

Although expectations were not formally specified, interviews with city officials and a review of documents suggest that the city hoped recreation vouchers would achieve four results. These were: (1) provide recreation services that were more responsive to citizen desires; (2) offer seed funds that would encourage the creation of new recreation organizations; (3) better meet the recreation needs of disadvantaged groups; and (4) resolve the council's annual difficulty in deciding which non-profit recreation groups should be supported with public funds.

Increasing Responsiviness. There was a concern that the city had become unresponsive in its allocation of resources for recreation services and supported the same groups year after year even though priorities had changed. The city had always subsidized the traditional, male-dominated, major Australian sports of football, cricket, and field hockey by developing capital facilities like playing areas and changing accommodations, along with general maintenance of these areas. Rented to private, non-profit clubs at nominal rates, these facilities typically have rates set at approximately ten percent of their maintenance cost. In the majority of cases, the clubs that rent them have exclusive use for the relevant season. Such financial arrangements meant that the city subsidized each active participant group member with twenty-three dollars.

However, other minor sports and recreation groups, such as those offering track and field, netball, badminton, baseball, surf lifesaving, lawn bowls, tennis, creative arts, and many others, received virtually no public support even though they provided similar recreational opportunities. Indeed, in total these minor clubs that got no assistance from public funds had a clientele similar in size to that of the substantially subsidized traditional sports clubs.

The voucher scheme was intended to alleviate this imbalance by enabling taxpayers to become active selectors instead of passive receivers of recreation services. With this plan, citizens can direct their allocation for the recreation subsidy to their chosen pursuit and not pay to subsidize someone else's recreation. Because they have more control over the delivery of recreation services, the system has to be more responsive to the wishes of the citizens.

The intent is that offerings that effectively meet people's perceived needs prosper, while those that do not are either redesigned or discontinued. Organizations receive public funds only to the extent that they can attract support from citizens.

Encouraging the Emergence of New Organizations. It was hoped that vouchers would introduce dynamism and encourage diversity in the recreation system by spreading the recreation dollar more evenly to meet the many interests that were not being served. There was a specific expectation that new recreation organizations would emerge:

> We could see new community organizations being formed and different recreational activities started. We could see families coming together to form Family Fitness Groups or participate in Family New Games. The money redeemed by Councils for the vouchers could be used by new groups to purchase equipment or hire a venue in which to stage their activities. A whole host of new recreation activities could be created.[12]

Serving Disadvantaged Groups Better. The South Barwon Council was conscious that too often the very young, the aged, the physically handicapped, and the socially and economically deprived were being neglected in favor of physically active people. The voucher scheme was conceived as "a possible stimulant to the 'recreationally inactive' to start them exploring the many lesser-known opportunities now available throughout the community."[13] The city recognized that it could justifiably be accused of an elitist approach to providing recreation services if it continued to subsidize

opportunities solely for the non-handicapped population.

Selecting Groups for Subsidies. The final expected effect of recreation vouchers was that the council would no longer have to select which non-profit recreation groups should receive public subsidies. These decisions often arouse controversy because some interest groups are inevitably passed over in favor of others. Using vouchers transfers the selection decision from council to citizens. With a voucher scheme it was expected that recreation organizations would no longer try to exert pressure on council members but instead recognize that public resources could only be obtained by offering services that people wanted. The voucher scheme enabled elected officials to say to all groups soliciting funds, "If your service is valuable, then the citizens will demonstrate their support by committing their vouchers to it." The scheme also permits subsidizing groups that may have a substantial constituency but be politically controversial.

Finally, the city recognized that one of the most difficult tasks facing any government is how to terminate a service that it has traditionally supported. Vouchers enable citizens to make this decision; therefore city officials cannot be subjected to the pressure that inevitably arises from terminating support of a special interest.

LESSONS AND LIMITATIONS

The simplicity of the voucher scheme implemented in South Barwon may be somewhat deceptive. While it is an exciting innovation, it has several limitations, and in the six years that they have operated this system, city officials have learned many lessons. These limitations and lessons are discussed here under six headings: opposition from entrenched interests, monitoring the scheme, ambiguity in defining recreation, the non-returned decision; imperfect communication; and the equity issue.

Opposition from Entrenched Interests. It was anticipated that if the voucher scheme was funded by taking money from the existing recreation services budget then traditional beneficiaries would vigorously oppose vouchers and make the scheme politically unfeasible. Therefore a supplementary appropriation was added to the recreation budget to fund the voucher scheme. This precedent has been followed each year.

The original intent was that the ratio of voucher funding to traditional funding would gradually move toward an equal division of the two financing methods over a period of years. This intent has not been realized because vigorous opposition emerged from those who saw that their share would decrease if this shift occurred, particularly in the major sports of cricket, football, and field hockey. Indeed, some counselors who are personally involved with these major sports are seeking to abolish the voucher scheme or reduce rather than increase its role. They perceive it as a threat to the financial support these major sports have traditionally received from the city.

Some of the council who are not fully supportive of vouchers have challenged their usefulness in reflecting the preferences of taxpayers. They suggest that while the vouchers give some indication of general support for particular recreation activities in the community, they should be interpreted with great care because "people are capable of taking a benevolent attitude and can issue vouchers to the clubs that need the most help, rather than to their first choice of recreational activity."[14]

Monitoring the Scheme. For a voucher scheme to work, it must be monitored from the outset. Groups that attempt abuses must be vigorously opposed to establish the legitimacy of the scheme. Although the city issued guidelines, some groups, while carefully following the written rules, sought to abrogate the intent of the voucher program.

A perceived danger was that recreation organizations would be tempted to spend great amounts of time, energy and money on public relations and propaganda activities. The general canvassing of taxpayers to request them to assign their vouchers to a particular organization is prohibited because of possible adverse reactions to solicitations or letterbox "junk mail" drops.

Vouchers are only accepted directly from taxpayers so they cannot be collected and handed in by a beneficiary group. This prevents the possibility of individual members getting unduly harassed by fellow members. It also precludes the possibility of vouchers being solicited by an organization through raffles or similar

methods. Before this rule was implemented, one imaginative organization announced a raffle for a vacation to the Fiji Islands. The entry ticket for the raffle was a completed recreation voucher assigned to that group!

The city believes that extra emphasis on promotion has some positive dimensions, particularly increasing citizens' awareness of the recreational opportunities available in South Barwon. The simple act of providing a list of organizations to citizens and asking them to select one or two to support has the spin-off benefit of improving awareness.

Ambiguity in Defining Recreation. When it was first introduced, a significant limitation of the South Barwon scheme was its failure to precisely and unambiguously define "recreation." Initially, the city did not recognize the importance of this issue. Consequently, the criteria for admission to the voucher scheme are fuzzy. This has created a continuing problem, for after criteria were established, efforts to amend them became controversial and had to be abandoned. The criteria are set out in item 2 of the guidelines. (See Figure 5.2.) They are generic rather than specific, requiring only that an organization be "non-commercial and recreational and/or sporting."

Lack of specificity in these criteria has caused the interpretation of what constitutes recreation to be incrementally broadened each year. It was noted earlier that fourteen community-service organizations were included among the 150 eligible groups. The initial justification for their inclusion was that they offered recreation services as part of their overall mission. These community-service groups include pensioners' clubs who use their voucher funds to provide activities such as a Christmas party for their senior members, and Coast Guard volunteers who man radios in the coastal area. In the future it is expected that other community-service groups such as St. John's Ambulance Brigade, the Red Cross, and various organizations that serve the handicapped will be declared eligible.

Although these groups constitute less than ten percent of all organizations in the voucher scheme, they secured thirty-six percent of the returned vouchers in 1982. This proportion seems likely to increase as more community-service groups are declared eligible. Their substantial support probably stems from a long-established tradition of voluntary community service and the associated heritage of donations from citizens. These organizations are worthy of support, but their inclusion in the voucher scheme clearly detracts from its original purpose — to encourage more responsive offerings and a greater diversity of recreation activities.

This is a difficult issue to resolve. In South Barwon, the definition is too broad. However, a narrow, restrictive definition could be similarly limiting because it might inhibit the emergence of new recreation opportunities.

The Non-returned Decision. In 1982, there was a fifty-three-percent return rate for the vouchers. (See Table 5.1.) This means than only 37,000 dollars of the 70,000-dollar voucher budget was expended. The redemption rate is likely to be influenced by what happens to the $4.50 if taxpayers do not complete and return their vouchers.

TABLE 5.1

Return Rates of Vouchers Issued by South Barwon During a Six-year Period

Year	Voucher Value	Vouchers Issued	Completed Vouchers Returned	Return %	Payments to Organizations (In Dollars)
1981-82	$2.25	30,704	16,384	53..3	36,864
1980-81	2.25	30,572	15,876	51.9	35,721
1979-80	2.00	28,978	14,838	51.2	29,676
1978-79	1.75	28,538	12,856	45.0	22,498
1977-78	1.50	28,062	10,487	37.3	15,730
1976-77	1.50	27,956	4,434	15.9	6,651

Note: When interpreting this table, it is important to note that the voucher value (e.g., $2.25 in 1981-1982) reflects the invitation to taxpayers to allocate their $4.50 to two groups. Hence, in 1981-1982, only 15,352 pieces of paper ($4.50 vouchers) were issued, one to each taxable property in the city. However, taxpayers could respond twice on each voucher.

Under the GI Bill, for example, servicemen and women forfeit their vouchers if they choose not to use the educational opportunity. The same rule was adopted in South Barwon. If the voucher is not returned, then the city does not spend the $4.50. Effectively, this non-response reduces the annual bill so it may appear that there is incentive for non-users not to return the vouchers. However, the individual taxpayer does not receive the $4.50 as credit. This savings must be shared with those who do return their vouchers. Therefore non-returners forego the opportunity to allocate $4.50 but, assuming that fifty percent of the vouchers are returned, only receive $2.25 in tax savings. Individuals who assign their vouchers allocate $4.50 and also receive the benefit of a $2.25 tax saving because fifty percent of the citizens did not assign their vouchers.

Other decision rules that could be considered include: (1) returning the unredeemed voucher money to the general fund and disbursing it for other uses; (2) returning it to the traditional budget for recreational services; or (3) distributing the unassigned dollars pro rata among the organizations receiving support from those citizens who did assign their vouchers.

Imperfect Communication. The communication issue consists of three dimensions. The first concerns the need to know how other citizens assign their vouchers. In South Barwon, people redeem their vouchers within a single time period. The city makes no interim announcements about the amount of money accrued by each organization, and this lack of information may lead to undesirable results.

For example, assume that a group of taxpayers wants to encourage the development of four organizations, but they are able to assign dollars to only two of them. If they all "vote" for numbers 1 and 2, then organizations 3 and 4 are left without support. However, if they have better information about how other taxpayers are assigning their vouchers, some might switch their dollars to organizations 3 and 4 in an attempt to ensure that they receive a minimum level of support.

The evidence suggests that a second source of imperfect communication was the difficulty in explaining the concept of recreation vouchers to citizens in the early years. Table 5.1 suggests that it was only in the third or fourth year of operating the scheme that many citizens understood the procedure. The very low first-year return of 15.9 percent was at least in part attributable to the fact that the vouchers were placed in the middle of an information booklet concerned with the city budget. This meant that many citizens overlooked the voucher. However this low first-year return did enable officials to gain some administrative experience gradually and permitted subsequent fine-tuning of the program with minimum disruption. For example, in subsequent years, vouchers were mailed as a separate inclusion with tax notices.

The third dimension of imperfect communication concerns the need for citizens to be familiar with the groups seeking their vouchers. Imperfect information causes inequities and inefficiency. When citizens do not possess sufficient knowledge to make intelligent choices among organizations, they become vulnerable to hucksterism. This concern is particularly important for poorer citizens who are notoriously hard to reach through printed material.[15]

One of the expectations of the recreation-voucher scheme was that it placed financial resources directly into the hands of the economically disadvantaged, enabling them to select recreational services most relevant to their needs. While this goal is laudable, its attainment may be chimeral because of the information-access inequities that may accompany a voucher scheme. Theoretically, affirmative dissemination efforts could be designed and undertaken with special attention to the informational needs of the economically disadvantaged. However, the empirical literature suggests that this task is too difficult and expensive to be practical.[16]

This was not a major problem in South Barwon because the city is one of the most preferred residential areas in the Geelong region of Victoria. Its population is generally considered upper-middle class, and a high degree of self-motivation is evident. However, in other contexts this issue cannot be dismissed cavalierly as a minor problem:

> Information imperfections are a problem that will not be solved easily, and may prove the fatal weakness of theoretically sound proposals to . . . achieve greater economic efficiency and social equity.[17]

The Equity Issue. Perhaps the most obvious limitation of the South Barwon scheme involved the weighting and distribution of the vouchers. To receive a voucher, residents have to pay real property taxes directly. This creates two kinds of inequities.

First, there are inequities among those who pay property taxes. Only residential property — not commercial property — is included in the scheme. Further, the absentee landowner, single-family homeowner, and one-hundred-unit-apartment owner each receive the same one-voucher allocation.

Second, inequities exist because some citizens do not pay property taxes directly. An initial expectation of the voucher scheme was that it might better serve disadvantaged citizens. However, no evidence indicates that this group has benefited. Since the disadvantaged are more likely to live in rental units, landlords in fact assume more control. This has the pernicious effect of successfully disenfranchising the poor from choosing the types and extent of recreation activities entitled to public financial assistance.

Before inequities of distribution can be resolved, there has to be some consensus as to what constitutes equity. Equity is a complex concept that different people interpret in different ways. However, from the perspective of allocating vouchers, there appear to be three primary alternative equity models that can be adopted.[18]

The equal-opportunity model is likely to gain easiest political acceptance. This would entail allocating an equal number of vouchers to all citizens regardless of need or amount of taxes paid. Such an alternative suggests that vouchers be distributed on a per-person or per-household basis. The South Barwon allocation most approximated the per-household approach, with the exception that households not paying direct property taxes were excluded.

Compensatory equity would require that vouchers with extra increments of value be given to disadvantaged individuals. This would be consistent with Jencks' suggestion that the value of vouchers should be inversely proportional to family wealth.[19]

Market equity would involve allocating services to individuals in proportion to the tax revenues they pay. Those paying the highest taxes would receive higher-value vouchers.

Because subjective, normative judgements are involved, there probably cannot be any "right" or "wrong" concepts of equity — only different opinions. Ideas about a fair and equitable voucher-distribution system are also likely to be tempered by background and social position. In South Barwon, city officials initially intended vouchers to create compensatory opportunities; however, the allocation system facilitated equal opportunity or even a tendency toward market equity for those who paid taxes directly.

USEFULNESS AND FUTURE DIRECTIONS

The usefulness of vouchers in the delivery of public services has generated substantial discussion over a relatively long period of time; however, there have been few opportunities to gain insights from their application at the local government level.

Generalizations and implications from the South Barwon experience can be suggested only with caution since it was limited in scope and funding amounts. Generalizing from a single experience in a specific jurisdiction with a high per-capita income and a highly educated population located in a different country with different traditions also presents obvious dangers. Nevertheless, it does illuminate several points of interest.

First, vouchers were introduced at South Barwon as an administrative innovation rather than as the product of a popular movement. This meant that in the early years the policy decision lacked constituent support and was particularly vulnerable to political opposition. To minimize trauma and opposition, officials introduced the voucher scheme gradually and concurrently with the traditional system. This is consistent with the advice in the professional literature. In addition to responding pragmatically to political realities, a gradual introduction gave administrators time to evaluate and correct the initial plan.

South Barwon was fortunate in being able to use additional funds to finance the voucher scheme. Considering the present financial climate in North America, implementing a voucher scheme would realistically require that existing money be reallocated rather than more money appropriated.

Like most Australian cities, South Barwon does not employ many recreation professionals. Community recreation has traditionally been facilitated with seed money or in-kind maintenance assistance to non-profit organizations. Thus there has been no opportunity to observe how an established professional staff would react to a voucher scheme. However, resistance that emerged from those representing traditional entrenched interests prevented the expansion of the plan that officials had originally envisioned. This resistance stemmed from its threat to the status quo.

Vouchers give citizens direct control over resource-allocation decisions and thus offer intriguing possibilities for demonstrating responsiveness and accountability to citizen demand. Implementation is likely to be more difficult in a larger jurisdiction because of increased lo-

gistic problems and greater difficulty in monitoring the procedure to minimize abuse. Success depends on a willingness to monitor the marketplace vigorously. If vouchers were used on a large scale such regulatory efforts might be uneven.

The voucher concept is flexible enough to support a wide variety of specific applications. Indeed, although the scheme operated by South Barwon is an exciting innovation, it represents a rather tentative application of the voucher principle. Other applications could lead to much more radical changes in the structure and type of service delivery.

For example, instead of limiting a voucher scheme to raising funds that encourage private recreation services, cities could broaden it to incorporate recreation offerings directly operated by a municipality — such as swimming pools and recreation centers. This would mean that citizens control the total recreation budget.

A future development may be that citizens retain vouchers and use them as directly redeemable coupons or certificates instead of returning them to the city. With this mechanism, citizens could directly contract for the services they desired. Vouchers to the city could be used to purchase specific types of recreation services from authorized public and private suppliers. The supplier would then return the voucher to the city for redemption at its face value. Redeemable vouchers could be used to remove the monopolistic impact of service delivery and deliberately stimulate competition both within the public and non-profit sectors and between public, non-profit, and private agencies. This may streamline the system and lead to increased accountability, greater cost efficiency, and more relevant service delivery.

Clearly there is a danger that resources may be allocated to the most persuasive rather than the most responsive organizations. In South Barwon, traditional voluntary agencies that had substantial name identification gained a disproportionately large share of the voucher resources without making any noticeable efforts to be more responsive. This suggests that image may be more important than substance. Thus organizations may decide to invest considerable time, energy, and dollars on promotion rather than service.

The method of disseminating information is a crucial consideration. In South Barwon this was limited to providing taxpayers with a list of eligible organizations, and naturally citizens had a higher awareness of long-established agencies. There must be a greater commitment to disseminating more detailed information as part of the voucher system if new organizations are to be encouraged — a particularly important commitment if groups with lower educational levels are to be reached. Reliance on traditional approaches to transmitting information to these groups is unlikely to succeed. Unless everyone has equal access to information, including an equal ability to understand it, it cannot be said that all citizens have "free choice," a fundamental premise of voucher schemes.

Government entities are frequently depicted as reluctant to introduce innovations.[20] When the environment is safe and predictable, they have little incentive to introduce new programs because personnel costs that would result from possible failure are often perceived to be greater than the benefits that would result from success.[21] However, in recent years the uncertain fiscal environment, increased concern for accountability, trend toward contracting out, and shift in emphasis from provider to facilitator have caused many agencies to become more innovative.

In this environment, further experimentation with voucher schemes seems likely. The South Barwon experience has demonstrated the feasibility of applying vouchers in the recreation field and has identified a number of areas for improvement. The next step would appear to be that some recreation agencies in North America implement voucher use on a small scale, incorporating the suggested improvements from the South Barwon scheme. This would enable professionals to further refine the principle and test its appropriateness in the North American context.

SOURCES:

[1]Milton Friedman, "The Role of Government in Education," *Economics and the Public Interest*, ed. Robert A. Solo (New Brunswick, NJ: Rutgers University Press, 1955).

[2]James M. Ferris, "A Theoretical Framework for Surveying Citizens' Fiscal Preferences," *Public Administration Review 42*, May/June 1982, pp. 213-219. Gregory A. Daneke and Patricia Kilbur-Edwards, "Survey Research for Public Administrators," *Public Administration Review 39*, September/October 1979. Brian Stipak, "Local Government's Use of Citizen Surveys," *Public Administration Review 40*, September/October 1980, pp. 521-525.

[3]Steven H. Flajser, "Revenue-Sharing Voucher Program (RSVP)," *Policy Sciences 5*, 1974, pp. 309-315.

[4]David W. Sears, "The Recreation Voucher System: A Proposal," *Journal of Leisure Research*, 7, No. 2, 1975, p. 142.

[5]Robert Beckham, "The Experimental Housing Allowance Program," *Journal of Housing*, January 1973, pp. 12-17. Flajser, pp. 309-315. Sears, pp. 141-145. Gary R. Bridge, "Cultural Vouchers," *Museum News*, March/April 1976, pp. 21-26, 64.

[6]Christopher Jencks, "Give Parents Money for Schooling: Education Vouchers," *Phi Delta Kappa*, September 1970, pp. 49-52.

[7]David K. Cohen and Elenor Farrer, "Power to the Parents? — The Story of Education Vouchers," *Public Interest 48*, 1977, pp. 72-97.

[8]Donald Fisk, Herbert Keisling, and Thomas Muller, *Private Provision of Public Services: An Overview* (Washington, DC: The Urban Institute, 1978).

[9]An Australian dollar is approximately equal in value to a US dollar.

[10]Sears, p. 141 *et seq.*

[11]Much of the information in this section was derived from four sources: (1) a personal interview with Mr. Laurie H. Miller, the city engineer for South Barwon who was responsible for developing and implementing the scheme; (2) an information package available from the city of South Barwon, "Recreation Voucher Grants: Capitation Grants to Sporting Organizations;" (3) Special Report #76/2, submitted by the city engineer's department to South Barwon City Council, July, 1976, which first proposed the voucher system, "Capitation Grants to Sporting Organizations: A Recreation Voucher Scheme;" and (4) Laurie Miller, "Recreation Voucher Scheme," *Recreation Australia*, Vol. 1, No. 1, September 1981, pp. 15-17.

[12]"Capitation Grants to Sporting Organizations: A Recreation Voucher Scheme," p. 6.

[13]*Idem*, p. 6.

[14]Miller, p. 16.

[15]Michael A. Olivas, "Information about Inequities: A Fatal Flaw in Education Voucher Plans," *Journal of Law and Education*, Vol. 10, No. 4, October 1981, pp. 441-465.

[16]Olivas, p. 441 *et seq.*

[17]Olivas, p. 447.

[18]John L. Crompton and Charles W. Lamb, "The Importance of the Equity Concept in the Allocation of Public Services," *Journal of Macromarketing*, Vol. 3, No 1, Spring 1983.

[19]Jencks, *op. cit.*, p. 50.

[20]Erwin Feller, "Public Sector Innovation as 'Conspicuous Production,' " *Policy Analysis*, Vol. 7, No. 1, Winter 1981, pp. 1-20.

[21]Robert L. Bish and Hugh O. Norse, *Urban Economics and Policy Analysis* (New York: McGraw-Hill, 1975), p. 184.

25

Mickey Mouse Marketing

The two articles reproduced here were originally published in American Banker *in its July 25th and September 12th, 1979, issues.* American Banker *granted permission for them to be reproduced in this volume. Author N.W. (Red) Pope was a bank manager in Orlando. He was cognizant of the outstanding reputation among customers, employees, and other businesses enjoyed by the Disney complex of attractions in Orlando, and recognized that the people who worked at Disney were major contributors to that reputation. In these articles he identifies reasons for the Disney success and wonders why banks have not adopted such techniques. The principles he discusses are equally applicable to public recreation and park agencies.*

The financial industry would do well to emulate the marketing acumen of Mickey Mouse.

The world's most famous character has become a respected and envied symbol of the very best there is in target marketing, salesmanship, and customer relations. The leader that sets the standards that others in the attractions industry seek to match is the Disney Organization.

And in that marketing magic initially concocted by Walter Elias Disney over fifty years ago there are some very valuable lessons for the financial industry. For while the business of entertainment and the business of finance appear as far apart as an X-rated movie and a Disney G release, there is one obvious and necessary common denominator both share.

People.

People inside, and people outside. Customers and employees.

How Disney looks upon people, internally and externally, handles them, communicates with them, rewards them is, in my view, the basic foundation upon which its five decades of success stands. The banking and thrift industry, conversely, has appeared to put more emphasis on results, solutions, growth, and problems than on the basic method for achieving results or growth or solving problems with solutions — i.e., people.

People. Inside and outside. Customers and employees.

Sitting as I do every day in the shadow of Cinderella's Castle (East), and exposed to the Pixie Dust that permeates the atmosphere hereabouts, I have come to observe closely and with reverence the theory and practice of selling satisfaction and serving millions of people on a daily basis successfully. It is what Disney does best. It is one of the things banking needs to improve on most.

If anyone better understood the direct relationship between employees and customers, I haven't heard about him or her. If ever there was an organization built on people interfacing with people, it is Disney.

For two articles I will relate to the financial industry some of the personnel policies and customer-relations theories of the late Walt Disney and his successors in

168

the theme-park business, with the obvious hope that our customers will someday be able to say what almost every person who has been to Disneyland or Walt Disney World has said: "It was everything I expected, it was worth every penny, and I was served to my satisfaction by people who were enthusiastic, knowledgeable, and pleasant."

The articles will dwell on the internal side — the people on the theme-park payroll — and the customers, those who pay. But to Disney the two are so intertwined it may be difficult to separate one from the other. As you follow the piece, always keep your bank's policies, theories, philosophies, and methods in mind in relation to how Disney does it. Compare your way with the Disney way.

Put aside the fact that the Disney organization has been at the entertainment business for more than fifty years and in the theme-park business for almost twenty years.

And don't consider the fact that Walt Disney Productions has an ample supply of cash and financial support to do some rather remarkable things now and again. In the early days the exact opposite was true. So the Disney strength of today grew out of some rather lean times of yesterday. My point has more to do with attitude, philosophy, direction, and execution than cash or credit.

The beauty of it all is that the "Disney Way" has been in effect since Steamboat Willie changed his name to Mickey Mouse. Success did not prompt Walter Elias Disney to establish specific consumer and staff procedures and approaches. Rather, his innovative, unusual methods of people management brought about Disney's overall success as an organization.

There's little question of the fact that Disney is in the entertainment business. So it is natural that show-business terms are employed. Instead of Personnel, there is Casting. That alone gets the average young man or woman in the right frame of mind when he or she goes in for a job. And that's important at Disney. The frame of mind is the difference between being an employee or being a Cast Member. Show biz, if you will.

At Disney if your job has you interfacing with the public in any way whatsoever, you're "on stage" when you do your thing. One is not better than the other. That is emphasized. It takes both to "put on the show," as Disney people say it, and they mean just that.

No little, insignificant jobs at all. That is emphasized. It takes many people, doing many types of jobs, to put on the show every day. No job is without its importance to the show. The first time a new Disney cast member goes to his or her job there is a feeling of being a part of the overall success.

The most obvious element at Casting is the professionalism. Those who interview and hire and place are pros in the personnel business. They know what they are doing and how to do it. An interview at Disney is impressive to thousands of people, most of them young, who apply for jobs. And there are up to fourteen thousand jobs at Walt Disney World in season. Be aware that the first impression of the potential employee is as important as that of the employer.

What kind of people are interviewing job applicants at your bank? Do they give the proper impression to applicants? Is your personnel function really professional?

The new Cast Member, once hired, is given written instructions as to the steps he/she will go through in preparation-to-work stages. Written information, not verbal. The person is told when to report, where to report, what to wear, how long he or she will be in that training phase. The individual is provided a booklet that explains what is expected in appearance, hair style and length, from makeup to jewelry, from clean fingernails to acceptable shoes. Regardless of age or sex or job to be performed, there is conformity to the code. Everything is in writing. No chance for misinformation, misinterpretation. Attention to detail.

Everyone must attend Disney University and "pass" Traditions 1 before going on to specialized or technical training. That's right, Disney U — a multi-level educational institution run on Disney property by a full-time staff. In addition to several basic Disney philosophy courses there are evening classes in Spanish or accounting or drama or disco dancing. All Cast Members are eligible to attend and college credits are given for many courses.

Traditions 1 is an all-day experience wherein the new hiree gets a constant offering of Disney philosophy and operational methodology. Every audio-visual and static presentation method is used. And no one is exempt from the course, from VP to entry-level part-timer. All must matriculate at Disney U before any time is spent on a job, backstage or on stage.

Here is where banks so often fail to take advantage of a marvelous opportunity. We don't have our policies in writing. We tell the new people to "report on Monday." That's it. When they show up, we often hand them benefits booklets that are out of date and expect them to decipher the material. If a briefing is given, it is boring, ill-produced, lacks imagination, and is usually way over the heads of those forced to sit through it. Our principal method of indoctrinating a new hiree resembles handing a new recruit a gun, explaining which end to hold, and then walking off, leaving the person to load, aim, and fire the best he or she can.

Disney expects new CMs to know something about the company, its history and success and management style before they actually go to work. Every person is shown, during Traditions 1, how each division relates to other divisions, and how each division — Operations, Resorts, Food and Beverage, Marketing, Finance, Merchandising, Entertainment, etc. — relates to "the show." In other words, here's how all of us work together to make things happen. Here's your part in the big picture.

Are you listening?

The new CMs show up their first day at Disney U. They are ushered into a room with round tables, four to the table. Coffee and juice and a Danish are offered. It is 8:30 am. A name tag is given each person, but we'll get into that later. The "instructor" is with that group for the next eight hours.

Everyone is introduced — not by the instructor, or by him- or herself. The four people at the table are asked to get to know each other and then all of them introduce each other. Immediately you know three other people by name, face, where they came from, and their future jobs. You are a part of a group now, not alone — one of the crowd.

All of you gather for a picture. You smile. When your Traditions 1 day is over at 4:30 pm, you are given a copy of the weekly Disney newspaper for the theme park, and there on the front page is your group photo, with your name in the caption! Impressed? Certainly.

For about half of your eight hours you're in a classroom setting, watching films or slides or listening to an enthusiastic young lady use magnetic elements to show how the company operates. The other four hours are spent on a guided tour of the park. On stage, backstage — you are exposed to it.

And at lunchtime you are taken to one of the many company cafeterias and treated to as much lunch as you desire. Free. Impressed? You begin getting the idea that this company wants you to be happy on the job, and knowledgeable.

How many banks take their new hirees throughout the facility, explaining each department's function and how all relate to the business of the park? Do we treat our new hirees to a lunch? Take their picture, give them the company newspaper, explain the benefits properly?

Sure, your bank isn't Walt Disney World and you don't have the people, the money to do that. Are you sure you don't? Have you tried?

Remember those name tags? Everyone at a Disney theme park wears one; every person who works for any Disney enterprise wears one. Everybody. From the chairman of the board of Walt Disney Productions to that guy sweeping cigarette butts off Main Street after the parade. The dishwasher few people see, the ticket-taker at the entrance, the secretaries, security people — everyone wears a name tag.

With only the first name on it. That's it. President of Disney Productions, director of marketing, popcorn vendor, cook — first name only.

And the rule is that when addressing each other, only first names will be used. No Mr. or Mrs. or Miss or Ms. First names, please. It is part of the oneness, the unity, the "no one is better than anyone else" policy.

Can you imagine the average teller addressing the chairman of the board as "Charlie?" Or the janitor calling the VP/commercial loans by his or her first name? Perhaps banks need to be more formal than entertainment entities. It is probably expected that banks not be too familiar, too folksy, for money and credit is perceived as a more serious business than the attractions business.

Or is it? Have we structured ourselves so stiffly; are we so status-level-position conscious that communication doesn't properly occur? Do we give the feeling that sometimes it is "them" and "us?" Do we demand formality, aloofness?

After a day to learn what's what, get the Pixie Dust, the name tag and the photo, the new CM is dispatched to his/her job-training assignment. Very little OJT occurs at WDW — Walt Disney World. On-the-job observing, perhaps, but very little training.

Example. My two kids, ages eighteen and sixteen, average intelligence, reasonably quick, are accepted to be Casual Temporaries — summer, Christmas, Easter, etc., employment.

They are to take tickets, either at the main gate or the Magic Kingdom entrance. Take tickets. That's it. How tough can that be?

Four eight-hour days of instruction are required before they can go "on stage!" They are paid to learn, but before a Disney CM interfaces with a Guest — Disney has no customers at theme parks, only Guests — the management must be absolutely certain that the CM can, and will, perform properly. After all, we are dealing with Guest Satisfaction, they say. Nothing is spared to assure Guest Satisfaction.

"Why," I inquired, "does it take four days to learn how to take tickets?" Waste of time, I thought.

My two Traditions 1 graduates, with his new haircut and her "a-little-lipstick-only" makeup, jump to the defense of thirty-two hours of education in the fine art of taking tickets.

I was informed that there are X varieties of tickets, each having special meaning. What happens if someone wants to know where the restrooms are, when the parade starts, what bus to get back to the campgrounds, what the park's hours are, where do we eat inside, what happens if I lose my child, how many bricks in the castle? Questions *ad infinitum*.

"We need to know the answers or where to get the correct answers quickly," I am advised. "After all, Dad, we're on stage and help produce the show for our Guests. Our job, every minute, is to help the Guest enjoy the park."

Wow! Can you imagine one of the bookkeepers, a proof operator, a secretary, a collector rising to the defense of four days of intensive pre-job training so they could better serve our customers? Well, why not?

After four days, they went on the line. First to observe, then to try it under careful supervision. After a few hours, they were put to the task. It is this way in every job throughout the park where some specific training is required and general knowledge demanded. Regardless of the time it takes or the instructional costs, no one interfaces with a Guest until he or she is proved ready to properly serve that Guest.

Stop and examine the average bank teller's training programs. The New Accounts person. Baptism under fire.

And so I said to my minimum-wage-to-start-with tycoons after the first day, "How does it feel to be ticket-takers?"

Again I was berated.

"Ticket takers? Dad, we're WDW Hosts."

I had forgotten. Everyone on stage and backstage in the theme park area itself has a title with the word "host" in it. There is no Policeman. There is a Security Host. There is no monorail driver. There is a Transportation Host. There are no street cleaners. There are Custodial Hosts. No French fries server, but a Food and Beverage Host. Guests have hosts, don't they? Certainly, so everyone at Disney is a Host or Hostess.

And everyone who interfaces with a Guest in the park is "themed" — costumed to fit the job. The world's largest laundry does all those costumes and uniforms every day, or all night, as the case may be. Come to work in the morning and after clocking in go to Wardrobe. Show biz again.

Mike Mescon, the incredibly provocative Georgia State professor/lecturer, says if he headed a bank he would drop almost all bank titles and use instead the term "salesperson." For, Mr. Mescon emphasizes, that's what it is all about. Selling. Low-key or hard-sell, salesmanship and customer service are two elements that separate banks from one another. The bank that can train its people properly, motivate its people, reward its people and have its people enthusiastically representing that bank on and off the job will win.

Walt Disney was a marketing magician, no doubt. But his keen insight into personnel and customer relations, separately and collectively, enabled him to create the world's most successful entertainment conglomerate by starting with a mouse he drew and named Steamboat Willie in 1928.

The next article, also keying on The Disney Way, will highlight customer relations and feature several marketing approaches banks might use to sell to their target groups.

MORE MICKEY MOUSE MARKETING

Nothing I've had published in thirty years prompted more mail or phone calls than "Mickey Mouse Marketing," the first of two articles concentrating on customer and staff relations as practiced by the Walt Disney organization.

While this could mean all my previous stuff was pretty bad, it might also mean this piece was particularly good. I don't think it was either. What I think prompted the cards and calls was that the gist of the article touched some of banking's exposed nerves.

A banker in New York wrote that he had known for years how good Disney was at customer relations, and how bad his bank was at it, but he hadn't been able to get money to do much about the latter. The Denver banker said he knew his bank's training was horrible, but management hadn't given that priority billing. The Pennsylvania banker remarked that until bankers cared as much about how well the customer was served as how well the bank was served, banking would never change its customer relations.

An Ohio banker wrote me stating that odds were pretty long on bankers looking upon their personnel as high priorities. His way of stating that was "human resources inside our banks are yet to be ranked as important as computers, branch offices, or, for that matter, the board of director's annual retreat. In the main, staff morale is not all that big a need to too many bank managers."

The good part about the letters was that people apparently were moved to critical introspection upon reading the piece. The bad part was that almost without exception everyone admitted management apathy or lack of commitment.

Incidentally, Disney does not make its programs or methods or manuals or personnel available, as a rule, to outsiders on a "for sale" or consulting basis.

Now, back to Part Two in the continuing saga of how Walt Disney World and other Disney entities look upon their bread (staff) and butter (guests). Remember, please, as you read on, to compare how your bank does things with the way Mickey Mouse and his associates do them.

Of the one hundred million people who have passed through Walt Disney World's turnstiles since October, 1971, a great many ask seemingly stupid questions about the place. Stupid to us, perhaps, but not to Disney. Like how many bricks are in the Castle, how many lights are there in the theme park, how many boats do you have here, how long did it take to build this place, how much did it cost, how many telephones are there in the whole place, how often do you have to paint the submarines, how many hot dogs do you sell here each year? *Ad infinitum.*

To many businesses this sort of barrage of trivial inquiry would lead to an abrupt, "How should I know, kid!" To Disney it is the sort of stuff dreams (and attendance) are built on. And if any employee (host or hostess) cannot give the answer to any question . . . that's right, any question . . . then there is a telephone exchange to call. Immediately. The minute the question is asked and the Disney staffer can't answer it, call that number and ask!

Twenty-four hours a day a cadre of switchboard operators with fact books to rival the largest phone books in American stand by to answer those "very stupid" questions on the spot. Like, the most meals served in a single day was 220,500 (12/31/75). And thirteen million ketchup packets are given out annually and twenty-four tons of French fries are sold every week and three-and-a-half million pounds of hot dogs were sold to the guests last year.

And if you add up all the boats and rafts and submarines and ferries and canoes and other floating material throughout the 27,400 acres, you'd have the seventh largest navy in the world, and that's a fact.

The bottom line is: serve the guest. If someone cares about hot dogs, tell 'em the answer. Whatever the guests want to know, get 'em the facts, now!

Sometime, stand in your lobby and watch your personnel attempt to answer basic, not stupid, questions. How much are your safe-deposit boxes? What are your CD rates? How much can I get for a Canadian dollar? Does your bank have a branch office in the south part of town? What's your best rate on an auto loan? What hours are your drive-ins open?

Maybe the person asked doesn't have the answers, or perhaps shouldn't try to give out rates, but how does he or she respond? How does he or she serve the customer?

One fast rule at Disney theme parks is that no employee will be served before a guest. In fact, Disney provides cafeterias, breakrooms, snack bars, and other facilities for its people "backstage." This includes special live and automated teller operations our Sun Bank runs for Disney employees so they can do their banking conveniently.

If you want a soft drink and you work at Disney, go backstage. If you want to buy a Minnie Mouse blouse, do it at the company store. Need a check cashed? Backstage. From toilets to parking, Disney makes sure its guests' needs are not slowed by staff use. While we in banks don't run theme parks, I'll have to admit I've seen our bank employees in teller lines ahead of customers.

Every week Walt Disney World's cast communications division of Disney University produces an eight-page, eight-and-a-half-by-eleven newspaper called *Eyes and Ears*. One glance at its contents and you know it was prepared for Disney people. It is a people publication featuring all sorts of activities, improved employment opportunities, special benefits, educational offerings, and even a complete classified section. The stories are very short, newsy, punchy. Lots of pictures of cast members. A brief feature perhaps. And I've never, never seen a single photo in that newspaper in seven years that showed anyone not smiling. Contrived? Maybe, but it got to me, didn't it?

Banks produce some of the worst employee publications possible. Poor writing, inadequate story selection, not enough photos and those published of poor quality, too much about the brass or the home office. And the reason is, I think, that we expect people in marketing or personnel or some other division to take on the paper as an additional job. We don't hire newspaper people to produce newspapers. We hire loan officers to make loans, and auditors to audit, and managers to manage, but we feel some obligation to assign the internal communications to someone as an afterthought, an extra job, assuming it is a simple, quick thing.

"Give it to the boss's nephew . . . he used to write for the high-school newspaper."

One evening during a BMA conference when some of us were "learning from one another," the subject of company publications, house organs, arose. Most of us agreed that poor quality was a standard. One member of the group admitted, blushingly, that his personnel director had decreed the bank would have some sort of newspaper to appease all the EEOC types, and to show some union that his bank "talked" with its people, regardless of content or quality. He said the bank president wanted to prove, if the need arose, that his bank had an ongoing communications vehicle, content notwithstanding.

Disney feels, on the other hand, that informed people are happier, less confused, more aware of benefits and opportunities, and more cognizant that management genuinely wants and strives to communicate. In addition to the weekly newspaper, Disney produces on a regular basis single-page bulletins for management, two-page "hot news" bulletins with promotions and transfers on a regular basis and, less frequently, an eight-page standard-size newspaper for all cast members.

The written word is most important to employees of any company. But it must be professionally done to properly communicate. A cheap, shoddy, and poorly constructed publication will be obvious to the intended readers. Perhaps they will take that to mean that management isn't all that interested in doing any better. And that publication is an extension of the bank. How we are perceived by those who see it, inside or out, is cause for concern.

Disney also cares what its staff members think about the theme park as a place to work. When your reputation and continuation in business depend on how well employees serve paying customers, then perhaps some attention should be given to the "care and feeding" of the employees. (Hear that, banks?)

There are several types of employees at a Disney theme park, from the permanent, year-round types to what Mickey terms "the casual, temporary cast member." This means summers and holidays and maybe weekends, when the attendance is greatest and staff needs are highest. Like my two kids taking tickets during peak seasons. Disney is a master at being able to use part-timers, keeping the higher-paid group at a minimum, a trick many banks are beginning to pick up, especially in the teller area.

As the summer ends and some three thousand casual temporaries return to school, Disney asks each to complete a simple questionnaire, anonymously. My job was, my division or department was, my age is, my formal education is, I live x number of miles from the park, etc. I am a: man/woman. Notice it didn't say male/female. They find out some basics first.

Then they ask the respondent to check one of five applicable answers, from very good to poor, to these:

— I think the reputation Walt Disney World has with the public is . . .

— Looking at how Walt Disney World compares with other companies, I would say it is managed . . .

— How did you feel when you told people what company you worked for?

— How did you feel your wage (salary) compared with wages (salaries) paid for similar jobs outside Walt Disney World?

— Inside Walt Disney World?

There are questions about hiring practices and procedures, the orientation program, the initial training given. Did you feel satisfied with your job? How important did you feel it was? Was it interesting?

For eight pages and eighty-four questions, Disney management wants to know — from those in the less glamorous jobs all the way to more outstanding positions — if its people are happy, treated fairly, trained properly, and communicated with. Why? Because the basis for operating a theme park dedicated to the happiness of all sorts of people must be . . . happy people. Inside. People with pride, respect for the employer. And to get these kids back next summer, Disney knows it has to offer the best surroundings, training, and opportunities.

Banks are beginning to pay some heed to what its employees think about working conditions and opportunities, too. Next to interest paid on time deposits, salaries and wages are the second highest cost in most banks. The cost of turnover is exorbitant. Our training has been inadequate. We have not been competitive in the personnel marketplace. And, like Disney, a bank is a service business which requires people to interface with the customer in so many transactions.

When the energy crisis hit Florida and California and gasoline became as precious as glass slippers, Disney realized its large contingent of people, working literally around the clock, might be hard pressed to get gas to come to work. Mobilization occurred. First, in all publications car pools were encouraged and, via computer, actually designed for everyone on the payroll. Large buses were contracted to run regular schedules from the largest neighborhood areas to the park for ninety cents. And if eight or more cast members arranged a car pool and would agree to pay for gas, oil, and maintenance, Disney would provide a van! Free! Finally, to assure some gas for work-oriented travel, Disney put in its own gas station!

Many banks have opted to reduce the lighting, raise the thermostat, or permit removal of jackets. But Disney, keying to employee needs, went further. It did the analysis, it made the decisions to lease vans, work

out car-pool schedules and set up bus routes, before it asked for employee cooperation. Many banks I'm aware of asked every employee interested in a car pool to contact personnel.

The obvious happened. Both people contacted personnel. Perhaps, had the banks leased vans, set up the routes, put the thing into service, and said, "Okay, we've committed ourselves and set it up, now you take advantage of it," more people would have done just that. Waiting for enough volunteers to come forth will seldom provide sufficient personnel to fight the battle, much less win the war.

I hope all bank vice presidents (and above) are sitting down to read the next two items.

Annually, all the "white collar" types at Walt Disney World — the management if you will — undertake a week-long program called cross-utilization. In essence it means giving up the desk, the secretary, and the white collar and donning a theme costume or an apron and heading for the frontline action. For a week the "bosses" sell tickets or popcorn, dish out ice cream or hot dogs, load and unload rides, park cars, drive the monorail or trains, or take on any of the one hundred "on stage" jobs that make the park come alive to guests.

According to my sources at Disney, the cross-utilization concept is designed to give management a better "hands on" view of how the guests need to be served and, at the same time, get a better understanding of what the cast member must go through to properly serve the guests. And assignments are made for Cross U, not selections offered. You take the job given you and head for wardrobe and a long eight hours on your feet with a smile on you face, ready or not.

Now, all the time you've been reading this you have been envisioning the VP installment credit in a drive-in teller cubicle, the VP/trust holding down a collector's job, perhaps the VP/marketing working in the proof department, the president of the bank handling the new-accounts desk and all those dumb questions. There's the commercial loan VP operating the mailroom, and somehow our operations VP is in marketing trying to handle a newspaper reporter's persistent questions about why the "little man" is being charged so much interest while at the same time attempting to compute market share for fifteen branch offices manually.

Kind of makes you smile, doesn't it?

Secondly, and I quote from a recent *Eyes and Ears*:

As many of you are aware, our vice presidents and directors (Note: A director at Disney is a level below a VP, in a management function such as director of marketing, director of finance, director of food and beverage, etc.) have been scheduling themselves to visit the Magic Kingdom to increase their awareness of both the guest experience and the work experience of our cast members. So don't be surprised if you're stopped during your workday to chat with one of our VPs or directors. They're genuinely anxious to see your operation and what you do each day!

Following that statement to the troops there is a schedule showing what day which VP or director will be in the park. Both day and night shifts are covered. And wouldn't you know . . . those VPs and directors are supposed to write a report on their findings!

What is all this mingling about? What is this orchestrated entry into the trenches with the folks doing the dirty jobs going to achieve? Well, for my money it is going to tell one heck'uva lot of hardworking people that "somebody up there cares."

How can you spend eight hours shoving out those fries alongside a couple of sweatin' and smilin' kids making $3.20 an hour and not be learning something positive about personnel relations and management?

How can you stand there for eight hours, smiling and saying "howdy" to sixty thousand people, trying to answer their questions in Spanish, direct them to the nearest restrooms, look at their faces of anticipation, and not learn something about the consumer public?

Perhaps periodically it would be most revealing and educational if the bank's brass, and some of our board members for that matter, came down to the lobby on a Monday morning. Or meandered out into the drive-in lanes on a Friday afternoon. Talked to the people in line. Or took the place of that person in the teller window. Chances are it wouldn't take many such trips for improved communications to come about, for some improved benefits to be put in, for some staff morale to improve and for productivity on both ends to get better.

Mutual understanding for each other's needs and problems. Mutual respect for each other— as people, and as fellow bankers.

To all those who say they are too busy, whose schedules won't permit them to idle away a couple of hours doing such things, I'd suggest the demands upon senior executives at Walt Disney World at peak season

are at least as compelling as those of most bankers. It is, I submit, a matter of priorities. He who sees the need, who wants to fill it, will. Case closed.

Disney has a private recreating area with lake, rec hall, picnic areas, boating and fishing and volleyball and family-outing opportunities *ad infinitum* for its cast members' exclusive use — professionally staffed.

There is a library, staffed, with everything from "how to do it" books to the latest fiction best sellers for the benefit of cast members.

There is a division of Disney University called cast activities. Its sole purpose is to provide educational, recreational entertainment and cost-saving opportunities to the employees.

Several women from casting make daily rounds of all work areas — offices, backstage and on stage — to check cast members' hair lengths, make-up, general appearance. Disney has rules about how to dress. You understand them when you report to work. You get one warning. The public sees fresh-faced, neatly attired people serving them, but that doesn't happen by accident.

There is no question that much of Disney's success with people, inside and out, stems from quite a bit of regimentation. Some say it is militaristic in fact. And in spite of all those smiling faces out there in Fantasyland, there are more than a few sour attitudes behind the braces.

But in spite of the rules, the regulations, the demand that everyone do everything the Disney way, there is no question that people who work there have a special feeling for that fifty-year-old mouse. They know the management overtly works at employee relations. They are cognizant that if they want a lifetime career, or a summer's employment, there is a cornucopia of possibilities within that organization. They know all this because the company management puts employee relations just under guest relations as a top priority, and not far under.

And that is, of course, the real answer.

When a company's customers are happy with the service and the product, and find enthusiastic and knowledgeable personnel who are anxious to help, chances are that company will continue to enjoy the lucrative patronage of those customers for a long time.

When a company's employees know, and are continually reminded, that their employer is genuinely concerned with and has interest in their personal well-being, and undertakes meaningful programs to manifest that interest, chances are things are alive and well inside the shop.

Hark! Could that be your bank's employees whistling as they arrive for the day's toil? Listen . . .

"Hi ho, hi ho, it's off to work we go . . ."

26

Think Strawberries:
Everybody Sells

This speech given by James Lavenson, president of the Plaza Hotel in New York City, was reproduced in the bulletin Twin Cities Lodging Industry *published by the Minneapolis office of Laventhal and Horwath. Many of the issues and principles raised by Lavenson in his discussion of sales techniques in the context of a hotel lend themselves to the context of delivering recreation services.*

I came from the balcony of the hotel business. For ten years as a corporate director of Sonesta Hotels with no line responsibility, I had my office in a little building next door to The Plaza. I went to the hotel every day for lunch and often stayed overnight. I was a professional guest. You know, nobody knows more about how to run a hotel than a guest. Last year, I suddenly fell out of the corporate balcony and had to put my efforts into the restaurants where my mouth had been, and in the rooms and nightclub and theatre to which I'd been adding my two cents.

In my ten years of kibitzing, all I had really learned about the hotel business was how to use a guest-room toilet without removing the strip of paper that's printed "Sanitized for Your Protection." When the hotel staff found out I'd spent my life as a salesman and that I'd never been a hotelier, never been to Cornell Hotel School, and that I wasn't even the son of a waiter, they were in a state of shock. And Paul Sonnabend, president of Sonesta, didn't help their apprehension much when he introduced me to my executive staff with the

following words: "The Plaza has been losing money the last several years and we've had the best management in the business. Now we're going to try the worst."

FRANKLY, I THINK THE HOTEL BUSINESS HAS BEEN ONE OF THE MOST BACKWARD IN THE WORLD. THERE'S BEEN VERY LITTLE CHANGE IN THE ATTITUDE OF ROOM CLERKS IN THE 2,000 YEARS SINCE JOSEPH ARRIVED IN BETHLEHEM AND WAS TOLD THEY'D LOST HIS RESERVATION. Why is it that a sales clerk at Woolworth's asks your wife, who points to the pantyhose, if she wants three or six pairs and your wife is all by herself, but the maitre d' asks you and your wife, the only human beings within miles of the restaurant, "How many are you?"

Hotel salesmanship is retailing at its worst, but at the risk of inflicting cardiac arrest on our guests at The Plaza when they first hear shocking expressions like "good morning" and "please" and "thank you for coming," we started a year ago to see if it was possible to make the fourteen hundred employees of The Plaza into genuine hosts and hostesses. Or should I say "salespeople?"

A TAPE RECORDER ATTACHED TO MY PHONE PROVED HOW FAR WE HAD TO GO. "What's the difference between your eighty-five-dollar suite and your 125-dollar suite?" I'd ask our reservationist, disguising my voice over the phone. You guessed it: "Forty dollars."

"What's going on in the Persian Room tonight?" I asked the Bell Captain. "Some singer" was his answer. "Man or woman?" I persisted. "I'm not sure," he said, which made me wonder if I'd even be safe going there.

Why is it, I wondered, that the staff of a hotel doesn't act like a family playing hosts to guests whom they've invited to their home? It didn't take too long after becoming a member of the family myself to understand one of the basic problems. Our fourteen hundred family members didn't even know each other! With that large a staff, working over eighteen floors, six restaurants, a night club, a theatre, and three levels of sub-basement including a kitchen, a carpentry shop, plumbing and electrical shops, a full commercial laundry — how would they ever know who was working there, and who was a guest or just a purveyor passing through? Even the old timers who might recognize a face after a couple of years would have no idea of the name connected to it. It struck me that if our own people couldn't call each other by name, smile at each other's familiar face, say good morning to *each other*, how could they be expected to say amazing things like "good morning, Mr. Jones," to a guest? A YEAR AGO THE PLAZA NAME TAG WAS BORN. THE DELIVERY TOOK PLACE ON MY LAPEL. AND IT'S NOW BEEN ON FOURTEEN HUNDRED LAPELS FOR OVER A YEAR. EVERYONE, FROM DISHWASHERS TO THE GENERAL MANAGER, WEARS HIS OR HER NAME WHERE EVERY OTHER EMPLOYEE, AND, OF COURSE, EVERY GUEST, CAN SEE IT. BELIEVE IT OR NOT, OUR PEOPLE SAY HELLO TO EACH OTHER — BY NAME — WHEN THEY PASS IN THE HALLS AND THE OFFICES. AT FIRST OUR GUESTS THOUGHT THE PLAZA WAS ENTERTAINING SOME GIGANTIC CONVENTION, BUT NOW EVEN THE OLD-TIME PLAZA REGULARS ARE ABLE TO CALL OUR BELLMEN AND MAIDS BY NAME. We've begun to build an atmosphere of welcome with the most precious commodity in the world — our names. *And* our guests' names.

A number of years ago, I heard Dr. Ernest Dichter, head of the Institute of Motivational Research, talk about restaurant service. He has reached a classic conclusion; when people come to a fine restaurant, they are hungrier for *recognition* than they are for food. It's true. If the maitre d' says, "We have your table ready,

Mr. Lavenson," then as far as I'm concerned, the chef can burn the steak and I'll still be happy.

When someone calls you by name and you don't know his or hers, a strange feeling of discomfort comes over you. When that person does it twice you *have* to find out that person's name. This we see happening with our Plaza name tags. When a guest calls a waiter by name, the waiter wants to call the guest by name. It will drive him nuts if he doesn't know. He'll ask the maitre d' and if he doesn't know, he'll ask the bellman, who will ask the front desk. Calling the guest by name has a big payoff. It's called a *tip* — (order).

At first there was resistance to name tags — mostly from old-time formally trained European hoteliers. I secretly suspect they liked being *incognito* when faced with a guest complaint. We only had one staff member who said he'd resign before having his dignity destroyed with a name tag. For sixteen years he'd worn a rosebud in his lapel and that, he said, was his trademark and everyone knew him by it. His resignation was accepted along with that of the rosebud.

Frankly, there are moments when I regret the whole idea myself. When I get on a Plaza elevator and all the passengers see my name tag, they know I work there. Suddenly I'm the official elevator pilot, the host. I can't hide, so I smile at everybody, say "good morning" to perfect strangers I'd ordinarily ignore. The ones who don't go into a state of shock smile back. Actually, they seem to mind less the fact that a trip on a Plaza elevator, built in 1907, is the equivalent of commuting to Manhatten from Greenwich.

There are six hundred Spanish-speaking employees at The Plaza. They speak Spanish. They don't read English. The employee house magazine was in English. So was the employees' bulletin board. So were the signs over the urinals in the locker rooms that suggest cigarette butts don't flush too well. It was a clue as to why some of management's messages weren't getting through. The employee house magazine is now printed one side in English, the other in Spanish. The bulletin board and other staff instructions are in two languages. We have free classes in both languages for departmental supervisors.

WITH FOURTEEN HUNDRED PEOPLE ALL LABELED AND SMILING WE WERE ABOUT READY LAST JUNE TO MAKE SALESPEOPLE OF THEM. THERE WAS JUST ONE MORE OBSTACLE TO OVERCOME BEFORE WE STARTED

SUGGESTING THEY "ASK FOR THE ORDER." THEY HAD NO IDEA WHAT PRODUCT THEY WOULD BE SELLING. NOT ONLY DIDN'T THEY KNOW WHO WAS PLAYING IN THE PERSIAN ROOM, THEY DIDN'T KNOW WE HAD MOVIES — FULL-LENGTH FEATURE FILMS WITHOUT COMMERCIALS — ON THE CLOSED-CIRCUIT TV IN THE BEDROOMS. AS A MATTER OF FACT, MOST OF THEM DIDN'T KNOW WHAT A GUEST ROOM LOOKED LIKE UNLESS THEY HAPPENED TO BE A MAID OR A BELLMAN.

THE REASON THE RESERVATIONIST THOUGHT FORTY DOLLARS WAS THE DIFFERENCE BETWEEN TWO SUITES WAS BECAUSE HE'D NEVER BEEN IN ONE, MUCH LESS ACTUALLY SLEPT THERE. To say our would-be salesman lacked product knowledge would be as much an understatement as the line credited to President Nixon if he had been captain of the Titanic. My son told me if Nixon had been captain of the Titanic, he probably would have announced to the passengers that there was "no cause for alarm — we're just stopping to pick up ice."

Today if you ask a Plaza bellman who's playing in the Persian Room, he'll tell you Ednita Nazzaro. He'll tell you because he's seen her. IN THE CONTRACT OF EVERY PERSIAN ROOM PERFORMER, THERE'S NOW A CLAUSE REQUIRING HIM OR HER TO FIRST PERFORM FOR OUR EMPLOY- EES IN THE CAFETERIA BEFORE OPENING IN THE PERSIAN ROOM. OUR EMPLOYEES SEE THE STAR FIRST, BEFORE THE GUESTS DO.

AND IF YOU ASK A ROOM CLERK OR A TELEPHONE OPERATOR WHAT'S ON THE TV MOVIES, THEY'LL TELL YOU BECAUSE THEY'VE SEEN IT — ON THE TV SETS RUNNING THE MOVIES CONTINUOUSLY IN THE EMPLOYEES' CAFETERIA.

OUR NEW ROOM CLERKS NOW HAVE A WEEK OF ORIENTATION. IT INCLUDES SPENDING A NIGHT IN THE HOTEL AND A TOUR OF OUR ONE THOUSAND GUEST ROOMS. THEY CAN LOOK OUT THE WINDOW AND SEE THE FORTY-DOLLAR DIFFERENCE IN SUITES SINCE A VIEW OF THE PARK DOESN'T EVEN CLOSELY RESEMBLE THE BACK OF THE AVON BUILDING.

As I mentioned, about six months ago we decided it was time to take a hard look at our sales effort. I couldn't find it. The Plaza had three men with the title "salesman" and they were good men. But they were really sales-*service* people who took the orders for functions or groups who came through the doors and sought us out. Nobody but nobody ever left the palace, crossed the moat at Fifth Avenue, and went looking for business. We had no one knocking on doors, no one asking for their order. THE PLAZA WAS SO DIGNIFIED IT SEEMED DEMEANING TO ADMIT WE NEEDED BUSINESS. If you didn't ask us, we wouldn't ask you. So there! Our three sales-service people were terrific once you voluntarily stepped into our arena. You had to ring our doorbell. We weren't ringing yours or anyone else's.

This condition wasn't unique to our official Sales Department. It seemed to be a philosophy shared by our entire, potentially larger, sales staff of waiters, room clerks, bellmen, cashiers, and doormen. IF YOU WANTED A SECOND DRINK IN THE OAK BAR, YOU GOT IT BY TIPPING THE WAITER. YOU ASKED FOR IT. IF YOU WANTED A ROOM, YOU WERE QUOTED THE MINIMUM RATE. IF YOU WANTED SOMETHING BETTER OR LARG- ER, YOU HAD TO ASK FOR IT. IF YOU WANT- ED TO STAY AT THE HOTEL AN EXTRA NIGHT, YOU HAD TO ASK. YOU WERE NEVER INVIT- ED. Sometimes, I think there's a secret pact among hotel people. It's a secret oath you take when you graduate from hotel school. It goes like this: "I promise I will never ask for the order."

When you're faced with as old and ingrained a tradi- tion as that, halfway countermeasures don't work. WE STARTED A PROGRAM WITH ALL OUR GUEST CONTACT PEOPLE USING A NEW SECRET OATH: "EVERYBODY SELL!" And we meant ev- erybody — maids, cashiers, waiters, bellmen — the works. We talked to the maids about suggesting room service; to the doormen about mentioning dinner in our restaurants; to cashiers about suggesting return reservations to departing guests. And we talked to waiters about strawberries.

A WAITER AT THE PLAZA MAKES ANY- WHERE FROM TEN THOUSAND TO TWENTY THOUSAND DOLLARS A YEAR. The difference between those two figures is, of course, tips. When I was in the advertising business, I thought I was fast at computing fifteen percent. I am a moron compared to a waiter. Our suggestions for selling strawberries fell on responsive ears when we described a part of the Everybody Sells program for our Oyster Bar restaurant. We figured with just the same number of customers in the Oyster Bar, that if the waiters would ask every customer if he or she would like a second drink, wine or beer with the meal, and then dessert — given only one out of four takers — we'd increase our sales volume by 364,000 dollars a year. The waiters were way ahead of the lecture — they'd already figured out that was another fifty thousand dollars in tips! And since there are ten waiters in the Oyster Bar, even I could figure out it meant five grand more per man in tips. It was at this point I had my toughest decision to make since I've been in this job. I had to choose between staying on as president or becoming an Oyster Bar waiter. But while the waiters appreciated this automatic raise in theory, they were quick to call out the traditional negatives. "Nobody eats dessert anymore. Everyone's on a diet. If we served our chocolate cheesecake to everybody in the restaurant, half of them would be dead in a week."

"SO SELL 'EM STRAWBERRIES, WE SAID! BUT SELL 'EM." And then we wheeled out our answer to gasoline shortages, the dessert cart. We widened the aisles between the tables and had a waiter wheel the cart up to each and every table at dessert time. Not daunted by the diet protestations of the customer, the waiter then went into raptures about the bowl of fresh strawberries. There was even a bowl of whipping cream for the slightly wicked. By the time our waiters finished extolling the virtues of our fresh strawberries flown in that morning from California, or wherever they think strawberries come from, you not only have had an abdominal orgasm, but one out of two of you order them. IN THE LAST SIX MONTHS WE'VE SHOWN OUR WAITERS EVERY WEEK WHAT'S HAPPENING TO STRAWBERRY SALES. THIS MONTH THEY HAVE DOUBLED AGAIN. SO HAVE SECOND MARTINIS. AND BELIEVE ME, WHEN YOU GET A CUSTOMER A SECOND MARTINI, YOU'VE GOT A SITTING DUCK FOR STRAWBERRIES — WITH WHIPPED CREAM. OUR WAITERS ARE ASKING FOR THE ORDER.

"THINK STRAWBERRIES" IS THE PLAZA'S NEW SECRET WEAPON. Our reservationists now think strawberries and suggest that you'll like a suite overlooking Central Park rather than a twin-bedded one. Our bellmen are thinking strawberries. Each bellman has his own reservation cards, with his name printed as the return address, and he asks you if you'd like him to make your return reservations as he's checking you out and into your taxi!

Our room-service order takers are thinking strawberries. They suggest the closed-circuit movie on TV (three dollars will appear on your bill) as long as you're going to eat in your room. Our telephone operators are even thinking strawberries. They suggest a morning Flying Tray breakfast when you ask for a wake-up call. "You just want a light breakfast, no ham and eggs?" "How about some strawberries?"

We figure we've added about three hundred salespeople to the three-person sales team we had before. But most important, of course, is that we've added five more sales people to our sales department. Four of them are out on the street calling — mostly cold — on the prospects to whom they're ready to sell anything from a cocktail in the Oak Bar to a Corporate Directors meeting to a Bar Mitzvah. The chewing-gum people sell new customers by sampling on street corners. The Plaza has chewing gum licked a mile. OUR SALESPEOPLE ON THE STREET HAVE ONE SIMPLE OBJECTIVE: GET THE PROSPECT INTO THE HOTEL TO SAMPLE THE PRODUCT. WITH THE PLAZA AS OUR PRODUCT, IT ISN'T TOO DIFFICULT. AND ONCE YOU TASTE THE PLAZA, FRANKLY, YOU'LL LOVE THE ROOMS.

In analyzing our business at the hotel we found, much to my surprise, that functions — parties, weddings, charity balls, and the like — are just about three times more profitable than all our six restaurants put together. And functions are twice as profitable as selling all one thousand of our rooms. Before we had this analysis, we were spending all our advertising money on restaurants, our night club, and our guest rooms. THIS YEAR WE'RE SPENDING EIGHTY PERCENT OF OUR ADVERTISING MONEY TO GET FUNCTION BUSINESS — WEDDINGS INSTEAD OF HONEYMOONS, BANQUETS INSTEAD OF MEALS, ANNUAL CORPORATE MEETINGS INSTEAD OF CLANDESTINE ROMANTIC RENDEZVOUS FOR TWO. We've added a full-time Bridal Consultant who can talk wedding language to nervous brides and talk turkey to their mothers. Retailers like Saks and Bonwit's and Bergdorf's have had bridal consultants for years. Hotels have Banquet Managers. Banquet Managers sell wedding dinners. BRIDAL CONSULTANTS SELL STRAWBERRIES — EVERYTHING FROM THE BRIDAL SHOWER,

THE PICTURES, THE CEREMONY, THE RECEP-
TION, AND THE WEDDING NIGHT TO THE
HONEYMOON AND THE FIRST ANNIVERSARY.

When you fight a habit as long-standing as the hotel
inside salesperson, you don't just wave a wand and say,
"Presto, now we have four outside salespeople." WE
WANT OUR NEW SALESPEOPLE TO KNOW
HOW SERIOUS WE ARE ABOUT GOING OUT
AFTER BUSINESS.

We started an Executive Sales Call program as part
of our "Everybody Sells" philosophy. ABOUT
FORTY OF OUR TOP AND MIDDLE MANAGE-
MENT EXECUTIVES, ONES WHO TRADITION-
ALLY DON'T EVER SEE A PROSPECT, ARE AS-
SIGNED DAYS ON WHICH THEY MAKE OUT-
SIDE CALLS WITH OUR REGULAR
SALESPEOPLE. PEOPLE LIKE OUR
PERSONNEL DIRECTOR, OUR EXECUTIVE
HOUSEKEEPER, OUR PURCHASING DIRECTOR,
AND OUR GENERAL MANAGER ARE ON THE
STREETS EVERY DAY MAKING CALLS. OUR
PROSPECTS SEEM TO LIKE IT. OUR SALES-
PEOPLE LOVE IT. AND OUR NON-SALES
"SALESPEOPLE" ARE GETTING AN EDUCATION
ABOUT WHAT'S GOING ON IN THE REAL
WORLD — THE ONE OUTSIDE THE HOTEL.

27

Promoting Recreation Programs with Low-Power Radio Broadcasts

The availability of increasingly sophisticated radio transmitting and receiving equipment has made it possible for agencies to consider using low-power radio broadcasts to promote their programs. These systems are relatively inexpensive to acquire, and they require minimal technical expertise to install and operate. This case explains how to purchase and operate low-power broadcasting and documents the experiences of some agencies who have used it.

Recreation and park departments have long been conscious of their limited ability to communicate knowledge of program offerings to their constituents. Awareness of an agency's offerings is important. Indeed, it can be argued that it is unethical for an agency to invest money in public programs without informing residents that such programs are available.

Recent technological improvements in radio broadcasting and receiving capability have made it possible to consider low-power radio broadcasts as a vehicle for promoting programs and events. These systems are relatively inexpensive to acquire and require minimum technical expertise to install and operate. A low-power radio broadcast system could communicate information to both local residents and out-of-town guests about such things as special events in parks, park and facility locations, traffic conditions and parking options, availability of tickets or campsites, and other safety, directional, or interpretive information.

A wide variety of businesses are currently using low-power radio broadcasts successfully. Examples are auto dealerships, car washes, banks, churches, drive-in theatres, driver-education classes, travel-information centers, racetracks and fairgrounds, real-estate developments, and shopping centers

FEDERAL REGULATIONS

Federal Communication Commission (FCC) regulations specify that low-power radio broadcasts can be made only from either of the extreme ends of the AM radio band (530 kilohertz or 1610 kilohertz). Not all AM car radios can pick up signals from the 530 kilohertz (kHz) and/or 1610 kHz dial positions, although good transmitting equipment properly installed and supplied with enough signal strength is likely to be receivable by over eighty percent of all automobile receivers. This proportion increases as more automobiles are equipped with digital-tuned radios, which are superior to traditional radio dials in their ability to pick up and hold a specific station. Thus departments can use a low-power radio broadcast system as an additional tool for reaching and informing potential clients about a service.

The licensing and regulation procedures delineated by the FCC make it clear that low-power radio broadcast authorizations are only granted when they do not interfere with primary (commercial) stations. Thus a local commercial station that operates at 540 kHz precludes the installation of a low-power broadcast station at 530 kHz (likewise for a 1610 low-power system when a commercial station exists at 1600 kHz). The FCC also reserves the right to reconsider the status of a low-power system if interference is reported by primary broadcast stations on the second or third adjacent frequency (550 kHz, 560 kHz, 1580 kHz, and 1590 kHz). Therefore agencies considering a low-power broadcast must take care to ensure that there are no possible conflicts with existing commercial stations in the area.

Limitations are placed upon low-power radio broadcasts' use of background music and commercial sponsorship in order to protect local commercial stations from direct competition from low-power transmitting stations. A low-power station is therefore limited to broadcasts of a descriptive or informational nature. A detailed account of low-power radio broadcast regulations should be obtained from the FCC before any system is put in place. Rule 90.242, which governs the licensing of travelers information stations, and Rule 90.17, which governs local government radio services, are both applicable to public-sector agencies operating low-power stations.

INSTALLATION COSTS AND OPERATING CONSIDERATIONS

A department interested in purchasing a low-power radio broadcast system should budget two to five thousand dollars for equipment and installation. It is likely to take four to six months between the time a decision to proceed is made and the time the system is on-line and functioning.

The quality of transmission received by the visitor is crucial to success. Given the relatively low cost of these systems compared to the potential benefits that may accrue, it may be wise for a department to consider spending extra money to purchase more technically sophisticated equipment than to buy the cheapest that is available.

A low-power radio broadcast system usually consists of one broadcasting station, but it may be comprised of a group of stations if a large geographical area is to be covered and/or the number or length of messages to be conveyed are substantial. A system that involves several broadcast stations is referred to as a co-channel system. The *Travelers Information Station (TIS) Planning Handbook* published by the National Park Service outlines several considerations that you must take into account to provide a quality service. The location and size of the area to be covered by each radio broadcast system are important. The maximum transmitting range of a low-power radio broadcast installation ranges from one to five miles. This range depends on such factors as the size and type of antenna employed, local topography, and presence of nearby commercial stations operating on a close frequency.

The position that you select on the radio band can also make a difference. Generally, stations operating at 1610 kHz have a slightly greater range than those operating at 530 kHz. Some localities may have no choice as to which end of the band to select if there are commercial stations in the area that operate at one or both ends of the band. For example, a department in a city with an existing commercial station operating at 1600 kHz would not employ a system at 1610 kHz because the commercial outlet would almost certainly be powerful enough to render the low-power system useless. The 530 kHz band location would be the only low-power option available in this case.

The speed of the vehicles to be reached is also a consideration. The motorist must have sufficient time to adjust his or her radio and hear the entire message at least once in its entirety before the vehicle passes out of broadcast range. This can be of particular concern when the broadcast range is small and/or traffic is moving rapidly, as it may be on an expressway. Placement of signage informing motorists of the radio station just prior to a major intersection may be a good strategy in urban settings because slow-moving or standing traffic is more likely to receive the message in its entirety.

The distance from other co-channel low-power radio broadcast installations, if they are needed, ground conductivity within the area being covered, and other environmental considerations must be measured before a system is installed. You can find introductory information on ground conductivity and its effect on broadcasts, as well as data on local conditions, in the National Park Service *Travelers Information Station (TIS) Planning Handbook*. Generally, the higher the elevation of the transmitter relative to surrounding topography, the better the range of the system.

In most cases, taped messages are used in low-power radio broadcast systems. One-, two-, or three-minute tapes that automatically repeat the message are preferred. For example, the Tampa International Airport has made eight different tapes that are used in response to the prevailing situation at a point in time. Included are the standard normal operations tape, several tapes that broadcast different parking situations, and an emergency tape. The airport has drafted a policy statement that dictates which tapes should be used and under what circumstances. The National Park Service *TIS Planning Handbook* (p. 10) states that,

> Drivers must encounter an audio signal in order to tune in on TIS as they enter an area. However, since music is not permitted, and a tone would be objectionable to those who have already tuned to the station, a repeated voice message without long silent intervals is the only way of providing a signal for tuning.

It is possible to use live broadcasts, but this is not time efficient since a message would have to be given repeatedly. This would ensure that each vehicle received the message instead of silence when it reached the TIS advisory sign "Visitor Information, Dial AM 1610." Low-power radio broadcast equipment is generally compact enough to be conveniently set up in a closet or similar small space in an office. This makes the equipment very accessible if and/or when tapes must be changed or live broadcasts made.

OPERATING EXAMPLES OF LOW-POWER RADIO BROADCAST SYSTEMS

Several federal and state recreation and park agencies are currently involved in low-power broadcasting. The National Park Service (NPS) Travelers Information Stations (TIS) have been on-line since 1967. Typically, the NPS places signs along the road at park entrances and at strategic points inside parks that urge motorists to "Tune your radio to 1610." The content of the messages within the NPS-TIS program is limited to non-commercial informational spots. By 1978 low-power radio broadcast facilities had been installed not only by the NPS, but also by other federal

agencies — including the Bureau of Land Management, Federal Highway Administration, National Aeronautics and Space Administration, United States Forest Service (USFS), and National Oceanic and Atmospheric Administration (NOAA).

The NOAA is the voice of the National Weather Service. National Oceanic and Atmospheric Administration broadcasts are transmitted at over 370 locations throughout the United States on seven VHF/FM frequencies. The FM band provides a greater transmission range than the AM band. This type of system provides NOAA with a broadcast range of thirty to forty miles from each transmitter. Generally, NOAA broadcasts cannot be picked up by motorists without the purchase of supplemental equipment since the transmitters employed operate between 162.40 and 162.55 megahertz (MHz), while the standard FM band available on most radios ranges from 88.00 to 108.00 MHz. However, the NOAA program is noteworthy because it has helped spread the word regarding the potential of low-power radio broadcasts as an informational tool.

In recent years, some recreation managers have purchased equipment with receiving capabilities in this higher range of the FM band. These managers then tape and rebroadcast this weather information with their own low-power broadcast stations on the AM band (*Woodall's Campground Management,* November 1983, p. 13). Such broadcasts serve the dual purpose of informing potential visitors of expected weather conditions while also acting as a promotional tool for the sponsoring facility. Despite the extra transmitting range that is gained by operating on the FM band, this system is not able to reach large numbers of people because they do not possess the necessary specialized receiving equipment.

Few municipal park and recreation departments are using low-power radio transmissions. The Department of Leisure Services in St. Petersburg, Florida, was one of the pioneers in this area. Target area for the transmitter was the St. Petersburg waterfront, a popular multiple-use area that includes attractions such as the city's large five-story pier, two museums, the Bayfront Center Arena and Theater, a professional baseball field, an Olympic sized swimming pool, and miles of waterfront parkland and white-sand beach. St. Petersburg's radio system served to direct visitors and residents to available parking areas during peak-use periods in the waterfront area, while also informing travelers on nearby roads and highways of both current and upcoming events. Informational signs that read "Visitor Information — Dial AM Radio 1610" were placed at strategic locations in the city within the area covered by the radio transmissions. A critique of the program circulated by the Department of Leisure Services shortly after the installation of the system noted that,

> Although in operation for a few weeks, the public response is gratifying. Local media have played up "the City's radio station," making public awareness high from the beginning. From the minimal costs involved, the positive impact potential is great through more efficient management of traffic and through encouraging more residents and passers-by to participate in community events and activities.

This early assessment proved to be overly optimistic. The St. Petersburg radio broadcast system is no longer in service because two major problems arose. First, the system was a co-channel operation consisting of several broadcast stations located throughout the city rather than a single one. Most successful low-power broadcast systems operate in situations where there is a single major entrance to the facility or program that can be served with a single transmitting station. Problems may arise when an agency attempts to blanket an entire city or region because the motorist often passes in and out of range of individual broadcast stations, resulting in interruptions in the message. This is annoying to motorists, and it usually results in low use of the low-power broadcasting service. A second problem encountered by St. Petersburg was the existence of a commercial station at 1590 kHz that effectively overpowered the 1610 kHz broadcasts done by the Department of Leisure Services in some parts of the city. When the St. Petersburg low-power radio broadcast program was discontinued after it had been immobilized by a storm that disabled the transmitter, it was not reactivated.

An interesting variation of a low-power radio broadcast system has been developed by the Jackson County (Missouri) Parks and Recreation Department. Jackson County reached an agreement with Gannett

Advertising to promote radio messages through "talking billboards." Gannett is a national company that is interested in pilot-testing the potential of such billboards. The billboards are situated on a major downtown traffic artery and read, "Support your Jackson County Park System. Tune in the 86.9 FM to find out today's information." The message is limited to fifteen seconds since that is the time period during which automobiles are likely to be within range. The probability of a response to this type of message is enhanced if the billboard is close to a traffic light or stop sign, where cars are required to slow down and drivers thus have more time to react to the sign. These billboards have generated more interest among residents than conventional signage, but it is too early yet to derive conclusions as to the relative effectiveness of this message system.

CONCLUSION

Low-power radio broadcasts present an interesting opportunity to park and recreation managers searching for effective methods of communicating with potential client groups. The large percentage of people who travel to and from recreation activities in private automobiles, combined with the availability of increasingly sophisticated radio transmitting and receiving equipment, suggest that use of low-power radio broadcasts by recreation and park agencies will become more common in the future.

SOURCES:

McFadden, Ralph, and John H. Shoaf, *Travelers Information Station Planning Handbook*, National Park Service Denver Service Station, March 1979.

Jackson County Parks and Recreation Department
22807 Woods Chapel Road
Blue Springs, Missouri 64015

Department of Leisure Services
PO Box 2842
St. Petersburg, Florida 33731

28

Promoting through the Use of Animated Characters: The Gus and Goldie Example

Private-sector businesses have incorporated animated characters into their promotional efforts. The most well-known of these is probably the McDonald Corporation's Ronald McDonald. The principles that explain the success of this character and his ilk have been adopted by El Paso's aquatics managers. Their Gus and Goldie characters are used to promote learn-to-swim programs. The extraordinary success of this promotional tool led to a franchise, so nearly twenty other agencies are now using the program.

Superstar Ronald McDonald made his debut in 1963 at Macy's annual Thanksgiving Day Parade in New York City. Ronald is probably the world's best-known clown. Since 1967 he has been the McDonald Corporation's "official spokesman" for children and is as well-recognized by American youngsters as Santa Claus. Ronald *is* the McDonald Corporation to many children, and he has become an ageless living entity for millions more. He has given McDonald's an extra dimension, providing a faceless corporation with an intelligent, sensitive, warm personality with whom people — especially children — can identify.

McDonald's has been as successful as any company in America in communicating with children, and the company has established an enviable loyalty among them. Ray Kroc, the founder of McDonald's, often stated,

"We're not in the hamburger business; we're in show business." He recognized that characters and fairy tales help children understand the world around them, and that characters like Ronald provide an exciting theatrical flair by creating a fantasy setting. Animated characters have a special feel and charm that enable the opportunities and messages they convey to stand out from the mass of messages to which people are exposed. They elicit smiles and laughter that enhance attention and recognition, heightening the company's name awareness, identity, and image.

Reasons contributing to Ronald's success are captured in McDonald's "official biography" of Ronald:

> Ronald does everything kids would like to do — skating, boating, flying around in the air, magic, riding on camels and best of all going to McDonald's to eat hamburgers, his favorite food. Ronald spends all his time going from one McDonald's restaurant to another to see his friends, the children. If his friends are sick he visits them at the hospital. Ronald's favorite thing to do is make children happy, to make everyone laugh.

The success of Ronald and other commercial characters of a similar genre has been replicated in local target markets by some creative park and recreation agencies. There is some historical precedent for using characters in this field. The most well-known example is Smokey the Bear, who was created by the US Forest Service over forty years ago as an identifiable figure who would communicate about the dangers of starting a forest fire. This is a major concern since careless Americans still start over ninety thousand forest fires every year. Smokey the Bear illustrates the success characters may have in building customer identification with the service or idea with which they are associated. During the period that Smokey has been telling us to be careful with fire, the number of forest fires in the United States has been cut in half, saving seventeen billion dollars in natural resources. At least part of this saving seems likely to be attributable to people paying attention to Smokey's message.

THE SPAWNING OF GUS AND GOLDIE

In 1979, Bill Cowan and Gayle Vokes, who are director of aquatics and aquatics program coordinator, respectively, for the city of El Paso, Texas, Parks and Recreation Department, recognized the potential of animated characters for communicating with children. They recognized that personification is essential to communicate effectively — children don't identify with an abstract concept like, "Learn to Swim," or with an organization like "The Parks and Recreation Department." Abstract concepts have no meaning for children, so they ignore them. Instead they orient strongly to people and animated person-like characters. They enjoy simple plot. For example, McDonaldland characters try to steal the fries, burgers, and shakes. The adventures, fantasies, and humorous sketches work by dramatizing the influence of the service or product being sold.

With this in mind, Cowan and Vokes conceived and developed the El Paso Aqua Puppets, whose role was to offer a water-safety instruction program under the guise of entertainment. The purpose of the hand puppets was to dramatize swimming-pool rules, basic water safety, and city aquatic programs, especially the Learn-to Swim program for school-age children.

The puppet stage represented a city swimming pool where the Aqua-Puppets cavorted and swam while a real-person lifeguard stood at one side of the stage. When a puppet broke a swimming rule, the lifeguard blew a whistle, issued a reprimand, and explained the purpose of the rule.

The leading Aqua-Puppets were the fish-kids, Gus and Goldie. Gus was a scrappy little blue guppy and Goldie was a cute gold-and-orange sunfish with valentine lips.

Rounding out the puppet cast were Dunkin, a playful green dolphin; Senor Gato, an elderly catfish who swims laps at the pool for his health; and Algie, a messy little monster who lurks in the canals and the Rio Grande (which runs through El Paso) but tries to sneak into the pool whenever he thinks the chlorine count might be low. (Algie, whose name comes from algae, is always spotted in the nick of time and a handful of chlorine thrown to chase him away.)

The stars of this show were Gus and Goldie, and the program name was changed from Aqua Puppets to the Gus and Goldie Learn-to-Swim Program. The hand puppets were also transformed into touchable, larger-than-life walk-arounds so children could touch and visit with them at promotional events. The characters were cheerful, personable, and colorful, and proved to have a whimsical appeal that attracted both children and adults. (See Figure 5.5.)

El Paso had a good aquatics infrastructure with excellent facilities, outstanding instructors, and a complete range of classes. However, despite the apparent excellence of the service, citizen response was apathetic. When Gus and Goldie's Learn-to-Swim program was initiated, it was the springboard that propelled the Aquatics Department into the public eye by providing a vibrant, fresh image and new allure for all its aquatic programs. With Gus and Goldie, Learn-to-Swim loses its "should" connotation and takes on one of entertainment and fun. There is a delightful beckoning appeal that is hard to resist. Substantial attendance and revenue increases were realized immediately in the first season.

The following results, recorded after Gus and Goldie were spawned, document the increase in attendance at El Paso pools:

Season	Increase over Preceding Season
1979-80	Up 25% over 1978-79
1980-81	Up 10% over 1979-80
1981-82	Up 15% over 1980-81
1982-83	Up 20% over 1981-82
1983-84	Up 6% over 1982-83
1984-85	Up 21% over 1983-84

During this period of impressive results, the El Paso economy was depressed. The city was hit hard by a

FIGURE 5.5

El Paso's Director of Aquatics Bill Cowan with Gus, Goldie, and Friends

very large devaluation of the peso and subsequent unemployment.

The Learn-to-Swim program is the anchor of a successful aquatics program because by teaching people to swim the size of the effective target market for aquatics increases.

IMPLEMENTING THE GUS
AND GOLDIE PROGRAM

The Gus and Goldie program consists of a three-month summer promotional campaign that uses three major communication avenues. They are:

1. ELECTRONIC MEDIA. The program's focus is on television commercials with strong radio-broadcast support.

2. VARIOUS SIGN MEDIA. Posters, billboards, and other available sign media support the main television and radio thrust.

3. PUBLIC APPEARANCES. Gus and Goldie go out into the community to schools, neighborhoods, civic events, parades, and local fairs.

The program is underwritten by sponsorship from the local business community. Sponsors receive high visibility for their investment in the program. All sponsors are publicly acknowledged on television and radio commercials, billboards, and any other outlets that are used. The department also identifies them in events or promotions that receive press coverage. In addition, Learn-to-Swim, with its connotation of caring for children's safety, is a positive image for businesses to be associated with.

In El Paso, the local Coca-Cola Bottling Company has been a major sponsor. They imprint cans with the Learn-to-Swim logo that features Gus and Goldie and session dates for the season, along with a Thursday free-admission offer in exchange for six specially marked cans. (See Figure 5.6.) This effort is supported by point-of-sales displays, commercials, and billboards that promote the concept. The company also painted walls in pool areas that are visible to the street. These proclaim that "Swimming is a life-preserver," and include logos for Coke and caffeine-free Coke.

In Shreveport, Louisiana, which has adopted the program, two major sponsors were a dairy that featured Gus and Goldie on their milk cartons, and McDonald's, which agreed to co-sponsor the program's commercials, billboards, and newspaper advertisements.

The effectiveness of the promotional effort is the result of using Gus and Goldie on television and radio as the primary thrust of the campaign. Television-watching is a major children's activity, and if children are not watching they are likely to be listening to a portable or car radio, or walking down the street wearing earphones.

In a child's mind, if you are on television, you are a star! And that is exactly the reaction Gus and Goldie get when they attend a community event or make a public appearance. They attain the status of real celebrities and their star quality reflects positively on the parks and recreation department.

The success of Gus and Goldie in El Paso has caused other cities to inquire about the program and request advice in implementing a similar effort. Given this interest, the city decided to franchise the program for others. That way many communities now have access to the expertise and promotional materials associated with Gus and Goldie, and the fee is surprisingly nominal. (See Figure 5.7.)

In addition to the managerial expertise of the El Paso team, the franchise agreement makes a full range of materials available, including:

— Gus and Goldie walk-around suits (El Paso also supplies the patterns as an alternative.)
— Gus and Goldie hand puppets
— Television commercials
— Print advertisements
— Posters
— T-shirts
— Progress cards
— Achievement certificates
— Suggested lesson plans

All the materials are copyrighted and registered by the City of El Paso. The number of cities now involved in the program enables the cost of new commercials and other promotional materials to be spread over a greater area.

The Gus and Goldie package is designed to work with a city's existing learn-to-swim program — not to substantially amend or replace it. It is intended to make existing programs more visible, exciting, and compelling at no extra cost to the city.

SOURCE:

Director of Aquatics
El Paso Parks and Recreation Department
Two Civic Center Plaza
El Paso, Texas 79999

FIGURE 5.6

Gus and Goldie Coca-Cola Imprint

THURSDAYS ARE COCA-COLA DAYS
AT THE CITY PARKS AND
RECREATION SWIMMING POOLS

Bring six specially marked Coca-Cola cans
to any city swimming pool and
receive free swim admission for one.
For more information call:

541-4594

SWIMMING: IT'S A LIFE PRESERVER!

FIGURE 5.7

**Gus and Goldie Learn-to-Swim
Franchise Agreement**

29

Staff Development and Recognition: Four Inexpensive Suggestions

Most of a recreation and park agency's budget is likely to be allocated as salaries for personnel. Consistent investment in staff development and recognition is central to improving an agency's efficiency and effectiveness. Staff development and recognition can increase productivity in two ways. First, new knowledge may accrue. Second, greater agency commitment and effort are likely to emerge as a result of attention to and incentives for staff. This communicates the feeling that elected officials and senior managers believe that everyone is an important member of the team.

Four relatively inexpensive suggestions for enhancing staff productivity through development and recognition are discussed here. They are: Team of Five, networking, Captain Clean, and revenue-incentive salary agreements.

TEAM OF FIVE

Senior managers in an agency usually have a variety of opportunities to interact with their peers, visit other agencies, and participate in training programs. However, staff at middle-management or lower levels often are fortunate if they can attend even a regional meeting of the state organization. The Team of Five proposal initiated by the St. Petersburg Department of Leisure Services was intended to help fill that void.

Each month a team of five employees is sent out to another agency for a two-day period. It is a voluntary program for which all employees may sign up, and they are notified if they are elected two months in advance of the visit. The program has two main goals. The first is to encourage interaction and networking, not only with people in other agencies but also within the department. This is done by having five people who may not have previously known each other must interact for two days. To encourage internal networking, efforts are made to select employees from different divisions with different interests and perspectives. The second objective is to encourage employees to become inquisitive and search for better ways of doing their jobs. This encourages people to strive to be better, and helps fight inertia and complacency. It also stimulates bottom-up and lateral dissemination of ideas because lower-level employees are more likely to make suggestions to peers and supervisors while discussing their experiences after such trips.

When the program started two years ago, the selected agency had to be from within the state of Florida; however, this was subsequently expanded to include neighboring states. For a number of reasons, five was selected as the optimal number of employees for each team. First, this is the maximum number that can travel comfortably in one car. Second, the department had five hierarchical levels, and the original intent was that one representative from each should be assigned to each team. This idea was discarded, though, after staff discovered that some people felt intimidated by the presence of more senior managers; better results were obtained when team members came from similar levels. Third, five people travelling together as a social gathering are likely to have more opportunities for sub-group exchanges than a group of four; that is, they can pair off into two's or three's.

Each group's mandate is to return from their visit with at least five services that the host agency performs better than their own department. Individual members each have to present at least one new idea. This specific charge is an important ingredient in the program's success. Before it was included, visiting teams tended to focus on what their own department did better instead of on what they could learn from the host agency to improve. In successful agencies especially, there is likely to be some feeling that "if we do it this way, it obviously must be better." This specific charge counters that reaction.

When a team returns from a trip, they meet with the department's director and report their findings. The ideas cannot be "pie-in-the-sky" suggestions requiring substantial capital investments or political realignments. Team members must present not only the idea, but also the detailed knowledge needed to implement it.

The director tries to give immediate feedback. Over fifty percent of the ideas are immediately put into action and the rest either investigated further or rejected. If immediate approval is not forthcoming at the debriefing meeting, then team members are informed about why their idea was rejected and what further investigation uncovers. One of the bonuses inherent in the program is the recognition accorded low-level employees by the opportunity for them to discuss their ideas with the director.

Two reward programs are associated with this program. First, the team that produces the best ideas with the most impact on the agency during the year is permitted to select a department from a list of thirty major agencies across the United States and visit that agency on a similar mission. Second, all recommendation that are implemented are eligible to be considered for each award out of the department's "Ideas Awards Program." Each year ten thousand dollars is solicited from corporations for this purpose. Out of the 150

ideas that have typically been implemented, about one hundred of them are likely to be rewarded by cash.

NETWORKING

Networking may be defined as the process by which individuals with common interests and concerns interact to exchange ideas, solve problems, and make contacts for future opportunities. A group of departments in the Kansas City area in association with the Missouri Recreation and Parks Association and the Kansas City Chamber of Commerce consciously formalized this process by hosting an informal public networking session. The success of the initial event has led them to repeat it, and it is anticipated to become an annual meeting.

The first three-hour program consisted of short presentations by twelve speakers on subjects of interest to park and recreation-related businesses and organizations. One local attorney addressed the topic of liability in recreation and parks. The public utility representative talked about power costs and conservation. The US Postal Service provided information on bulk mail and obtaining non-profit postal rates. An established concessionaire discussed buying power and pricing.

Other topics included market programming, fund raising, direct marketing, and advertising and promotion. Speakers were stationed at booths placed around the room and presentations were conducted simultaneously. Participants could visit the booths and attend the presentations in which they were interested.

Individuals and businesses involved in the parks and/or recreation market or those simply interested in working with local departments were invited to the meeting through advertisements in local newspapers. The chamber charged a fee of ten dollars per person, and approximately 450 attended. These individuals included representatives of ski shops, travel agencies, marine retailers, the Girl and Boy Scout organizations, professional ball teams, playground-equipment dealers, beer and soft-drink companies, radio stations, and others.The cost of catering and renting the hotel room was divided among sponsors of the event.

The networking social provided an opportunity for the public agencies' staffs to meet staff members of other departments. Corporate contacts were made that later led to sponsorships. The departments received business cards from companies who wished to be considered for various bid proposals.

CAPTAIN CLEAN

The city of St. Petersburg initiated an annual program with their sanitation department that they called "Captain Clean." The program clearly lends itself to adaptation to the parks field, where it might be implemented to recognize park laborers and called "Captain Green."

The typical St. Petersburg sanitation worker is in his mid-thirties, with a sixth-grade reading level and twelve years employment with the department. He has little direct contact with the public since the city has a highly automated garbage pick-up system.

The city had never managed to build an *esprit de corps* among its sanitation employees. Yet everybody likes to feel important and part of a team, so the Captain Clean program was intended to contribute to this end. The goal was to increase productivity by creating a greater sense of pride in the work done. Police and fire departments commonly achieve this with widely publicized policeman- or fireman-or-the-year awards, but this type of recognition generally has not been extended to sanitation workers or park laborers. To remedy this situation, the city launched a competition to let the residents of St. Petersburg identify who was the best garbage collector in the city. They were to pick Captain Clean.

A Captain Clean logo was developed, and for two months all sanitation workers wore Captain Clean hats and orange T-shirts emblazoned with the yellow symbol. Each sanitation worker's picture was taken and included as part of a special inset in the main city newspaper, which announced the competition. In addition to listing all thirty-six sanitation workers, the insert included a map and route description for each employee. (See Figures 5.8 and 5.9.) Hence friends and family saw their pictures, too.

The insert also included information on the sanitation program and a ballot for residents to use to cast their votes. City merchants were persuaded to contribute prizes to the winner and two runners-up, and these were also listed in the insert. (See Figures 5.10 and 5.11.)

In addition to sponsoring the newspaper inserts, the city had posters advertising the program applied to all the garbage trucks. As a result of this publicity, 3,374 votes were cast by residents in the Captain Clean competition and the winner received 487 votes with twenty-four percent of his two thousand clients voting. Another newspaper insert announced the winner (Figure 5.12), and he was recognized at a meeting of the city council. Council members were photographed with him alongside his truck.

It was a very successful motivator. Workers became much more visible and anxious to establish a personal rapport with residents. They became more people-oriented because those residents represented potential votes for them in the annual contest. If they didn't win, they at least wanted enough votes to gain the respect of their peers.

REVENUE INCENTIVE SALARY AGREEMENTS

Over one half of the Jackson County Park and Recreation Department's ten-million-dollar-a-year budget is generated through revenue-producing programs, facilities, sports leagues, classes, campgrounds, trips, a golf course, two marinas, and various special events and festivals. Each revenue-producing program is operated through a separate enterprise fund. Enterprise funds create an awareness of the need for quality programs and effective pricing among employees since their programs are supported only by the revenue they produce.

The department has built employees' salaries into their budgets and partially based some of them on a percentage of the revenue the programs produce. Under the terms of their contracts, if an employee does not cover his or her salary with revenue that programs generate, then he or she may be terminated or have the number of work hours reduced to match the income generated. This way, if someone is hired at thirty thousand dollars a year and only makes twenty-five thousand in revenue toward that salary, the county can cut them back to a ten-month instead of a twelve-month appointment. If the market shifts and the activity they are hired to develop loses popularity, then they must either find replacement revenues from another program or have their position terminated. Some positions are not twelve-month jobs but seasonal ones. In these cases the department only pays full salary for the months employees are fully engaged. However, they do provide year-round benefits for their recreation employees. They

FIGURE 5.8

Newspaper Insert of Sanitation Workers

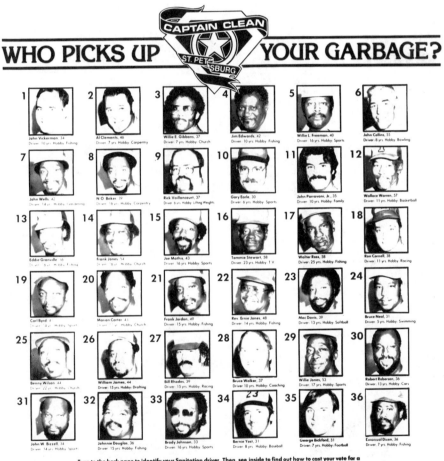

FIGURE 5.9

Map and Route Description

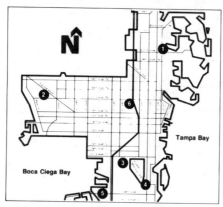

City of St. Petersburg
BRUSH MAP INDICATOR

Tampa Bay

Boca Ciega Bay

BRUSH SITE LOCATIONS

1. 62nd Ave. NE, east of 4th St. N. (east of St. Louis Cardinals ball field by the Sewer Treatment Plant).
2. 77th St. & 26th Ave. N. (near NW Sewer Treatment Plant).
3. 26th Ave. S. & 26th St. S.
4. 40th Ave. S. & 9th St. S.
5. 54th Ave. S. & 41st St. S. (near SW Sewer Treatment Plant).
6. San Avalon-25th St. N. & 20th Ave. N. (entrance off 22nd Ave. N.).

HOURS OF OPERATION

May through November
Mon.-Fri. 10:00 a.m. to 6:30 p.m.
Sat.-Sun. 8:00 a.m. to 6:30 p.m.

December through April
Mon.-Fri. 9:00 a.m. to 5:30 p.m.
Sat.-Sun. 8:00 a.m. to 5:30 p.m.

CITY OF ST. PETERSBURG
Do Your Part For A Cleaner St. Petersburg

4.

RECOGNIZE YOUR SANITATION DRIVER?
Find his route description here:

NORTH

1.	Mon.	4 St -16 St N. 83 Ave -94 Ave N
	Tues.	4 St -Tallahassee Dr. N.E. 83 Ave -99 Ave N.
2.	Mon.	4 St N.-Meadowlawn Dr. N. 70 Ave-83 Ave N.
	Tues.	Bayou Grande Blvd.-16 St N.E. 50 Ave N.E.-Tanglewood Dr. N.E.
3.	Mon.	4 St -9 St. N. 42 Ave -54 Ave. N.
	Tues.	4 St -Birch St. N.E. 58 Ave -83 Ave. N.
4.	Mon.	16 St N.-I-275 62 Ave-83 Ave N.
	Tues.	Birch St N.E.-Shore Acres Blvd. N.E. 35 Ave -49 Ave. N.E
5.	Mon.	4 St -17 St N. 62 Ave -70 Ave N.
	Tues.	Shore Acres Blvd.-Mass Ave. N.E. Delaware Ave.-Arrowhead Dr. N.E
6.	Mon.	4 St -16 St. N. 54 Ave -62 Ave. N.
	Tues.	Mass Ave. N.E.-Carolina Ave. N.E. Shore Acres Blvd.-Mich. Ave. N.E.
7.	Mon.	9 St N.-I-275 42 Ave -50 Ave N.
	Tues.	4 St N.-Birch St. N.E. Brightwaters Cir. N.E.-41 Ave N.E.
8.	Mon.	16 St N.-I-275 30 Ave -45 Ave N.
	Tues.	4 St -Bayshore Dr. N.E. 15 Ave -30 Ave N.
9.	Mon.	4 St -16 St. N. 34 Ave -42 Ave N.
	Tues.	4 St -Birch St N.E. 41 Ave -58 Ave. N.E
10.	Mon.	4 St -12 St N. 22 Ave -34 Ave N.
	Tues.	Snell Isle Blvd.-Arkansas Ave. N.E. Eden Isle Dr.-Brightwaters Blvd. N.E
11.	Mon.	9 St. N.-I-275 22 Ave -30 Ave N.
	Tues.	22 St -31 St S. 15 Ave -22 Ave S.
12.	Mon.	9 St N.-I-275 9 Ave -22 Ave N.
	Tues.	28 St N.-I-275 5 Ave -22 Ave N.
13.	Mon.	1 St -9 St N. 9 Ave -22 Ave N.
	Tues.	7 St -22 St S. 18 Ave -22 Ave S.
14.	Mon.	34 St -40 St N. 1 Ave -11 Ave. S.
	Tues.	4 St N.-North Shore Dr. N.E. 6 Ave N.-15 Ave N.E

SOUTH

15.	Mon.	1 St -9 St S. 5 Ave -2 Ave S.
	Tues.	4 St N.-I-275 5 Ave -9 Ave N.
16.	Mon.	1 St -9 St S. 7 Ave -18 Ave S.
	Tues.	16 St -34 St S. 5 Ave -15 Ave S.
17.	Mon.	34 St -49 St S. 11 Ave -18 Ave S.
	Tues.	9 St -22 St S. 11 Ave -18 Ave S.
18.	Mon.	16 Ave -26 Ave S. 9 St -Beach Dr. S.
	Tues.	49 St -58 St N. 4 Ave -9 Ave N.
19.	Mon.	16 St -40 St S. 22 Ave -28 Ave S.
	Tues.	16 St -Beach Dr. S. 26 Ave -38 Ave S.
20.	Mon.	Caesar Way S.-34 St S. 30 Ave -54 Ave S.
	Tues.	Pompano Dr.-Coquina Dr. S.E. Dolphin Ave.-Manatee Ave. S.E.
21.	Mon.	34 St -51 St S. 34 Ave -62 Ave S.
	Tues.	Alhambra Way S.-4 St S. 3 Ave -54 Ave S.
22.	Mon.	22 St -31 St S. 58 Ave -Pinellas Point Dr. S
	Tues.	9 St -22 St S. 54 Ave -66 Ave S.
23.	Mon.	9 St -22 St S. 66 Ave -Pinellas Point Dr. S.
	Tues.	9 St -Bahama Shores Dr. S. 54 Ave -Pinellas Point Dr. S.

WEST

24.	Mon.	Sunset Blvd S.-81 St S. Causeway Blvd N.-13 Ave N.
	Tues.	20 St -31 St 5 Ave N.-5 Ave S.
25.	Mon.	34 St -49 St S. 18 Ave -26 Ave S.
	Tues.	34 St -49 St N. Dartmouth Ave.-9 Ave N.
26.	Mon.	58 St -Sunset Dr. N. 1 Ave -7 Ave S.
	Tues.	49 St -58 St N. 22 Ave -30 Ave N.
27.	Mon.	58 St -70 St N. 1 Ave S.-5 Ave N.
	Tues.	43 St -55 St N. 30 Ave -40 Ave N.
28.	Mon.	Country Club Rd. N.-Park St. N. 1 Ave S.-25 Ave N.
	Tues.	49 St -58 St N. 13 Ave -22 Ave N.
29.	Mon.	70 St -Country Club Rd. N. 5 Ave -22 Ave N.
	Tues.	40 St -55 St N. 1 Ave -7 Ave N.
30.	Mon.	Tyrone Blvd -70 St N. 5 Ave -18 Ave N.
	Tues.	34 St -46 St N. 26 Ave -34 Ave N.
31.	Mon.	58 St -Tyrone Blvd. N. 9 Ave -22 Ave N.
	Tues.	28 St -43 St N. 9 Ave -17 Ave N.
32.	Mon.	58 St -66 St N. 22 Ave -30 Ave N.
	Tues.	28 St N.-I-275 22 Ave -40 Ave N.
33.	Mon.	56 St -62 St N. 30 Ave -40 Ave N.
	Tues.	31 St -43 St N. 34 Ave -40 Ave N.
34.	Mon.	62 St -68 St N. 30 Ave -40 Ave N.
	Tues.	35 St -46 St N. 17 Ave -26 Ave N.
35.	Mon.	66 St -78 St N. 30 Ave -40 Ave N.
	Tues.	43 St -58 St N. 9 Ave -17 Ave N.
36.	Mon.	80 St -Pelham Rd. N. 25 Ave -40 Ave N.
	Tues.	34 St -58 St N. 1 Ave -4 Ave N.

FIGURE 5.10

Sanitation Program Information

CLIP AND USE
SANITATION DEPARTMENT SERVICES GUIDE

Service	Phone Number
1. For free repair of automated container	893-7334
2. For information about residential collection	893-7309
3. For free curbside removal of residential furniture, appliances and carpeting	893-7398
4. To report overgrown, unkempt yards or vacant lots.	893-7360
5. For locations/hours of six free brush sites	893-7398
6. For rodent control	893-7360
7. For free removal of cardboard packing cartons for new residents	893-7398

Sanitation Department
City of St. Petersburg
P.O. Box 2842
St. Petersburg, FL 33731

DID YOU KNOW?

- It takes only 36 drivers to service St. Petersburg's residential refuse collection routes, thanks to the City's one-man automated system. Before automation, 84 drivers were required to do the same job every day.
- Your Sanitation driver services an average of one home every 21 seconds.
- The average St. Petersburg family generates 70 pounds of garbage each week.
- Each Sanitation driver services an average of 1,080 homes every day.
- A Sanitation truck carts off some 20 tons of garbage every day.
- More than 27 million pounds of brush have been removed from the city since last winter's freeze.

2.

Follow these
TIPS FOR TIDINESS

- Cool fireplace and bar-b-que ashes completely before disposing.
- Remind your neighbors politely that St. Petersburg now has a pooper scooper law for pets.
- Wrap your trash and close your container lid to deter animals and insects.
- Place your 90-gallon automated containers at the curb by 7 a.m. on collection day.
- Use your alley or curbside containers for disposal of normal household waste, kitchen garbage and yard trimmings that are less than 4 feet long.
- Report the sighting of rodents immediately. Use the number listed in the Services Guide.
- Do not dispose of household chemicals, darkroom chemicals, motor oil or old batteries in your City-supplied containers. These items contain toxic substances. For information on how to dispose of hazardous waste, call toll free 1-800-342-0184.
- Old furniture and appliances left in your yard attract animals and termites. Call 893-7398 for free curbside removal.
- Report stray dogs to Pinellas County's dog control office by calling 530-6500.
- Don't be a litterbug. And help maintain our city's future cleanliness by teaching your children to use refuse containers.

FIGURE 5.11

Captain Clean Contest Announcement

Cast Your Vote for a Cleaner St. Petersburg.

ELECT CAPTAIN CLEAN

We need your help to select our City's most conscientious and courteous Sanitation Driver. By casting your vote for your route man, you will encourage his continued good service — and recognize his diligence in helping to clear our city of 27 million pounds of extra debris that resulted from last winter's damaging freeze.

There's another way that you can help create a cleaner St. Petersburg. Don't jam into your dumpster throw-aways such as furniture, building materials, large pieces of carpet, appliances — or tree limbs greater than six inches in diameter or longer than four feet. Those bulky items cause equipment problems, which may provoke service delays. For information about their disposal, consult the Sanitation Services Guide on page 2.

Captain Clean will be the driver who receives the most votes from his customers. He'll win valuable prizes — all donated by leading St. Petersburg businesses that want to help strive for an even cleaner city, too.

CAPTAIN CLEAN COMPETITION PRIZES include . . .

- A Weekend-For-Four at the lush Tierra Verde Resort — with an extra bonus of two-for-one tickets to Giggles Comedy Club.
- A navy blue Captain's blazer from men's clothier Egerton & Moore.
- A Seiko quartz watch from Bruce Watters Jewelers.
- A candlelight dinner for two at Ten Beach Drive Restaurant.
- Free movie passes from Tyrone Square Six Theaters.
- Four dinners at JoJo's Restaurant.
- An Instamatic camera from Madeira Camera AV Center.

TO CAST YOUR VOTE: Find your Sanitation Driver's picture and enter his number on the ballot. Or, identify your driver by the large number that appears on his truck door.

Then, send us your vote for courteous service. Or, if you're dissatisfied with your Sanitation Department service, use the ballot to tell us why. Or call 893-7332 between 7:30 a.m. and 4 p.m. to register your vote for Captain Clean. Winners will be announced on September 10 in the St. Petersburg Times and Evening Independent.

OFFICIAL BALLOT FOR CAPTAIN CLEAN

In appreciation for good service,

I vote for

Driver No. [ ]

I think Sanitation Services could be better ☐. Here's my suggestion for improving service and a cleaner St. Petersburg: _____

_____

Clip and send this ballot to: CAPTAIN CLEAN COMPETITION, City of St. Petersburg, P.O. Box 2842, St. Petersburg, Florida 33731. Or CALL 893-7332 (between 7:30 a.m. and 4 p.m. weekdays).   Deadline for ballots and calls: Friday, August 24, 1984.

FIGURE 5.12

Newspaper Insert Announcing Captain Clean Winners

ANNOUNCING THE WINNER!

Willie L. Freeman is CAPTAIN CLEAN

Mr. Freeman was elected by 13 percent of 3,734 votes cast by St. Petersburg residents to select our City's most courteous and conscientious Sanitation Driver.

A Sanitation route driver for 16 of his 40 years, Mr. Freeman is proud to be elected Captain Clean from among the city's 36 residential drivers, men who serve 78,000 households by averaging a garbage pick-up every 21 seconds.

Willie said, "I'm really proud to be Captain Clean. I want to thank the people of St. Petersburg for their votes for all of us drivers. We're proud of the work we do for you."

As Captain Clean, Mr. Freeman has won valuable prizes donated by leading St. Petersburg businesses. So have runnerup Bruce Walker and third place driver Brady Johnson.

Their election was part of a campaign that asked citizens to CAST A VOTE FOR CAPTAIN CLEAN AND A CLEANER ST. PETERSBURG.

And although the votes have been counted, our war against grime continues.

Captain Clean wants you to know...

■ It takes only 36 drivers to service St. Petersburg's residential refuse collection routes, thanks to the City's one-man automated system. Before automation, 84 drivers were required to do the same job every day.
■ The average St. Petersburg family generates 70 pounds of garbage each week.
■ Each Sanitation driver services an average of 1,080 homes every day.
■ A Sanitation truck carts off some 20 tons of garbage every day.
■ More than 27 million pounds of brush have been removed from the city since last winter's freeze.

See reverse side for handy telephone numbers and a brush site locator map.

 CITY OF ST. PETERSBURG

have the same rights and benefits as all other merital personnel in the county.

The department is committed to doing everything possible to help these staff members attain their revenue goals. The forty-seven full-time staff members in the recreation division are hired under this type of agreement. Before an employee is hired to operate an enterprise program, he or she must sign a salary agreement affirming understanding of the department's policy. Some potential employees are frightened away by such a salary arrangement. This aids the department in selecting people who are confident in their ability to effectively operate an enterprise program.

This approach provides added incentive for staff to become aware not only of costs and pricing, but also other possible target markets, new and better programs, and effective promotions. The department regards this type of contract essential if an enterprise fund operation is to work successfully, for there is no tax support to subsidize the operation.

A second employee-revenue incentive plan used by the department involves a bonus program implemented in lieu of merit. Each recreation employee is scored on a number of criteria, and the point total determines the bonus level. Criteria include such items as service, quality control, number of complaints, speed of inventory turnover, gross sales, and net profit. Each of the twenty-nine recreation-program and facility cost centers used by the department has its own uniquely formulated set of criteria geared to its particular operation since the goals and opportunities associated with each are different.

In some facilities where the object is to maximize revenue return, exclusively financial criteria are used. Managers at those facilities receive a percentage of the income they produce in addition to their base salaries. For example:

— The golf professional is a department employee. He receives a base salary and in addition a percentage of the annual greens fees in accordance with the following formula:
    $50-125,000 = 5% of gross greens fees
    $125-200,000 = 7.5%
    over $200,000 = 10%
This bonus yields approximately twenty-five thousand dollars.

— The manager and assistant manager of the marina divide between them three percent of the net and two percent of the gross revenue up to 500,000 dollars a year and seven-and-a-half percent of gross above 500,000 dollars per year. From this arrangement they receive approximately ten thousand dollars.

The bonus criteria for the recreation-program staff enable most of them to accrue between fifteen hundred and five thousand dollars annually. When establishing a bonus system that relies heavily on financial performance, the department has learned the importance of using both gross and net income bases. If performance is based only on net income, there is a temptation for employees to concentrate on achieving short-term gains by cutting back on cost items crucial to long-term customer satisfaction. At the same time, if gross revenue only is used as a basis, then there is no incentive to keep costs under control.

The incentive bonuses are awarded at the end of each financial year when accounts have been finalized. These incentives encourage managers to reach out and seek new opportunities for producing revenue for the department. They are intended to offer extra encouragement to retain existing customers and attract new ones. For example, incentives have encouraged golf and marina managers to host major special events such as golf and fishing tournaments that generate large amounts of revenue as well as publicity for the facility and the department.

Enterprise funds and employee incentives work by giving employees a sense of ownership. The department believes it benefits from having employees who feel as if they are operating their own business.

SOURCES:

Department of Leisure Services
PO Box 2842
St. Petersburg, Florida 33731

Jackson County Department of Recreation and Parks
22807 Woods Chapel Road
Blue Springs, Missouri 64015

OTHER BOOKS FROM VENTURE PUBLISHING

Leisure In Your Life: An Exploration, Revised Edition, by Geoffrey Godbey

Planning Parks For People, by John Hultsman, Richard L. Cottrell and Wendy Zales-Hultsman

Recreation Economic Decisions: Comparing Benefits and Costs, by Richard G. Walsh

Leadership Administration of Outdoor Pursuits, by Phillis Ford and James Blanchard

Acquiring Parks and Recreation Facilities Through Mandatory Dedication: A Comprehensive Guide, by Ronald A. Kaiser and James D. Mertes

Recreation and Leisure: Issues In An Era of Change, Revised Edition, edited by Thomas L. Goodale and Peter A. Witt

Private and Commercial Recreation, edited by Arlin Epperson

Sport and Recreation: An Economic Analysis, by Chris Gratton and Peter Taylor (Distributed for E. and F. N. Spon, Ltd.)

Park Ranger Handbook, by J. W. Shiner

Playing, Living Learning - A Worldwide Perspective on Children's Opportunities to Play, by Cor Westland and Jane Knight

Evaluation Of Therapeutic Recreation Through Quality Assurance, edited by Bob Riley

Recreation and Leisure: An Introductory Handbook, edited by Alan Graefe and Stanley Parker

The *Leisure Diagnostic Battery-Users Manual and Sample Forms,* by Peter Witt and Gary Ellis

Doing More With Less In The Delivery Of Recreation and Park Services - A Book of Case Studies, by John Crompton

Behavior Modification In Therapeutic Recreation: An Introductory Learning Manual, by John Dattilo and William D. Murphy

Outdoor Recreation Management: Theory and Application, Revised and Enlarged, by Alan Jubenville, Ben W. Twight and Robert H. Becker

International Directory of Academic Institutions In Leisure, Recreation and Related Fields (Distributed for WLRA)

Being At Leisure-Playing At Life: A guide to Health and Joyful Living, by Bruno Hans Geba

Venture Publishing, Inc.
1640 Oxford Circle
State College, PA 16803
814-234-4561